MW01141495

Management for Professionals

For further volumes:
http://www.springer.com/series/10101

Klaus Solberg Søilen

Exhibit Marketing and Trade Show Intelligence

Successful Boothmanship and Booth Design

 Springer

Klaus Solberg Søilen
School of Business and Engineering
Halmstad University
Halmstad
Sweden

ISSN 2192-8096   ISSN 2192-810X (electronic)
ISBN 978-3-642-36792-2   ISBN 978-3-642-36793-9 (eBook)
DOI 10.1007/978-3-642-36793-9
Springer Heidelberg New York Dordrecht London

Library of Congress Control Number: 2013939355

Printed on acid-free paper

Springer is part of Springer Science+Business Media (www.springer.com)

Dedicated to:

Leipzig
Old city of trade shows

and

University of Leipzig
Alma Mater

Preface

This book is about trade shows, which is a function studied under the heading of *exhibition marketing*. Some readers may wonder about the title "*trade show intelligence*". That is an aspect of exhibition marketing which focuses on information gathering and analysis. It is a consequence, we might say, of the *Information Age* and the realization that trade shows, to be truly effective and profitable today, need to take full advantage of the information opportunity which a trade show is.

Trade shows have become increasingly sophisticated and complex just over the past 20 years. That itself has resulted in part from advances in the study of marketing, which has given company managers many more choices. People who attend these occasions today have much higher expectations for the exhibition and the behaviour and performance of exhibitors than they had only a few years ago. That in turn has created a demand for more education in this field. Students and budding professionals need a thorough understanding of the different roles and functions of a trade show; the days of just showing up and doing one's best are over.

The aim of this book is twofold: to survey the research literature in the field, and to show how successful boothmanship and booth design is achieved at trade shows. The book is not written from any individual national perspective, but sets out to address a truly international audience. This has meant drawing on cultural elements and citing examples from trade shows all round the world.

To date, trade shows have been neglected in the literature of marketing. Philip Kotler, for instance, devotes only a few paragraphs to the topic in his *Principles of Marketing*. At the same time, these events continue to prove themselves to be a highly significant function within the marketing profession, indeed one of its leading activities. That is reflected in the figures for spending on trade shows.

Statistics for 2010 show that there are now more than 30,000 exhibitions with a size of over 500 m^2 annually, attended by 2.8 million companies and 260 million visitors.[1]

---

[1] See UFI, *2011 Exhibition Industry Statistics*, p. 14. The UFI organization, based in Paris, is the largest interest organization for trade shows; the acronym originally stood for *Union des Foires*

The project of writing this book has stemmed from the experience of taking part in a number of different international trade shows with dozens of companies for over a decade now, initially with smaller IT companies and with Swedish furniture manufacturers.

The aim has been to write a university textbook for students who plan to specialize in the field of *event marketing* and more particularly *exhibition marketing*, while at the same time producing a book that might be of interest to practitioners. As such, it is very much a do's-and-don'ts book, but not like the bulk of the existing literature: for instance, it does not contain as many checklists as other books on this topic tend to include. Checklists are unavoidable in the practical activity of exhibition marketing, but they are not a necessary element of *marketing theory*. Also, this book does not go down to the same level of detail as many other books; for instance, it will not tell you what voltage to use in different countries, or how to fill in the registration form for a particular show. Rather, it offers you different ways of organizing your exhibit or booth, and it outlines the particular sales behaviour and managerial challenges required to make trade shows both efficient and successful. To help the reader in the task of learning exhibition marketing, all keywords important for a thorough understanding of the theory are given in italics. Thus you can check your knowledge by seeing what you are able to remember and explain. This is also done in order to help employees in company training sessions, and teachers in finding good exam questions.

Many people imagine that selling at exhibitions is just like selling at home; that the skills and requirements are more or less the same. One of the aims of this book is to show that people who think like that are mistaken.

The book adopts the exhibitor's perspective. The emphasis is on exhibition behaviour. Exhibitors often overlook the fact that exhibitions give them the opportunity not only to distribute information, but also to gather information from customers, from their competitors, and from stakeholders. Exhibition behaviour draws on the study of *market psychology*, the *psychology of marketing*, and *behavioural economics*. All of these subjects are explored here as we set out to present the trade show in each of its aspects.

One problem in writing a book on trade shows is that little research is available, even though there are plenty of books on event marketing in particular, and things have improved over the past decade. A large majority of existing studies have been carried out by trade associations and interest groups; fewer by academics. Most of the books available are written by consultants, who often carry their own personal views over into the conclusions in the hope of fostering business opportunities. That is only to be expected; it is understandable enough.

Internationales. It is now the Global Association of the Exhibition Industry, but the old acronym is still used. The second largest interest organization is the Society of Independent Show Organizers (SISO) in the USA, with about 2,700 events, according to its homepage. In Latin America there is AFIDA, and in Southern Africa EXSA.

I first became acquainted with trade shows when I worked as an auditor with KPMG at the Norway Trade Fair in Oslo in 1996. Since then I have had the opportunity of attending a number of the largest exhibitions around the world as a consultant, working for more than two dozen companies, mostly in Europe and the USA. This took me to events such as the International Furniture Fair of Milan (*Salone Internazionale del Mobile*), the world's largest interior-decoration trade fair, and the *Consumer Electronics Show* (CES) at Las Vegas, one of the world's largest technology-related trade shows. Much of the content for this book began as notes I made in order to help those companies understand how to get the most out of the trade shows we attended, either as exhibitors or as visitors. At the same time, I have very much remained an academic with a keen interest in marketing and later also in *intelligence studies*. I hope the book will appeal to both practitioners and academics alike.

I would like to express my thanks to the staff members of all the various companies I have travelled with over the years. They are too many to be mentioned individually here, but some of their names will crop up in the book. Special thanks are due to Prof. Per Odenrick of the University of Lund, Georg Gärdh of Träriket, Lars E. Thon, Chief System Architect at Aeluros Inc., The Knowledge Foundation, Per Jenster Chairman of NIMI, Paul Woodward Managing Director of UFI, Annette Fink of AUMA, Gordon Nary and Jim Wurm at E2MA, Richard Liden of Karskrona Municipality, UNIVA in Lund, Charles M. Orgish of Stanford University and to Prashanth Mahagaonkar and Barbara Bethke at Springer.

Completed in Blumenau and Porto Belo, Brazil

Halmstad, Sweden   Klaus Solberg Søilen
January 2013

Contents

Introduction

What is a *trade show*? In this introduction, we set out to offer the reader a relatively complete historical answer to that question. Let us just start by saying that the purpose and essence of trade shows is person-to-person information exchange and selling (Chapman 1993: 36–38). Information exchange covers both distribution and gathering of information. If trade shows are viewed as a means of information exchange between exhibitors and visitors (in the form of advertising and PR), no category of marketing activity is more expensive to undertake. When they are viewed as personal selling, no form of selling is more effective. But that is looking at the short run. In the long run, an information edge leads to increased sales, and hence to greater profits. So the question quickly becomes, how do you gather information effectively in connection with a trade show – before the show opens and after it is over, but in particular while the show is under way? If we can learn to use trade shows to gather information not only from our visitors, but also from our competitors and stakeholders, then we are beginning to exploit the full potential of a trade show for making a worthwhile return on our marketing investment. That is the core message of this book, a message we shall describe from different angles and in much more detail in the chapters to come.

According to a report from the Center for Exhibition Industry Research (CEIR), it costs US\$233 to acquire a sales lead at a trade show, versus \$303 in the sales field (CEIR 2003: #sm17). This is despite the substantial cost of building and transporting an exhibit around to various shows. If these figures are correct, our marketing money can hardly be put to better use in any other category of sales activity. We may not make the sales during the show, but we might get an order later from someone who saw us and visited our booth at the show.[2]

What are the other reasons for attending a trade show? The commonest reasons quoted, apart from the fact that attending leads to more sales, is that a trade show

---

[2] There are different terms for the structure which a particular exhibiting company or organization erects on a specific area of floor space at a trade show: British writers would commonly call it a *stand*, Americans a *booth*. This book will use the latter term.

represents an opportunity to test the market for our products, it is a place to learn about the latest designs and trends, appearing at a show strengthens our brand, it gives us a great deal of potential publicity, and it is a place where we can find new suppliers and form closer relationships with existing agents in our industry (suppliers, people of influence, trade organizations).

From a marketing perspective, fairs or exhibitions have become ever more important for an organization's *marketing mix*. We see this as companies are investing more money in building larger and more extravagant booths. They are also putting more time into preparing their staff for these events. For many companies, exhibitions have become the single most important milestone among all their various marketing activities. And that explains why it is so important to get shows right.

In *business-to-business* (B2B) marketing, industrial trade shows are frequently seen as more important than advertising in trade publications (Godar and O'Connor 2001: 77). Trade shows are important not only for sellers but also for buyers (despite the perceived threat from advances in internet technology creating virtual substitutes for real shows). Trade shows are shaped by buyers' needs. If buyers want to shift towards more virtual solutions, that is how the industry will go. Many of the concepts and ideas discussed here will still be valid, since they are rooted in the same observations of human nature, whether we choose to operate offline or online. There will be technical adaptations and hybrid solutions mixing offline and online modes. But, more important, research to date confirms that the internet, and new technology in general, have not in fact become a substitute for face-to-face meetings at trade shows. Rather, they have become a greatly appreciated support technology, making the running of meetings more efficient. For example, we now often scan visitors' conference tags electronically, and plan meetings using SMS. We use e-mail to exchange contracts. According to UFI statistics, 73 % of exhibitors set up *matchmaking meetings* with visitors on-site, versus 19.2 % online.[3] Twenty-five percent charge visitors a fee for these meetings.

With all this new technology, what do we see overall? Are companies being effective in their trade show activities? Ten years ago, the answer was a clear no.[4] The answer today is still no, but great improvements have been achieved thanks to increasing willingness on the part of researchers and professionals to take trade shows more seriously.[5] Despite the relatively sparsity of research articles in the

---

[3] See "UFI matchmaking survey results 2012", p. 8.

[4] Research by Margit Weisgal (1999) suggested that 83 % of prospects were not contacted by a company representative within a 1-year period after a show had closed, and that 80 % of exhibitors failed to follow up on their leads.

[5] In terms of sales versus costs, 65 % of companies feel participation in shows is worthwhile, while 24 % think it is wasteful (Weisgal 1999: 56). In terms of industry contacts companies are much more satisfied. Thirty-four percent identify trade show participation as first in line to be cut down if marketing budget is reduced, 25 % identify advertising (Weisgal 1999: 59). See also Johansson (2001), a study which examined 175 national tourism organizations of various sizes and organizational structures in Sweden.

field of exhibition marketing (which may in turn explain why the more popular marketing books frequently avoid the topic), there are many good how-to books about exhibition marketing available today, mostly books of a fairly practical nature. Barry Siskind's (2005) is still one of the better ones overall. And some other how-to books which are well worth reading include Huckemann, Seiler, and ter Weiler (2005), and Ruth Stevens (2005). A classic "how-to-do-it, step-by-step" book is by Christine Christman (1991). For the pre-show phase there is a good book by Judy Allen (2002); and a truly enjoyable and comprehensive book on events from a managerial perspective is by Joe Goldblatt (2002), who is regarded as one of the pioneers in this field. In Germany, a number of useful books have been produced by Elke Clausen (1997, 2005). Apart from these authors, trade show interest groups such as the Global Association of the Exhibition Industry (UFI)[6] and the Association of the German Trade Fair Industry (AUMA) continue to provide useful statistical data (see Kirchgeorg et al. 2007). That kind of information is necessary in order to get an adequate overview of the trade show industry and to understand recent trends.[7]

Statistics from trade shows are not only relevant for the purposes of the industry itself. Trade show budgets are also a good indicator of expected economic growth in a country, hence they are used by many economists and central banks. For example, despite continuing economic uncertainty, 30 % of German exhibitors planned to increase their trade show budgets in 2012, while 55 % planned to spend the same amount as in the previous year. Statistical data showed us that trade show budgets fell after the economic crisis of 2008, and that continued into 2010, with a 3 % drop. These changes were reflected in the *overall economy*. Then in 2011 there was a 3 % increase in trade show budgets, which was again reflected in the German economic recovery.

Figure 1 shows the proportion of companies declaring an increase in their turnover year-on-year.

From a July 2012 UFI report we learn that:

- Three to five companies out of ten, depending on the region, declare an increase of their annual profit of more than 10 %, and this proportion has been rather stable for the last 3 years now.
- It shows that a majority of respondents from all regions consider, for the second time in a row, that their business is affected by the 'economic crisis'. The significant decrease of confidence outlined 6 months ago in Asia/Pacific is confirmed, with 71 % declaring that the impact of the 'economic crisis' on their exhibition business is not over.

---

[6] UFI statistics for Europe are mainly gathered in collaboration with other national trade-show organizations, including AEF in Italy, AFE in Spain, OJS in France, SFC in Scandinavia, and FKM in Germany.

[7] Most of the data come from surveys sent only to members. The best data are collected and analysed from a large number of trade-show interest organizations.

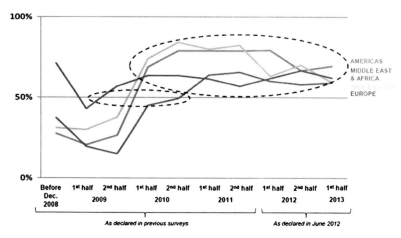

Fig. 1 Trends in trade show budgets (Source: UFI, Global Exhibition Barometer, July 2012, p. 5)

- The only new element appears to be the slowdown in the growth of turnover for both the Asia/Pacific region, where this started a year ago, and for the Americas, where it was more recent.[8]

A closer look at the single largest market for trade shows, Germany, shows that most companies expect to spend the same amount on trade shows this year as they did last year. Twice as many companies are planning to increase their spending as those planning to spend less (Fig. 2).

After a few troublesome years for exhibition activities early in the twenty-first century, mainly because of the financial crisis and uncertainties related to potential applications of new internet technology, trade shows are becoming a priority again. Just a few years ago, there were voices which announced the death of the traditional trade show. Since then we have seen a revival of interest, even if at a slow pace. Whether this is only temporary, so that we may face further hardship in the years to come in the form of reduced interest, is not for this book to say. What we can say is that to date, at least, the correlation between advances in internet technology and decline in exhibition activities has been exaggerated. Research on the effects of the internet on trade shows suggests, rather, that (quoting Li 2010: 272):

- While a website's capability in providing quality information facilitates the usage of the company website for pre-show promotion, an exhibitor's legitimacy motive of using its website to build up the company image contributes to the usage of the company website for at-show selling, and the firm's inter-functional coordinating capabilities that capitalize on internet connectivity in support of superior customer services encourage the usage of company website for post-show follow-up, and

---

[8] UFI, Global Exhibition Barometer, July 2012, pp. 6–7.

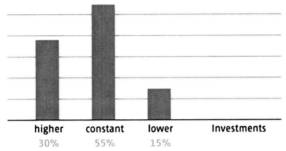

AUMA_MesseTrend 2012

Investments in participations
Compared to 2010/2011, ...% of German exhibition
companies* are planning worldwide in the period 2012/2013:

higher	constant	lower	Investments
30%	55%	15%	

Trade fair budget per company: 2012 + 2013: 376,600,- €

* representative survey conducted by TNS Emnid commissioned by AUMA
among 500 companies, which exhibit at trade visitor-oriented fairs; October 2011;
to 100 remaining percent: n.a.

Fig. 2 Expectations of trade show budgets for 2012 in Germany (Source: AUMA 2012)

- The key lesson for exhibitors is to adopt the right approach to internet marketing – using the internet primarily for "informational and communicational purpose" in pre-show promotion, and for "customer service and support purpose" in post-show follow-up.

For the moment, we seem to be moving towards integration more than towards substitution. Certainly, in the future we are going to see more technical solutions at trade shows, such as creation of virtual realities and *virtual trade shows*. We will also see creation of more *hybrid events*, combining real and virtual solutions. But, even with virtual solutions, most of the points discussed in this book will still hold true.

Furthermore there will be new problems, such as how to simulate human behaviour using virtual solutions, and how to create that most important ingredient in business life, trust. Despite everything we can glean from experts' and customers' reviews, environmental brandings, and business intelligence software, we still prefer to meet the people we are doing business with, especially if we are a company.

By now the reader will have noticed that this book uses a number of apparent synonyms. For example, what is the difference between trade shows, fairs, exhibitions, and expos? The short answers are "not much", and "it depends". However, the differences that do exist deserve our attention. These differences are best explained by looking at the terms in a historical context and across a number of Western languages.

Exhibitions and *expos* are, as the words suggest, more about showing products and services than about selling them. *Trade shows* or *industry shows* are business-to-business events, whereas *consumer shows* are business-to-consumer and open to the general public. There are also *association shows*, shows open only to a particular association. To put it simply, some trade shows are open to the public, some are

Table 1 Distinguishing elements for different types of trade shows (See also Pepinski 2003: 9)

Distinguishing element	Pole 1	Pole 2
Marketing	Sales	Information
Reach	National (regional, local)	International
Goods and services	Consumer	B2B
Season	Early in the year (e.g. CES)	Autumn
Trade show intervals	Annual	Irregular

not. There are a number of ways to distinguish between different trade shows (Table 1). The most common are:

In the USA the locations for trade shows are called *convention centres*, in Britain often *exhibition centres*. Sometimes trade shows are held in *conference centres*, which are much smaller, and contain lecture halls and other meeting rooms.

Trade show is a relatively new term, and did not appear in standard dictionaries until quite recently. The usual English phrase has been *trade fair*. "Fair", as a periodical gathering of buyers and sellers, appeared in the English language as early as the thirteenth century; it comes from old French *feire*[9] (which has given the modern French form *foire*). Fairs, or *feriae* in Latin, started out as religious festivals, and developed into markets. As a market, the fair would be accompanied by entertainment and amusements. Thus, we can draw a line of development from markets, to fairs, to trade shows.

Trade fairs were organized at regular intervals, generally at the same location and in the same period(s) of the year, and they usually lasted for several days or weeks. More importantly, in mediaeval times they were protected by the city's laws and exhibitors were exempt from customs and other taxes for the duration of the event.[10]

The word *exhibition* was first used in the sense "public display of objects" in the eighteenth century; in the specifically commercial context relevant to this book, it was popularized by the Great Exhibition of 1851 in London (see below). In recent times Americans have tended to use "exhibit" for what in Britain is called an "exhibition". (In Britain, an "exhibit" is a single item displayed at an exhibition. In this book, "exhibit" will sometimes be used for the display in an individual company's booth at a show.)

Expo, which is short for *exposition* (the usual French term for exhibition, first used in a commercial sense in 1565) is a newer term in English; the French use of *exposition* became known in Britain through the Paris *Exposition Universelle* of

---

[9] The same Indo-European root has given us *feast*. We find the same logic in the development of the word *holiday*, from holy day.

[10] Part of the so-called *Meßfreiheiten*, the freedoms to attend fairs, which also included free entry for any traveller, the right of exhibitors to use their own exchange, and the right not to be persecuted without due cause. To safeguard the exhibitor's rights, a special trade-fair court was set up which lacked the tedious formalities of the normal court. All this was a part of the *Meßordnung*, the trade-fair rules and regulations.

1867. In German the term is *Ausstellung*, which etymologically is equivalent to *exposition* – both mean "setting-out".

Most famous are the *Universal Expositions*, or *World Fairs*, organized by the Bureau International des Expositions (International Exhibitions Bureau) based in Paris. Participants are countries, and participation requires total design of pavilion buildings from the ground up.

Earlier fairs were entirely focused on sales. Modern fairs also focus on information exchange and the building of relationships. During the last decade of the twentieth century focus shifted back towards sales, but information exchange and relationship building have regained importance over the past decade. And at the same time, trade shows have also been developing in the direction of more entertainment and amusement facilities. This trend is likely to continue.

Fairs today are normally either arranged for (1) one special segment of an industry, (2) one industry, or they are (3) more general exhibitions. The historical development of fairs has gone from more general displays with a broad range of products and a diverse range of visitors (*horizontal fairs*), to increasingly specialized displays assuming more in terms of visitors' propensity to purchase, and stiffer competition among exhibitors (*vertical fairs*). Some research suggests that horizontal shows are preferred when participants have a lower selling volume and buying propensity and/or a greater breadth of product interest, or where the industry is more innovative.[11]

Exhibitions, which are considered an aspect of sales promotion, can be defined as *standardized fairs*. As such, they are nothing new. When we go back in history we find that most major European cities started as nothing more than a marketplace, a crossroads where buyers and sellers would meet because that particular geographical place turned out to be convenient for a number of merchants. The city of Leipzig is one such example, sited on the road between Western and Eastern Europe, the old Roman *Via Regia*, and on the North–South *Via Imperii*. Another important trade city along the *Via* Imperii was Frankfurt-am-Main. For a long time after the collapse of the Roman Empire the most important section of the road, between these two trade cities, was known simply as *Hohe Straße* ("the High Road").

What is new with trade shows as compared to the old fairs is the efforts we make and the relative importance these markets have acquired as a part of our overall range of marketing activities (1), the resources and the amount of organization we bring to those activities (2), and the professionalism by which we are attempting to understand them as socio-economic realities (3).

---

[11] See Wu et al. (2003: 23–4). The same empirical research suggests that, after selling and buying, product breadth is the most important factor for participants. Earlier research by the same group (Wu et al. 1997: 25–6) showed that neither vertical nor horizontal trade shows give the best overall financial outcome for participants, but that this results from an most optimal match between attendees' and exhibitors' expectations. Short-term profit-seekers may be best advised to choose vertical shows. Since larger firms often have more strategic goals, they may be better off choosing horizontal shows. See Williams et al. (1993).

Exhibitions are different from the simple marketplace in terms of:

- *Duration*: an exhibition usually lasts only for a few days and is normally held annually or twice a year. (The average duration for exhibitions in Europe in 2010 was 4 days.)
- *Extent*: attracting a substantial number of companies nationally and often even internationally.
- *Organization*: attending an exhibition takes up to a year of preparation and planning.
- *Investment*: since there are costs connected not only to attending, but also to building booths, staffing them, and providing for all kinds of promotional material.
- *Skills*: exhibitions are not like direct selling or serving in a store; they are a special situation in terms of selling, relationship building, and information exchange.

Well-organized vertical markets have existed for hundreds of years. These evolved not only for *economic* but also for *sanitary* reasons. Sellers would stand together in one corner of the market, for instance the authorities preferred to have all the meat sellers in one place, so that the sanitary conditions of their trade could be easily monitored and controlled. Later, sellers of fresh food would be placed out of the sun and inside buildings, or under large roofs. Today, we still see these simple open pavilions when we visit old city centres around Europe, especially in smaller villages where they have not yet been torn down, such as many places in Italy.

Economically, sellers discovered that even though they experienced more direct competition when they stood together, they also drew larger crowds. We see the same mechanism in China today: the same area of a town will have one street for pet shops, and another for safes. This looks strange when you first encounter it, but in the long run it makes good sense. If you want a dog or need a new safe, you know exactly where to go. Why these two industries ended up together is another question. In some cases it may just have been a coincidence. Safes are often bought by wealthier businesses, which were located in a certain part of town. In today's China pets, such as dogs, are seen as something of a luxury too, a status symbol, thus more popular in affluent areas.

The tacit knowledge and conclusion of the sellers who gathered together in this way was that the disadvantages of more intensive direct competition were more than outweighed by the greater number of new customers, or overall quantity of customers, resulting from co-location. Soon, new sellers had to be willing to come to the buyers' turf if they wanted to do business. This increased competition led to lower prices and hence attracted even larger groups of new customers. Vertical markets of the old type still flourish in many cities, not only in Asia. A visitor to Paris today will, for example, find that mushroom sellers are located in one of the city squares, and booksellers in another.[12] When the customer base in a given area

---

[12] The weekly magazine *L'Officiel des spectacles* for 23–29 August 2006 (pp. 99–100) offers a list of 77 markets within the city of Paris in that 1 week.

cannot support a market for 6 or 7 days a week, the sellers will decide to come only on certain days. Thus a single marketplace may be home to different products on different days, for instance the same marketplace might be selling cheese on Tuesdays and Thursdays, and flowers on Saturdays. The concentration of sellers in specific locations also helps to boost tourism, giving some squares a special character. The flower market at Place Louis Lépine on the Île de la Cité in Paris is one such example.

Present-day trade shows operate according to very much the same logic. True, their booths have become more sophisticated, they meet less frequently, and they are not allowed to shout out their offers these days (as they still do in many specialized French food markets), but those things apart, the mechanisms of this *pull marketing* activity has remained much the same.

In modern management literature, suffering as it does from inadequate historical perspective, academics are rediscovering the same long-established truths about the advantages of selling and living together. Today's mega-clusters and science parks are to a large extent an extension of the same idea. Examples include the science parks of Silicon Valley, or the less well-known example of Chengdu International Trade City with over 60,000 shops (yes, that number is correct). These are all different forms and degrees of concentrations of people doing the same or related activities. A trade show is basically the same thing.

Before the rise of any strong State that could dictate where merchants should stand (as certainly happens in the case of Chengdu International Trade City), people used to meet and trade very much as they pleased. They typically decided to meet at a particular place and time. This predictable regularity would allow a larger number of both buyers and sellers to attend and know what to expect. In the beginning they were often chased away by local rulers or hordes of bandits who wanted to take control of the trade themselves, or simply to rob. Or the travelling traders were taxed so heavily by officialdom that it failed to make commercial sense to come at all. That is pretty much the story of trade in the Mediterranean area more than a 1,000 years ago, for example among the Phoenicians, the Carthaginians, and later the Greek city-states. However, rulers gradually came to see the economic benefits of letting traders into their cities and offering them protection.

The turning-point came when local rulers understood that one of the chief creators of the wealth from which they benefited was in fact *free trade*. Instead of chasing the tradesmen away, or taxing them so heavily that they did not want to come back, rulers started instead to establish special rights, which included a special protection under the law, and tax and customs exemptions, for a certain fixed period of time. These terms might be specified in the city charter. An example of such a charter for the city of Leipzig is shown in Fig. 3.

Figure 3 shows the city charter (*Stadtbrief*) of the German city of Leipzig, dated 1165. It announces the initiation of the city's trade-fair rights.[13] The city of Leipzig

---

[13] The full trade-fair privileges for Leipzig were granted by Maximilian I at Worms on 20 July 1497. These were confirmations of earlier privileges conferred by the emperor Friedrich III in 1469. See Zwahr et al. (1999: vol. 1, p. 10).

Fig. 3 Leipziger Stadtbrief
(Source: http://www.
europeana.eu (2012-12-05))

has played an important role in the development of trade shows in Europe in general
and hence also in the world. The first modern trade fair (*Mustermesse*) was
established in Leipzig in 1895. Another early trade show city was Lyons in France,
with the Lyons Trade Fair. This was founded in 1916; it was needed as a counter-
attraction to the Leipzig fair when war broke out between the two countries. Milan,
Prague, and Utrecht followed with international fairs in the 1920s.

In the United States the first trade associations appeared in the mid-nineteenth
century along the eastern seaboard of the country. In 1895 a group of Detroit
businessmen set out to attract these organizations to come and do business in
their city, as it was now generally understood and accepted that these events
would attract a great deal of additional business to whatever city could secure
their presence (Gartrell 1988). Other cities were quick to follow when they
appreciated the economic benefits of these events for selling their own city, so to
speak. In this we also see the natural connection that exists between the organization of events like trade shows, and tourism. We see the same logic linking events
and tourism today in cities like Las Vegas, and with sporting tournaments like the

Olympics or the FIFA World Cup. Events have taken their place as part of a standard economic strategy for most cities and regions.

The real commercial breakthrough for the trade fair came when companies stopped bringing all their stock, but instead only displayed samples or prototypes. The new concept meant more exhibitors, more rapid organization, a better overview of the different products, and eventually higher receipts. In Germany this new type of fair was called a *Mustermesse*. The first was held in Leipzig in 1895.[14] The word for "trade fair" in German is *Handelsmesse*[15] or just *Messe*.[16] The *Mustermesse* made Leipzig one of the wealthiest commercial cities in the world. For centuries the city was the capital of the book trade. But, with defeat in the Second World War and the inclusion of Leipzig in East Germany, the book industry quickly shifted to Frankfurt, where it remains today. The editors moved out, bookbinding was gradually forgotten; even the old books were gradually sold to foreign libraries for the sake of obtaining hard currency. The Frankfurt Book Fair (*Frankfurter Buchmesse*) is now the world's largest trade fair for books in terms of the number of publishing companies represented, as well as the number of visitors. After the reunification of Germany, Leipzig has again become one of the leading trade show locations in Europe, but the city still lags far behind its competitors. Leipzig is today the 52nd largest trade city by indoor exhibition space. The 20 largest are listed in Table 2.

We see that of the six largest exhibition spaces, four are located in Germany. On the other hand, the country with most square footage available is the USA, with more than twice as much space. Large exhibition areas are distributed relatively widely across the USA, rather than concentrated in a few places as in Germany and elsewhere in Europe.

China also stands much higher in Table 3 than in Table 2. So too does Brazil. While China represents 72 % of total trade-show sites in Asia, Brazil accounts for 54 % of those of Latin America. In Europe, Germany has most exhibition space (22 %), followed by Italy (14 %).

The most popular trade shows are motor shows, followed by computer shows. These are organized as broad events which attract a large and varied public. The following list of the most visited shows is ranked according to the organizers' own reported figures (Table 4).

Up to the end of the nineteenth century, trade fairs were merely national marketplaces. In other words, it took a long time before marketplaces developed into anything like today's *international trade shows*, with participants from all over the world, both exhibitors and visitors. The first of these may be said to be the *Great*

---

[14] This was the *Leipziger Buchmesse* (Book Fair), before the Second World War the largest in the world. Today the Leipzig Book Fair ranks second, after the Frankfurter Buchmesse.

[15] In German the specialized fairs are called *Fachmesse*, the general fairs are *Universalmesse*.

[16] The German word *Messe* derives from Latin *missa*, "mass", i.e. part of Christian divine service: specifically, the consecration by the priest of the elements of Communion. This came to mean a day of celebration in the church, a Christian holiday. There would originally be an annual mass to celebrate the dedicatee or patron saint of a given church.

Table 2 The 20 largest trade-fair sites in the world

				Indoor exhibition space (sqm)	Europe	North America	Asia	Middle East
1	Messe Hannover	Hanover	Germany	466 100	1			
2	Messe Frankfurt	Frankfurt/Main	Germany	345 697	2			
3	Fiera Milano (Rho Pero)	Milano	Italy	345 000	3			
4	Chinese Export & Import Commodities Fair Ground - Pazhou Complex	Guangzhou	China	338 000			1	
5	Koelnmesse	Cologne	Germany	284 000	4			
6	Messe Duesseldorf	Duesseldorf	Germany	262 704	5			
7	Paris Nord Villepinte	Paris	France	241 582	6			
8	McCormick Place	Chicago	USA	241 524		1		
9	Feria Valencia	Valencia	Spain	230 602	7			
10	Porte de Versailles	Paris	France	228 211	8			
11	Crocus International	Moscow	Russia	226 399	9			
12	Fira de Barcelona: Gran Via venue	Barcelona	Spain	205 000	10			
13ex	BolognaFiere	Bologna	Italy	200 000	11ex			
13ex	Feria de Madrid/IFEMA	Madrid	Spain	200 000	11ex			
13ex	Shanghai New International Expo Centre (SNIEC)	Shanghai	China	200 000			2	
16	The NEC (Birmingham)	Birmingham	United Kingdom	198 983	13			
17	Orange County Convention Center	Orlando	USA	195 077		2		
18	Wuhan International Expo Center	Wuhan	China	190 000			3	
19	Las Vegas Convention Center	Las Vegas	USA	184 372		3		
20	Neue Messe Muenchen	Muenchen	Germany	180 000	14			

Source: UFI, The 2011 world map of exhibition venues, December 2011, p. 5

Table 3 The ten leading countries by indoor exhibition space

		Indoor exhibition space (sqm)	WORLD	North America	Europe	Asia / Pacific	Central & South America	Middle East	Africa
1	USA	6 712 342	21%	86%					
2	China (*)	4 755 102	15%			72%			
3	Germany	3 377 821	10%		22%				
4	Italy	2 227 304	7%		14%				
5	France	2 094 554	6%		13%				
6	Spain	1 548 057	5%		10%				
7	The Netherlands	960 530	3%		6%				
8	Brazil	701 882	2,2%				54%		
9	United Kingdom	701 857	2,2%		5%				
10	Canada	684 175	2,1%	9%					

Source: UFI, The 2011 world map of exhibition venues, December 2011, p. 6

Exhibition, also known as the *Crystal Palace Exhibition*. It was held in Hyde Park in London in 1851, and was inspired by the French *Industrial Exposition* of 1844 in Paris, which was one in a series of 11 French national industrial expositions.

To sum up, we may identify five different kinds of fairs through history (Table 5):

In the years following the Second World War, trade shows faced a number of problems. There was basically no empirical research to draw conclusions and learn from, organizers had few if any statistics from previous shows to build on, and kickbacks and free riders were a common phenomenon (cf. Thain 1955). It is only in the

Table 4 Trade shows with most reported visitors

Title	Description	Dates	Location	Visitors
Bologna Motor Show	Motor show	7 December 2006	Bologna, Italy	1,200,000 in 2006
Buenos Aires International Book Fair	Books	23 April–11 May 2009	Buenos Aires, Argentina	1,240,000 in 2008
Trade Show Video	Computer	11–15 August 2010	Toronto, Canada	1,240,000 in 2009
Mondial de l'Automobile	Motor show	30 September 2006	Paris, France	1,400,000 in 2006
Tokyo Motor Show	Motor show	22 October 2005	Tokyo, Japan	1,512,100 in 2005
AgQuip	Agriculture	19–21 August 2008	Gunnedah, New South Wales, Australia	100,000 approximately in 2005
EuroShop	Retailing	February/ March 2011	Messe Düsseldorf, Germany	104,766 in 2008
Bread Basket	Sustainable agriculture	12–16 May 2010	České Budějovice, Czech Republic	104,565 in 2008
NAB (National Association of Broadcasters)	Broadcasting	18–23 April 2009	Las Vegas Convention Center, Nevada	105,000 in 1999
Interclima + elec	Efficient energy use	9–12 February 2010	Paris, France	1,050,128 in 2008
COMPUTEX Taipei	Computers	3–7 June 2008	Taipei, Taiwan	106,517 in 2008
imm Cologne	Furniture	18–23 January 2011	Cologne Trade Fair, Germany	106,677 in 2008
International Tourism Exchange (BIT)	Tourism	17–20 February 2011	Fiera Milano, Italy	109,571 in 2008

Source: UFI, List reviewed on 30 August 2011

last few decades that trade shows have become more efficient and professionally managed through the introduction of better quality control.

In the 1960s and 1970s, the general focus at trade shows changed from *goods transactions* to information and communication. In the 1990s, it shifted back somewhat to a renewed focus on sales, as demand for return on investment increased and more managers started to question whether these events were really worth their cost. Since the early 2000s there has again been an emphasis on *information exchange*, even though harder times over the last few years, since the start of the financial crisis in 2007–2008, have forced companies to focus more on immediate returns. Thus, the question whether trade shows are worthwhile has popped up again, as it repeatedly does at times of crisis (hence, at frequent intervals).

Table 5 Types of fairs/trade shows (see Leitner 1980)

Types of fairs/trade shows	When began	Concept
Exchange fairs	Antiquity	Non-monetary, markets
Goods fairs	Medieval	Monetary, markets
Prototype trade shows	Nineteenth century	Placing orders
Universal expos	Nineteenth century	General exhibition by country
Industry trade shows	Twentieth century	Particular industries, or even industry segments

Studies show that trade show costs, in general, are a good investment (see for instance Gopalakrishna, Lilien, Williams, and Sequeira 1995), especially in the long run (Sharland and Balogh 1996). Others have pointed out that, for trade shows to be financially worthwhile, exhibitors need to become better organized with respect to prospecting and intelligence gathering (O'Hara 1993). That is also very much the refrain in this book, which includes an entire chapter on *trade show intelligence*. Other studies have shown that even though visitors do not buy at a show, or immediately afterwards, the shows nevertheless yield positive effects for *customer purchase intentions* (Smith et al. 2004). This element is seldom taken into consideration when evaluating the effectiveness and costs of trade shows – in part because it is difficult to measure, but also because it is less well understood.

Research suggests that perceptions of the value of trade shows depend on company size. Top management in smaller firms are thought to be more in favour of using trade shows than their counterparts in larger companies (Pitta et al. 2006: 159). Larger companies often feel less certain about the financial benefits of participating in these events, especially in the short term. It is not clear whether that is because their managers are further removed from the actual activity, or because they look at more short-term reports.

What to some people may look like a wasteful and expensive show can be the most cost-effective way of reaching customers and prospects when conducted properly (Pitta et al. ibid.). Industry figures have shown that on average 70 % of trade show attendees plan to buy one or more products displayed at the exhibition, and 75 % actually do so. Ninety-three percent say that trade shows influenced their buying decisions.

Figure 4 shows the breakdown of costs of participating in trade shows.

The numerals in Fig. 4 represent the following categories of cost:

1. Booth hire
2. Energy supply and other basics
3. Booth construction
4. Standard service and communications
5. Transport and handling
6. Personnel and travel costs
7. Other costs

We see that 35 % of costs relate to booth construction. The second largest category is personnel and travel cost. Booth construction costs will depend heavily on how may exhibitions you can attend while re-using the same booth set-up.

Trade Show Costs

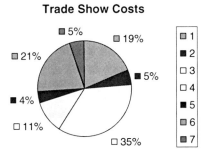

Fig. 4 Trade show costs (From Huckemann et al. (2005: 192)). Compared to costs in the late 1980s, space hire and transport have gone down (by 5 % and 8 % respectively) while exhibition construction has increased considerably (by 12 %). Personnel costs have remained roughly constant. See Siskind (1993: 47)

Normally, a new year will require a new stand, mainly because of the heavy wear to which exhibition equipment is subjected, and to changes in design; but in most cases there will be some parts of the booth which can be re-used – if nothing else, then at least the electrical equipment and whatever you have backstage. The logic of booth design is a bit like the logic for new cars. Each year, customers expect you to come out with something new, something different, to show that you are on the ball (so to speak), that you know what is going on in your industry. If you retain the same booth, then your most enthusiastic followers – the early adopters – and your competitors too will think you are starting to fall behind. Consequently booth design is very much about the signals we are sending out to the market. Whatever we choose to do, it will all be analysed by our competitors as implying something about our current position and future expectations. This was very clear in the case of Samsung a few years ago, as that company was preparing to step up to the position of largest technology company in the world.

It may come as a surprise to the reader to know that companies have always spent a great deal on shows.[17] It seems odd, therefore, that companies have not in the past paid greater attention to the professionalism of these events – to the science of it all. Attending trade shows has instead traditionally been seen as a reward, something like a holiday, for loyal and hard-working employees. Managers would until quite recently typically bring their "favourite people" with them to the trade show to "have a good time". No wonder it was expensive and ineffective! Professional training was practically unheard of. Instead it was normally enough just to show up at the airport.

The competitive climate that most industries find themselves in has changed dramatically over the past two decades. During the Cold War period, many Western companies felt secure about their place in the market, at least for some years into the

---

[17] Chapman (1995) estimates that trade shows accounted for between 16 % and 20 % of marketing budget a decade ago. Today's figure is well over 20 % (Barker 2004).

future. Since then, and especially over the past decade when competition from China has been running at full force, and South Korea and Taiwan have become major high-tech players, it has become very easy for any competitive advantage a firm might possess to be eroded; in some cases that happens over just a few years. In the mobile phone industry, every new product launch is a moment of truth. Companies in that industry can often fail between one financial quarter and the next.

When one reads about the historical development of trade shows and fairs, it is easy to get the impression that they were predominantly a Western phenomenon, initially at least. That is not true. From early times the Arabs had their "souks", the Persians and the Turks their "bazaars", with industry-like divisions; potters in one area of the market, fruit in another, blacksmiths in a third, and so forth. Rural markets have an even longer tradition in China (Skinner 1964). In Europe, the Phoenicians set up fixed markets with regular market dates all along the Mediterranean shores long before the Greeks colonized the area. As with many of the sciences, for instance astronomy and mathematics, we are discovering that the famous achievements of the ancient Greeks were essentially developments drawing on inspirations from the Middle East, India, and China. Much the same is true for the development of trade shows.

On the other hand, the development of the modern trade fair as a *distribution channel* has to a large extent been a German phenomenon. Germany has also played the leading role in the global trade-show industry, even though China has now surpassed Germany in terms of numbers of shows and visitors. For example, Germany houses five of the world's ten biggest trade-fair organizations.[18] Thus, CeBIT (standing for *Centrum der Büro- und Informationstechnik*) is the world's largest IT fair, with 339,000 visitors in 2012 (and 400,000 visitors in 2009), as compared to e.g. 113,000 for CES, the (American) Consumer Electronics Show, for 2009, and 150,000 expected in 2013 (all according to the organizers' own figures).[19] If we consider the 40 largest trade shows which have taken place over the last 5 years, ten of them were German. About 20 % of the world's trade-show capacity, in terms of floor space, is located in Germany. Germany attracts large numbers of foreign exhibitors to their own trade shows, and also exports its shows to other countries, as in the case of CeBIT. In 2008, only around 51.5 % of exhibitors attending trade shows in Germany were companies based within the EU. Out of a total of nearly 250 initiatives supported by the German government in other countries, around 60 % are organized in Asia. This has been a strong trend.

In Europe, in general, there was a downturn of between 5 % and 20 % in the number of trade shows in 2009, but this mainly affected the smaller trade shows.

---

[18] The combined turnover of these organizations was €2.5 billion for the 2003 financial year. They organized between 140 and 150 international trade fairs annually, with about 160,000 exhibitors and nine to ten million visitors.

[19] The author used to audit such trade-show figures while with KPMG in Oslo; hence he is aware that, if organizers wanted to manipulate the numbers, it would not be that hard to do.

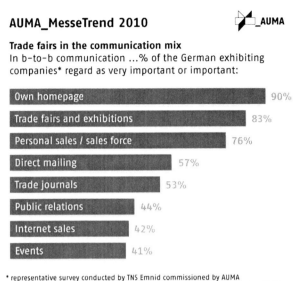

Fig. 5 Trade shows in the communication mix for German companies, 2010

That shows the extent to which it is important to be a major player in this industry, or at least one of the larger shows in one's industry sector, in order to survive. The industry is concentrated in a handful of countries. According to UFI figures, five countries (the USA, Germany, China, Italy, and France) account for 58 % of the world's total of indoor exhibition space.[20] There seems little prospect of the regional shares of total world indoor exhibition space changing greatly in the immediate future. But some countries are likely to increase their exhibition space considerably. In Europe, that will probably be the case in Russia, Spain, and Italy. In Asia, it promises to be the case for China, India, South Korea, and Singapore.

As to the issue of the relative importance of trade shows for marketing, we see from Fig. 5 that among German companies trade shows rank second in the marketing mix, after the construction of company websites, but before personal sales (i.e. sales involving active intervention by a salesperson) and direct mail.

Compared to previous years, we saw a slight downturn in trade show activities in 2010. The number of exhibitors in Germany dropped by 3.5 % from 2008 to 2009. Most alarming was that the number of visitors was down by 8 %. Part of the reason was that trade shows are now competing for attention with other forms of media, in particular with the Internet. People also have far more amusements and distractions today than they had a few years ago, in terms of more numerous television channels (cable, streamed TV) and video games. Domestic exhibitors may feel the same obligation to go to trade shows, but many visitors are finding other uses for their time (Fig. 6).

---

[20] For "UFI", see footnote 1 of the Preface.

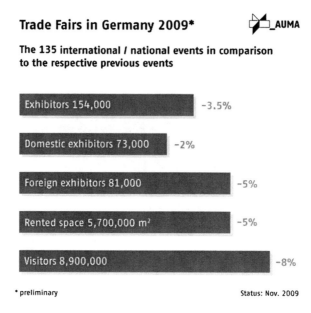

Fig. 6 Trade fairs in Germany, a comparison 2008–2009

Over a 5 year period, we see that there has been no drastic change in visitor numbers; in fact they have been gradually increasing. With international trade shows the increase in visitor numbers has been considerably more marked, especially in Asia; for instance, the number of visitors to fairs abroad run by German organizers increased by 73 % from 2004 to 2008. According to UFI, the number of visitors on average at European trade shows in 2011 was 30,462 (Fig. 7).[21]

Trade shows organized by Germans in Asia have been growing strongly for several years.

The number of events increased by 44 % over the period illustrated above (Fig. 8).

These are important indicators from the world's leading trade-show market for the global trade-show industry. Underlying these figures are growing business contacts between, in particular, Germany and China.

A number of other countries count as major players within this industry. The leading trade-show centres in the world today are Milan, Paris, Birmingham, Zurich/Basel, Vienna, Chicago, Las Vegas, New York, Orlando, Tokyo, Osaka, and Singapore. In the future it is anticipated that more locations will develop in Asian countries (Table 6).

Almost half of the total floor-space capacity at trade shows is located in Europe (48 %). Second comes North America (24 %), closely followed by Asia (20 %). The rest of the world (Africa, Middle East, and South America) accounts for only 8 % of trade-show capacity. There are many reasons for this. In the first place, it is difficult

---

[21] See UFI, 2011 exhibition industry statistics, p. 18.

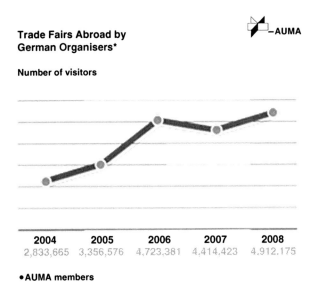

Fig. 7   Trade fairs abroad run by German organizers

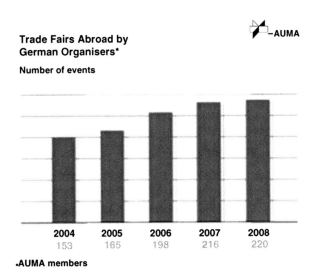

Fig. 8   Trade fairs abroad run by German organizers

to compete with the established trade shows. Once an industry has established a location for its shows, most companies tend to go there each year. As companies do not have unlimited marketing budgets and as time is scarce, they are forced to choose at the most a few meetings per year. In consequence, newly-established trade shows are consistently disfavoured (Fig. 9).

Table 6 World's largest exhibition centres

Exhibition Centers Worldwide 2006

AUMA

Hall Capacities* (gross in m²)

Location	
Hanover	495 265
Milan (Rho Pero)	345 000
Frankfurt/Main	321 754
Cologne	284 000
Düsseldorf	252 214
Valencia	230 837
Paris expo	227 380
Chicago	204 461
Birmingham	200 000
Orlando (Orange County)	190 875
Paris-Nord	190 669
Las Vegas (L.V. Convention Center)	184 456
Bologna	180 000
Munich	180 000
Berlin	160 000
Nuremberg	152 000
Madrid	150 000
Guangzhou (GICEC)	149 200
Bangkok (IMPACT)	140 000
Basle	131 100
Atlanta (GWCC)	130 112
Verona	122 000
Bari	120 000
Houston (Reliant Park)	119 258
Brussels	116 137
Barcelona (Montjuk)	115 000
Milan (City)	115 000
Barcelona (Gran Via M2)	114 000
Bruno	113 544
Poznan	113 100
Essen	110 000
Moscow (WZ)	108 500
Bübao	108 000
Shenzhen (SZCEC)	105 000
Lyon	104 000
Shanghai (SNIEC)	103 500
Geneva	102 470
New Orieans	102 230
London (Earis Court/Olympia)	101 300
Leipzig	101 200
Parma	100 000
Singapore (Expo)	100 000
Utrecht	100 000

Status: 1.1.2006
* with more than 100 000 m² Hallspace
   The figures refer - if not otherwise noted - on the main
   exhibition center in the individual city, not on the total capacity.

Source: AUMA (2008) http://www.auma.de

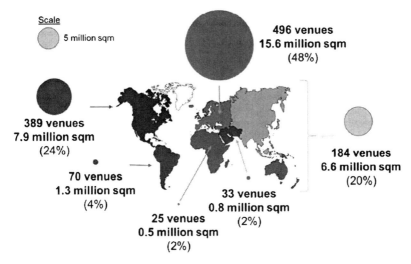

Fig. 9 Venues and indoor exhibition space in 2011 – numbers and capacity (Source: UFI, World map of exhibition venues, December 2011, p. 4)

It may be appropriate to give some further relevant statistics in this Introduction. In Table 4 we show shares of space rented, by industry sectors. The most popular trade shows in terms of square footage hired are "leisure, hobby, and entertainment". This is a consequence of the fact that people have more free time at their disposal and are living longer. The second-largest trade-show category is general, non-specific trade shows, with products from all kinds of industries. That reflects the trend towards seeing trade shows as entertainment in their own right – as giant shopping precincts. Third comes furniture and interior design, an industry which (like the fashion industry in general, indeed) depends on frequent changes in consumer tastes to increase sales (Table 7).

To understand the trade-show industry in more depth, we need to look at the economic logic underlying these activities.

In the first place, trade-show facilities are in essence large areas of real estate. Those who run them can be seen as estate agents. Their aim is to rent out as much space as possible at the highest price. Their decisions about what shows to support depends on the size of the audience expected for particular shows. Nowadays, this business is truly global, since businessmen are no longer hindered by geographical constraints but routinely travel to every corner of the world to attend those trade shows they consider the best in their industry.

Secondly, to draw really large crowds you need participation by the leading players (companies, industry associations) in your industry. These players will only come provided they believe that you can actually attract the largest crowds – that is, larger than those at competing shows. Once initiated, a trade show will attract a large number of smaller players. The bigger the show, the more reluctant any of the parties are to withdraw, and the larger players are sure to come. As the size of our trade show – and thereby also its barriers to entry – continue to increase, it becomes

Table 7 Trade shows by industry sector

Industry sector (UFI code)	Rented space		Number of events
	sqm	%	%
Leisure, Hobby, Entertainment (3)	2914301	13%	312	14%
General (27)	2112045	9%	139	6%
Furniture,Interior design (12)	2023406	9%	148	7%
Construction, Infrastructure(5)	2007775	9%	156	7%
Engineering, Industrial, Manufacturing, Machines, Instruments, Hardware (19)	1943482	9%	141	6%
Agriculture, Forestry, Fishery(1)	1693754	8%	127	6%
Textiles, Apparel, Fashion (25)	1595371	7%	176	8%
Food and Beverage, Hospitality (2)	1307993	6%	179	8%
Transport, Logistics, Maritime (26)	1242149	6%	74	3%
Automobiles, Motorcycles (16)	1022872	5%	70	3%
Premium, Household, Gifts, Toys (13)	967350	4%	52	2%
Health, Medical Equipment (22)	675619	3%	114	5%
Business Services, retail (4)	622019	3%	114	5%
Travel (6)	513074	2%	26	1%
IT and Telecommunications (21)	424059	2%	42	2%
Energy, Oil, Gas (9)	406841	2%	38	2%
Electronics, Components (18)	395266	2%	34	2%
Environmental Protection (10)	381127	2%	46	2%
Education (8)	377257	2%	141	6%
Printing, Packaging (11)	302692	1%	28	1%
Beauty, Cosmetics (14)	222915	1%	28	1%
Jewelry, Watch & Accessories (24)	217336	1%	30	1%
Security, Fire Safety, Defense (7)	211009	less than 1%	28	1%
Real Estate (15)	153000	less than 1%	51	2%
Chemistry (17)	139541	less than 1%	19	less than 1%
Optics (23)	23796	less than 1%	2	less than 1%
Aviation, Aerospace (20)	16748	less than 1%	2	less than 1%

Source: UFI, Euro fair statistics for 2011, p. 4

more difficult for new trade shows to compete with us in our *industry segment*. As we have seen, companies feel they can only be at so many trade shows per year, and they will select the larger ones, sometimes just one or two. This again ensures a considerable degree of stability for the trade show owners, but it also leads to lack of competition in the trade-show industry, and at worst to a sort of monopoly position for the trade-show organizers.

Trade-show organizers also face a number of current challenges. For one thing, globalization tends to favour virtual solutions. Trade shows are by definition closed environments, and many are limited to a local or regional purview, by custom or habit if not by regulations.

To further understand how trade shows work, we need to study each of the actors playing roles in the business. As listed by Morrow (2002: 20), these include:
- Exhibition management organizations
- Exhibition halls

- General service contractors
- Exhibition designers and manufacturers
- Specialist contractors
- Transport services
- Industry-specific publications
- Industry-specific associations

Each of these will be treated in detail in due course in this book.

The initial focus of the book adopts the marketing theory perspective, according to which trade shows are often handled as a *promotional channel*. Exhibitions are physical locations where groups of companies create an opportunity for customers to come and inspect their products. We might say that they are the revenge of *pull marketing*. Push marketing, for instance phone sales, magazine advertising, and television commercials, has become increasingly ineffective as customers have developed a more sceptical attitude towards these channels. People are simply tired of being harassed by salespeople. What began as the novelty of the *travelling salesman* quickly developed into pushy call centres and e-mail spam. As a result, consumers are also becoming increasingly concerned about *privacy* issues.

Exhibitions have much in common with *event marketing*, and the two are often treated together. Event marketing also includes activities like company anniversaries, openings, receptions, and kick-offs. These events are held:

- To create a consciousness and build an image around a company or a product
- To create emotions and enthuse the actors in our business, through activities like get-togethers and incentive events
- To inform and communicate with the actors, through congresses, forums, official statements, symposia, and workshops
- For product communications and sales, for instance through product presentations, promotional events, and all kinds of exhibitions and trade shows

As research on trade shows has developed, especially over the past decade, they are now often considered separately from events as a broader category, even though trade shows are still regarded as one part of what falls under the heading of event marketing. Similarly, only 20 years ago trade shows were treated under the same heading as *tourism*. Today, trade shows and tourism are two separate areas of study, even though they still have much in common as marketing phenomena. For example, many cities seek to develop their trade-show capacities as part of their tourism strategy, in order to attract more visitors to the city. Both areas of study also deal extensively with issues of travel and accommodation.

The distinction between trade shows and tourism is blurred by the fact that some trade shows are more "festival"-like than "sales"-like (we speak of *festival-intensive* versus *sales-intensive* trade shows). In general we can say that the more "festival" aspects there are to an exhibition, the more emphasis will be placed on *corporate identity* and image. Some exhibitions have developed into more of a "show" than others, and the opinion as to how much "show" should be included in an exhibition varies; less for B2B, more for B2C and for entertainment and leisure goods.[22]

If the show element has become more important in recent years this is partly because of an escalation in the use of marketing techniques to secure attention at exhibitions. In an environment where outstanding booths and excellent boothmanship are no longer unusual, the show element becomes another and a necessary way of making your company and your products stand out from the competition. The situation may be compared to the way that, at traditional open-air markets, stallholders would shout their offers out (as still happens today in many smaller markets, for instance in France). If someone on the next stall had a really loud voice, you had to bellow even louder to be heard. When you are really loud, the others have to be louder still, and so it goes on. This vicious circle of attention-grabbing has a number of adverse consequences (as the reader will well understand by now), and we shall discuss these in more detail later in the book. For the customers, the situation becomes hard to tolerate, and it risks ending up by making the company look less serious, especially in the B2B context and in more conservative industries, where the use of rational argument has always been the preferred strategy.

Trade shows can be a powerful marketing tool when correctly used. We will typically see more potential customers over a few days at a show than we will see over a whole year at the office. Shows can be an excellent opportunity for us to demonstrate our products and meet influential people in the industry. If we are attending a major international trade show, the chances are that everyone will be there. This is a place for hands-on demonstrations and for face-to-face conversations. It should not be a place where we simply hand out brochures. After all, we can do that back at home, from our office. If we are new to the business and do not know any of the key players, this will be our chance to begin building a network, to mingle, participate in evening events, and get to know stakeholders better. It is also a chance to get to know what is going on behind the scenes in our industry, behind the highflown rhetoric of the glossy magazines and often quite uninformative newsletters.

Considering all these opportunities, it may come as a surprise to many readers that the study of marketing has largely neglected the topic of trade shows. In its defence, one could point out that marketing as a subject of study is as a whole less than a 100 years old. But over that period the subject has been much more successful in studying other topics; advertising, for instance, despite lack of a theoretical foundation has got off to a far better start as an area of study. Both topics are frequently seen as un-academic, that is, not suited for university-level courses, in part because of lack of theory and rigour. The present author hopes that, in the case of trade shows, this book will persuade sceptical readers otherwise.

In view of its economic importance, the topic of trade shows is an aspect of marketing that has been unjustly neglected. We saw some interest in empirical

---

[22] For instance, Susan Friedman (2005: 17) wants to develop exhibitions as mini-Disney showcases with clowns and magicians, but also as educational seminars.

research on trade shows in the 1970s and 1980s which later faded out (Pitta et al. 2006: 158), but now we are seeing renewed interest, in particular from Asia, as will be apparent from the literature citations in this book.

It is surprising how many people still think that exhibiting is just something you "do" (cf. Walls 1998: 49). Even now, very few employees get any actual training in exhibition marketing, whether at university or in their jobs. Planning is often poor, not to mention the performance and the follow-ups. Previous research show that 83 % of prospects are not called on by company representatives within a 1-year period after the show. Eighty percent of exhibitors never follow up on their leads (Weisgal 1999). Only 29 % of firms that participate in trade shows have evolved specific trade-show objectives, and only half of those actually pursue these objectives (Dallmeyer 1998: 4). These findings are all reasons to insist that exhibitors ought to pay more attention to the theory that already exists.

Research shows that companies who have visited a booth at a trade show purchase more often than those who have not (see e.g. Gopalakrishna et al. 1995). We should remember that not all companies are there to sell. Some are there just to meet people, others simply to show that they are still in business and have not gone bankrupt. In other words, if you do not attend a show, that too sends a signal. To attend you do not necessarily need to have your own booth. Often it will be enough to move around meeting suppliers, media, and stakeholders.

From a macro perspective, trade shows are a major concentration of businesses, media, and customers, all coinciding at a particular place and time. The larger the shows are, the more impact they have on the industry. Thus, they have also become *indicators of seasonal trends* and a *barometer for industrial and economic activity.* If, say, Apple has the most expensive, most elaborate, most heavily-staffed booth at a trade show, people will register that as an indicator. The inference will be that Apple is doing well and is likely to do better still in the year to come. Companies can even exploit this by signalling such a situation to others before it is a reality. This can operate as a self-fulfilling prophecy. That was the case for Samsung at CES 2008. The size of their booth was exaggerated in relation to their market share at the time, but not in relation to their performance in, say, 2010, or today. Signals are not necessarily true. It might be that the company with a bigger and better booth is in fact in trouble, losing market share, and that all its extra spending represents an attempt to get back in the game. In such cases, trade-show expenditure should be seen more as an advertising investment than an accurate reflection of actual performance. However, that kind of misleading signalling is not the general rule. In general, there is usually a correlation between an increase in this year's spending on a trade-show booth and the company's performance, particularly if the company is one which has been around for a number of years.

As we begin in what follows to get into the specifics of trade shows, the first lesson of exhibition marketing will be to understand that trade shows are an integral part of the organization's total marketing efforts, and should be treated accordingly. The potential success of trade show participation is a question of the extent to which a company's activities conform to its overall marketing and exhibition strategy. That is the topic of the first chapter.

"Exhibition organizers and venue managers must have a thorough knowledge of their customers and they must be very close to the industries they serve. We must react rapidly to their changing needs and even be ahead of the curve in providing the tools and services which they'll need to successfully meet their business objectives. This book, Exhibit Marketing and Trade Show Intelligence, will assist all those in the exhibition industry to stay on top of trends and changes as we work to improve our customer's ROI and at the same time strengthen our own bottom line."

Paul Woodward
Managing Director
UFI, the Global Association of the Exhibition Industry

The Exhibit and Event industry has been rapidly expanding over the past several years and offers many global opportunities for a fascinating and rewarding career. Exhibit Marketing & Trade Show Intelligence provides those interested in a career in Exhibit and Event Management a solid foundation on how to become a valuable asset to any organization.

Jim Wurm, Executive Director
Exhibit & Event Marketers Association (E2MA)

Dr. Klaus Solberg Søilen's book is a vital handbook for all marketers who work with exhibitions as a marketing tool. The book provides clear and extremely useful recommendations for actions before, under and after the exhibition has taken place.

Svend Hollensen, author of "Global Marketing"(Pearson) and Associate Professor of International Marketing at the University of Southern Denmark.

Klaus Solberg Søilen is Associate Professor at Halmstad University, Sweden. He is the Editor-in-Chief of the Journal of Intelligence Studies in Business (JISIB) and Senior Editor of the International Journal of Innovation Science (IJIS). He has published half a dozen books and scientific articles for journals like Journal of Business Research, European Business Review and Knowledge Organization. Prior to his academic career he worked for ten years in industry, the last three at KPMG Oslo. He is often invited to speak at international conferences and fairs and has been a consultant to more than 60 companies.

Integrated Marketing Communications (IMC)

1

Trade fairs are more than just a matter of paying for space and showing up at the fair site, participation is a long-drawn-out and often repetitive process. It is a specialism and for some people it is a profession; and, like any other profession, it requires study and planning.

Exhibition management, or exhibition marketing as it is often called, can be regarded as part of the study of marketing and sales. The *exhibition marketing plan* or *trade show plan* is part of your advertising and marketing strategy. Among the various aspects of marketing, we could describe it as the one that is most closely related to the study of *logistics* (which can defined as the flow of resources between points). At exhibitions so much happens, over such a short period of time, involving so many resources, that it is easy to get things wrong if we are not prepared. And yet we learn that (according to research by Dallmeyer 1998) only 29 % of firms that participate in trade shows have developed specific trade-show objectives, and only half of those actually do what their plan specifies. In somewhat sarcastic vein we might say that this is no surprise either, if you wander round a trade show and count the mishaps you spot. Unfortunately, we do not live in an ideal world where everything goes according to plan, and there will always be some things that do not work even with the best plan. But simple observation makes it obvious that, for a majority of companies today, their "plan" can be nothing more than a few points jotted down on a slip of paper not many weeks before the show. That is not planning. Thus, there is a large margin for improvements.

A well-prepared plan should answer both strategic and operational questions. Just how you organize the plan is a matter of individual choice and not something we will cover in this book, where the primary emphasis is on research. On this issue, I suggest you consult any of the step-by-step books mentioned in the Introduction, for instance Christman (1991: 1–49).

When choosing a trade show to exhibit at, make sure the one you pick fits in with your selling season. A good time to exhibit at a trade show is often a few weeks or months ahead of a new product launch. That will give you the chance to test and perhaps modify your product before it is actually launched. In this way, a trade show can be a fantastic *marketing research laboratory*, and an important part of the

K. Solberg Søilen, *Exhibit Marketing and Trade Show Intelligence*,
Management for Professionals, DOI 10.1007/978-3-642-36793-9_1,
© Springer-Verlag Berlin Heidelberg 2013

product development stage, enabling you to set up focus groups and conduct surveys with key people from your industry.

Trade fairs are great places for so-called *tie-ins*. Since booth visitors are busy people, they will have to be given something in return for their time and effort. This issue can be treated as a classic *marketing tie-in*. The idea with a tie-in is to construct a *mini-event* in such a way that everyone involved sees it as a win–win situation and is keen to participate. We use tie-ins when we know (or at least have reason to suspect) that the people we would like to invite would otherwise decline. The tie-in normally involves at least three parties: a customer, a charitable organization, and our company. The booth visitor we would like to induce to fill in our survey or take part in our test is given something of real value for his or her effort, perhaps a nice warm sweater carrying two logos, one for our company or product and the other for the charity. And we may donate a few dollars to the charitable organization in the visitor's name; the sweater will then function as a reminder of a good deed done. In return we can ask for 15 min of the visitor's time, examining our new product and giving us his or her feedback. Often it is not realistic to ask for much more time at a trade show. For a mini-event like this, we also need a small room with a table and chairs. If we have a staff room, we can make sure it is free at certain times in the day and use that. The idea with tie-ins is that we help people to do good by helping us, bringing three or more parties together in a scenario where each party gains something of value. As a marketing tool, a tie-in does not need to cost much, but it is unlikely to come in at less than 8–10 euros (10–13 dollars) per person, including the donation and the giveaway.

Whatever research we do at the booth, it is important that it is co-ordinated with everything else we are doing in the company in terms of *marketing research*: it should blend into our *ongoing research*. It is from ongoing research that we define the research we carry out at the trade show. Bear in mind that there will never be time to do more than collect data at the trade show – and even that will feel hectic. Analysis of the data is done when we come home, as part of the *post-show follow-up*. The results of our ongoing research will in turn influence our future *strategic planning*. All in all, this takes a great deal of work and effort. That is why we need to go to business school to get it right (Fig. 1.1).

As a practical matter, we want our physical booth to be constructed so as to lend itself to multiple uses. But we also need to make sure that it does not become boring and merely functional. That could scare away visitors, who might see our booth as external to or not coherent with the rest of the show. There is a general shift at trade shows nowadays away from *product demonstration* towards *brand management*. The difference between trade shows, *shopping precincts* (which may contain *pop-up stores*), *flagship stores*, and *amusement centres* is gradually disappearing, as we seem to be moving away from trade shows that focus on products, towards service, dialogue, and entertainment (see e.g. Jensen 1999). In this way we might say that trade shows have actually come to resemble parties, often with *VIP entrances* and *VIP rooms*. The ingredients are much the same: the guests, the conversations, the entertainment, the food, the accommodation. We often go to a booth because it is fun, it looks interesting – not because it is "professional": not at B2C trade shows,

Fig. 1.1 A framework for strategic management of exhibition marketing (From Weisgal 1999, reprinted in Pitta et al. 2006: 159)

not these days. As an exhibitor, if you can manage to combine both of these functions, entertainment and professional marketing, you will have come far in the art and science of successful trade-show participation. Even larger companies make blunders in this respect. Some are so focused on the "fun" part that their products or services are scarcely visible. Others leave the visitor confused about what they are actually selling. We shall offer examples of both traps in the mini-cases we shall discuss.

Exhibitions are becoming ever more important for companies, and we might say metaphorically that the software is replacing the hardware. In principle the size of the stand is becoming less important, whereas clever marketing programmes are becoming more important. The demand for *return on investment* (ROI) is being voiced ever more loudly. We discussed this problem at some length in the Introduction, but without giving examples. Earlier research on ROI for trade shows, so called *return on trade show investments* (ROTSI), has shown that it is only the larger distributors which have a positive ROTSI in the short run.[1] They have a positive ROTSI not because they have larger booths, but because they are better organized. In other words, the size of the booth is itself a consequence of better organization. This suggests, then, that an equally high quality of organization would be feasible in a smaller booth. Ultimately it often boils down to a question of how many man-hours you can put into the planning, and of competence levels.

Steve Miller (1999: 16) offers the following quick method of calculating ROTSI:

---

[1] Calculated as Incremental Total Gross Profit less Cost of Exhibiting. See Smith (1998: 110, Table 3).

	Total show hours
×	Total staffers during each hour
=	Total staff hours
×	Number of contacts/hour
=	Total show contacts
×	% of attendees fitting your target market
=	Total number of targets reached
×	Closing %
=	Total number of sales
×	Average size of sale
=	Total sales figure
×	Length of relationship
=	Long-term ROI or ROTSI

Good organization or planning begins very early in the marketing process. We do not start by deciding to exhibit at a particular trade show, but by asking some critical questions:
- What is our target market?
- Which trade show (if any) attracts our potential and current customers?
- How much will it cost?
- Are there better ways of reaching that target market and of spending marketing money than participation in this trade show?

A trade show has three phases, *pre-show*, *at-show*, and *post-show*, each with its own objectives and specific requirements. We ought to spend most of our time on pre-show and post-show work. That means, if a show lasts 4 days, that we should probably spend, at a minimum, about 2 weeks planning it and 2 weeks following it up and drawing conclusions for next year's show, if we want to maximize our potential return. The follow-up part may take as much time for smaller as for larger companies. The at-show stage goes by so quickly that we will scarcely have time to think about what we ought to be doing. While we are at the show, that is it: you roll with what you have got. If you try to make plans during the show to make up for planning that you did not manage beforehand, the chances are that all you will achieve is to miss out on important parts of the actual show, the at-show activities. If it should come to that, then you would do better to adopt some kind of *organic strategy* and go with whatever seems best at the time.

So, what are the most important planning documents for a trade show? There are four:
- The *marketing plan*
- The *exhibition marketing plan*

Table 1.1 The planning documents

Document	What is it?	Provider
(Overall) marketing plan	Strategic plan for all operations	Exhibitor
Exhibition marketing plan	Strategic plan for exhibition	Exhibitor
Exhibition schedule	Tactical plan for exhibition	Exhibitor
Exhibitor manual	Tactical document for all exhibitors	Organizer

- The *exhibition schedule*
- The *exhibitor manual*

Each of these plans has its own specific function. The first three we have to prepare ourselves (Table 1.1).

All the planning documents may be assembled into an *exhibition planning book* or folder and distributed to everyone involved, according to need. Of course today this can all be done electronically, indeed even with a special smartphone app if we wish. In the years to come what is readable on a smartphone will have a better chance of being read, especially when we are on the move, as when we travel to a trade show.

The link between trade shows and marketing is sometimes called *integrated marketing communications* (IMC). As a company, we want to make sure that what we do at the exhibition is thoroughly integrated with the rest of our marketing activities. For instance, we will want to be sure of using the same colours, the same logo, the same design as in all our other communications. Visitors will get confused if they receive one impression of our company and products through television commercials and a different impression at the booth. To make certain that does not happen, we need to check to ensure that all design is co-ordinated. It is shocking to see how many mistakes are made in this area, considering the resources that are allocated to these events. Sometimes the booth will be painted in a slightly different shade from the company colours, or there will be chairs in the booth of an entirely different style, breaking with the overall colour impression and distorting the *company image*. Of course this is often easily explained: the manager was not there when the painter started work, or the painter simply brought the wrong shade of paint with him. The chairs were wrong because we forgot to bring them and had to run out and get some quickly; it was either these chairs, or no chairs at all. A detail, you say? Mistakes like these will often lead today's market-connected visitor or passer-by to feel that something is wrong. People are more sensitive to such details than we often suppose. It is all about consistency, and ultimately about company image.

The *Exhibitor Manual* includes schedules, co-exhibitor information, floor plans of all halls, location and content of services, registration contractors, as well as advertising and promotion. It can be a good exercise to read through the exhibitor manual with all the exhibition staff before going to the event, making sure that everyone can use it and knows how to locate key information (toilets, food, competitors, administration, assistance with electrical supply, etc.). The less time we need to spend on such issues while at the events the better. Being well-prepared will give our visitors the feeling we know the place, that we have been here before; and that will transfer to our business, giving the visitor confidence that we know our business too, even if they are asking us a trivial question like "Excuse me, do you know where I can find a toilet?". The logic is "If you are lost within the trade show, perhaps you are lost within your business as well". This may be a trick of association, but that seems to be the way human beings work.

The overall *Marketing Plan* is written to cover a whole year, and is normally updated once a year. It states the marketing and sales objectives, identifies the target market, specifies the appropriate market segmentation, and lists a number of milestones, one of which should be our exhibition. In exhibition marketing, many of the sales come in the post-show phase, when the company can follow up on the leads they made while they were at the show.

The marketing plan should also tie promotional products in with our strategy – items like bags, badges, pens, umbrellas (excellent products when rain can be expected during the show), memory sticks, cups, and so forth. We should aim to come up with useful items, preferably things that visitors can use while they are at the show, such as a bag, a water bottle, or a pen. It takes time to order and make such items, so we need to plan them well in advance. The function of promotional items is to inform, remind, persuade, and support other company efforts (Table 1.2).

Research shows that 66.3 % of visitors spent no more or less time than average in booths which gave them a promotional product. As many as 21.1 % actually spent less time, and only 12.6 % spent more time. But we also learn that, on average, attendees found the products very useful (5.4 on a Likert scale running from 1 to 7). The product is not what attracts people to a booth or keeps them there, but then that is not what we are mainly trying to achieve with these items. If people came to the booth for the sake of the giveaways, we would probably be attracting them for the wrong reason. A similar point applies to the way promotional products are given. They ought not to be placed in a stack for visitors to take as they please, as they pass by, but so far as possible they should be handed over individually, after conversation, as something to remember us and our generosity by. If you put a bowl of sweets at the entrance, then most likely people helping themselves from it will get in the way of prospects interested in coming into the booth. A bowl inside the booth, though, is a very different matter, preferably one placed in a corner out of sight to passers-by.

Again, the tip is to find promotional products that are meaningful, that say something about the company and what you are doing, and that are useful – ideally, something novel, to show that you are up to date. So you should take time to study the great variety of promotional products offered by different e-stores, or have something made to order for your company. If you are in the sports business you might give a golf ball with your logo on it; if you are in the car industry you could give an ice scraper; more originally, you could give a bottle of wine with your logo on the label if you are in the food business. Well-thought-out gifts tell people that you have made a special effort. The psychological association we are aiming for is for our visitors to think that that is the kind of company we are: not merely fair and generous, but rather smart too.

Take the time also to arrange little competitions between visitors, and also between your booth staff; and give out awards in the form of plaques, badges,

Table 1.2 Results of the use of promotional products at trade shows (Gruben 2003)

Question	Percentage at show	Percentage post-show
Attendees received promotional products while attending a show	62.6 %	
Declined to accept a product	17.5 %	
What products come to mind	Bags: 22 %	Bags: 26.1 %
	Personal/pocket–purse products: 17.3 %	Personal/pocket–purse products: 17.4 %
	Badges, ribbons, stickers, magnets: 12.7 %	Badges, ribbons, stickers, magnets: 4.3 %
	Houseware/tools: 11.6 %	Houseware/tools: 17.4 %
Remember the company that gave product	71.6 %	56.9 %
Found products extremely useful	43.5 %	43.5 %
Plan to use the product	84.7 %	
Company sent pre-show mailing	77.5 %	
Mailing informed about the promotional product	26.9 %	
Type of information received	Contact information: 60.1 %	
	Customer service number: 21.1 %	
	Info on company/services: 18.6 %	
	About products: 11.8 %	
What info accompanied the product	Booklet about products/ services: 40.7 %	
	Booklet about company: 29.7 %	
	Price list: 27.9 %	

diplomas, or statuettes. Specify everything in the *Exhibition Marketing Plan*. The exhibition marketing plan should be no longer than about ten pages. It should be fully integrated into your overall marketing plan. Competitions among staff can be a great way to get to know one another better, to have fun and relax and take one's mind off work for a while. A competition among visitors is a way to keep them remembering us, to keep them coming back, if only to see how they did. Give everyone a prize, even if it is just for participating. The same logic is followed at many dog and cat shows with those rosette award ribbons. They cost next to nothing, but feel like hitting the jackpot.

The *Exhibition Schedule* may be only a few pages long. It is commonly just a timetable showing, hour by hour throughout the period of the show, what is happening that is considered important for our company. It is a timetable for all staff: when to be where, why, and with whom, also possibly what to wear. It should also specify who covers what: who is manning the booth, who is at lunch, who is going to a meeting, who is checking out competitors, etc. Sometimes, a board of some type with a magnetic marker for each staff member will be better than keeping the information on a sheet of paper. That way, others can see at a glance who is where, and it will be easy to set up opportunities. Place the board out of visitors' sight, below the front desk or in a private room. The exhibition schedule may cover pre-show, at-show and post-show activities, but its main focus will be on at-show activities.

As a rule, the fewer plans the better, but you must have plans. You may also need some checklists. Lack of any plan, and failure to appreciate that trade shows are something that must be trained for and must be part of the company strategy, are the main reasons why so many companies feel frustrated with their trade show performance. Let's face it, trade shows are anything but easy; they are complex, exhausting processes. Furthermore, shows can be quite different from one another, making it hard to draw on previous experience. That is always the case for trade shows in different countries, but it can hold even as between regions within one country. Other reasons for failure are that exhibition management sets unrealistic goals, that they do not know how to measure results, that they do not know what to do, and that they spend more on the hardware (booth) than on the software (personnel). A lot of it boils down to lack of training and education: one might say that the most basic reason why trade shows fail is because they are difficult as a marketing activity. We typically underestimate the effort that goes into them, especially the planning effort.

Traditionally, trade-show practitioners have received little help from academics. Academics have often seen it as unimportant to study trade shows in detail, preferring to concern themselves with broader and more general theories of economic behaviour. But that has meant that they have often failed to be useful in practice; this has been a general problem with the study of business for most of the period since the Second World War. A general problem for academics in connection with trade shows is that one cannot make useful theoretical contributions without actually attending shows. In other words, trade shows are not easily studied from behind a desk, with just a dataset and techniques of correlation analysis. Rather, it is an area of study which requires extensive fieldwork. Fortunately for all of us, there has been increasing interest in this kind of research over the past 5–10 years.

Trade shows also concern people outside the marketing department or the marketing field, in top management. For their concerns we have the area of study called *exhibition management*. Exhibition management is a larger and broader topic than exhibition marketing. It includes legal issues and risk management. One special topic relating to trade shows that is included under exhibition management is the topic of contracts, comprising areas such as:

- Exhibition management contracts
- Hotel contracts
- Insurance policies
- Contracts of employment

The risks that have to be considered fall into two groups, the relatively likely and the relatively unlikely (Morrow 2002: 508–511). Among the relatively likely we find:

- Fire
- Labour issues, including trades unions, strikes
- Personal damage and health risks
- Crime, such as theft, robbery, vandalism
  Relatively unlikely are:
- Natural disasters, such as earthquakes, hurricanes, and other forms of extreme weather
- Terrorism (in certain areas of the world, e.g. the Middle East and some African countries)

As an extension of *risk management*, for some trade shows a *crisis management plan* should also be developed. This is intended to answer what-do-we-do-if questions. Most of these issues, however, lie outside the scope of the present book, where the focus is on marketing. (Nevertheless, they need to be mentioned.)

Trade shows do not represent a single form of marketing, but are themselves a mix of different activities, part of what we call *integrated marketing communications* (Kotler 2000: ch. 18).

These activities can be divided into subgroups (Hansen 1999: 2–3):

Behaviour-based:

Information-gathering activities:
The conceptual domain of the information-gathering dimension includes all activities related to the collection of information about competitors, customers, industry trends, and new products at the trade show.

Image-building activities:
The conceptual domain of the image-building dimension includes all activities related to building corporate image and reputation at the trade show.

Motivational activities:
The conceptual domain of the motivation dimension includes all activities related to maintaining and enhancing the motivation of company employees and of customers.

Relationship-building activities:
The conceptual domain of the relationship-building dimension includes all activities related to maintaining and developing relationships with established customers and establishing relationships with new customers.

Outcome-based:

Sales-related activities:
The conceptual domain of the sales-related dimension includes all activities related to on-site sales and sales immediately following the trade show.

Trade shows usually include advertising, direct marketing (mail, phone, e-mail), public relations, sales promotion (short-term incentives), and relationship marketing, or personal selling. Conducting a successful trade show means finding the right mix of these different activities. Take advertising as an example: we may want to consider advertising in the trade-show publication(s), at the airport, at the hotel, in local taxis, along the route from major hotels to the trade show (on fixed or mobile hoardings), in local newspapers, in trade magazines and journals. If so, all these advertising efforts must be integrated with the trade show, and they must be co-ordinated with the rest of the company's advertising. The same goes for direct marketing, public relations, and sales promotion.

Mobile ads can have a great effect at trade shows. When you get off your plane you will find them in the airport, on hoardings along the route from airport to hotel, inside and on the outside of taxis, in the sky on hot-air balloons and banners towed by small propeller planes. *Aerial advertising* can be very effective if you succeed in dominating the sky above the fair site.[2] Or we can simply have people walking around dressed up in the company logos or in amusing costumes. Cute or funny costumes break the ice. No-one can resist the temptation to accept a flyer from a person in an elaborate rabbit costume. Some companies employ penniless street people to hand out company brochures. It is highly questionable whether this creates good PR for a company, if it is obvious that the people employed are miserable. Most visitors feel sorry for them, and see them as exploited. That affects the company image negatively. It is better to pay happy-looking students to do the job properly. Be aware also, that if everyone else is using balloons too, then the idea is no longer a smart one. I have seen the sky filled with a crowd of balloons so numerous that the only impression was of a gigantic air balloon party; no-one was likely to register the individual logos on the balloons, because there were just too many of them. A spectacular idea is often spectacular only provided that no-one else is using it.

1.1   Event Marketing

Trade shows are part of what we call *event marketing*, or "time-based events", which covers everything from sports events to company celebrations. From the perspective of top management the area is sometimes referred to as *event management*, and often involves requirements for decision-making in special areas such as fairs, festivals, conferences, sports events, and tourism.

Event marketing activities are to a large extent a logistic challenge: large amounts of resources are assembled for a short period of time, which demands considerable planning and specialized skills. Events are attempts to link corporate messages to useful information, fun, and positive feelings. They are seen as the boosters and jet engines of the marketing trade. When used properly they can speed up the sales process. As such, they can never function well alone, but have to be followed up with other, more regular marketing activities, the sorts of things we do in the marketing department all year when we are not at events.

---

[2] Further special products would include skywriting or helicopter advertising, or one can put on a show with skydivers.

The reason we put on events is that people do not enjoy merely receiving information. People have also tended, in general, to become increasingly bored with existing types of meeting as they are presented with more and more invitations. A catalogue is easily forgotten and thrown away; but a show, an experience, is not.

Event services are often outsourced. This depends on the nature of the event and on what we are able to do ourselves as a company. For many companies, it is easy to outsource events, say balloon trips at a fair or a dragon-boat race, because they require little knowledge about the company and the industry. By contrast, the core activities of the trade show usually require deep knowledge of the company, its products, and the relevant industry; this is especially true for B2B shows. Thus, another reason why we might choose to outsource can be that we need our existing company resources for other activities. Each to his own, as it were; we do what we are best at. Events are often a specialism, just as advertising is, and as such they are often entrusted to those who specialize in events. It may also be a matter of cost. To return to a previous example, a well-made rabbit costume does not come cheap. Since the rabbit does not have to say much, but is mainly used to distribute information, perhaps in the form of flyers, or to wave a sign, this may be an activity that can be outsourced. A demonstration of a technical product, however, cannot be.

Most people in our company who get involved with trade shows will have other assignments for most of the year; for instance, if it is the marketing people who attend shows, or even more obviously if it is technical staff from R&D, then trade-show activities will be a minor part of their total duties. Only the largest companies, most of which are multinationals, can afford to have people working all year round just on exhibitions, and even in those companies this is not common. Sometimes it can even be a disadvantage to spend too much of one's working time on trade shows; one can find staff losing touch with what is actually going on in marketing overall, or in production, and starting to operate as though the shows are the reference-point for all the company's other activities. They are not; there are many other ways to sell. At B2B shows you will often want the actual engineers who created the product to be there, to give expert answers to questions. They cannot easily be replaced by trade-show specialists.

Trade-show activities can also be seen as part of *sales* and of what the *sales department* does. Selling objectives are becoming ever more important at trade shows, as public companies are pressed by their shareholders to deliver more short-term results because of increased competition.

The first mechanism to understand in an analysis of sales at trade Shows is the relationship between direct contacts, leads, and sales.

The model of Fig. 1.2 is a general one. It is impossible to put a precise figure on how high the conversion rate of leads into sales needs to be in all cases, because this will depend on the industry, the product, and the individual company. What we can say is that, for most companies, the proportions of contacts to leads and of leads to sales resemble something like a funnel, as portrayed in the figure. Hence the model can be useful to illustrate a general idea.

A rule of thumb suggests that you need 20 contacts per sale. The model suggests that the ratios of contacts to leads even at trade shows are much less extreme,

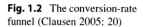 **Fig. 1.2** The conversion-rate funnel (Clausen 2005: 20)

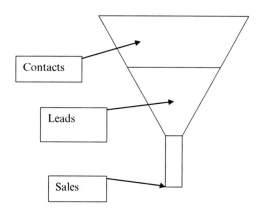

perhaps on the order of 2:1 or 3:1. Each company should set its own goals, depending on its own particular situation, and should define its goals in terms of contacts, leads, and sales. This then makes it much easier to discuss what went wrong afterwards, and to analyse why one underperformed (if that is what happened).

As we get down to work, we shall undoubtedly need to generate a set of good leads, or a "lead sheet". We ought not to rely on our memory here, but need to build up some type of list of potential customers. Don't try to press people to add their names to your list. If you do that, all you will have achieved is to generate a list in which some names are good leads but others are poor leads. In order to distinguish the most promising leads from those who seem less keen, you might use some symbol by their name. If you use a number, the lead may ask what it represents, and you might not want to explain that they are a "hot lead". You could also note when would be the best time to contact the visitor, what he was promised in the follow-up conversation, and details on what he was looking for in the product. Then when we get back to the lead we can provide him with better information. If the visitor receives all the information he was looking for, the chances are that he will be impressed. He will feel that you remember him.

Before getting involved with all the detailed considerations in this book, it is worth asking yourself if you really need to have a booth in order to attain your objectives at a trade show. For many companies, the most important thing is just to meet key players in their industry. That can easily be done by hiring a conference room rather than having one's own booth. Some companies will have a specialist *meeting planner* at the show, or they may send just a meeting planner rather than setting up a whole booth. The meeting planner may be an internal person or a consultant from outside. Having a meeting planner can be of particular help when one is dealing with a different culture, as for instance in the case of a Western company in China. Many Chinese companies will not meet you at first, simply because they do not know you. This is basically a question of trust and culture.

For most exhibitors, it will be natural to define two kinds of objectives: *selling* and *non-selling*. Non-selling objectives include relationship building with key players, exhibition intelligence, brand building, and product testing.

The following chapter takes us a step further in our understanding of what trade shows are, by identifying the most effective exhibitor behaviour at a trade show.

People-at-the-booth skills is an area of exhibition management which has been seriously neglected both in theory and in practice. Research by Susan Friedman (2004: 23) shows that half of all companies say they provide training only immediately prior to an exhibition. At the same time, there are significant differences among companies' lists of dos and don'ts (Pitta et al. 2006: 162). Research also suggests (Tanner 1994) that booth staff training is inefficient. Another finding suggests that current training leaves a great deal to be desired, which comes to much the same. In other words, this is an area with great potential for improvement.

Research also show that much current formal training functions so as to reduce contact time between booth staff and visitors, but does not lead to higher sales. That could be because training often focuses mainly on technical aspects of products rather than on relational aspects. Booth staff are often unable to distinguish between visitors who are seeking to buy the product and those who have come to the booth for other reasons. Or, putting it another way, the trainers themselves do not always understand the complexity of booth staff behaviour.

Ordinary sales training does not offer much help to those who staff exhibition booths. Booth staff have to practise two kinds of behaviour, selling and non-selling/promotional, and they need to be able to distinguish between a number of different types of agent with different needs. These are things that ordinary sales training does not cover. They imply that the company should have at least two sets of objectives: one for its selling and one for its non-selling activities.

A trade show is a performance. And, as in show business, many performers, especially the less well-prepared, tend to forget what they have learned once the stage lights are switched on. Putting it differently, a problem for exhibitors is that booth staff do not always seem to behave as they are trained to behave. This type of *boothmanship failure* has been confirmed by research (Tanner 1995: 257–264). A leading reason for this failure is that booth staff are seldom allowed time for practice. Instead, they are put in the position of actors who are asked to read a script at home and then go straight on stage to perform. There is another major difference between the two situations. In a theatre there is only one stage; at a trade show there are multiple stages, each requiring the playing of a specific role.

K. Solberg Søilen, *Exhibit Marketing and Trade Show Intelligence*, 15
Management for Professionals, DOI 10.1007/978-3-642-36793-9_2,
© Springer-Verlag Berlin Heidelberg 2013

Table 2.1 The five different stages on which trade-show staff perform

Location	Behaviour	Dress code	Identity and description
In booth	Active verbally	High profile, professional	Employee, sincere
In aisles	Active physically	Low-profile marketing promotion	A "fan", informative, humorous
In others' booths	Passive, observing	Blend in	A stranger or a representative of your own company, neutral
Social event (either at show or hotel)	Active physically and verbally	Dress up	A possible partner, congenial and trustworthy
Outside	Active verbally	High profile, professional	Serious, performing a survey, engaging in events marketing, etc.

There is the in-booth role, and a number of out-of-booth roles. When we are out of the booth, sometimes we are working in the aisles, or we may be at a conference or an oral presentation, or carrying out a survey, or we may be busy away from the trade fair arena, for instance at the hotel. Each individual location represents a different project with a different environment demanding different roles. In view of this complexity, it is no wonder that things do not always go as planned (Table 2.1).

Each location is associated with particular objectives, and these require the appropriate behaviour and dress code.

Visitors to a trade show, otherwise known as *attendees*, are often divided into *qualified attendees*, describing people who have a real business reason to be at the trade show, and *non-qualified attendees*. There will always be some attendees who are there as husbands, wives, friends, or children of *qualified attendees*.

Most of the contents of this book concerns behaviour within the booth, but we will also talk about the other "stages" here. Walking up and down the aisles, you have plenty of opportunity to do some discreet marketing on your employer's behalf. However, if you overdo promotional activity in the aisles, this is likely to create negative reactions on the part of organizers and/or other exhibitors. It might also conflict with exhibition policies, and end up in negative publicity for your company. That said, you might want to use the opportunity to attract attention to your booth and your products in a tactful way. For instance, while walking around the aisles, you could wear a T-shirt with a joky message saying "Visit *XYZ* and get this T-shirt for free", or "Find me at *XYZ* when I've finished lunch". Humour is in short supply at trade shows. Everyone is too busy being serious, to the point of being constantly on edge. So humour offers a form of relief. And in that way it becomes good marketing too.

Do not enter other companies' booths while wearing your promotional clothing. If you enter a competitor's booth, make sure you have taken off any kit that explicitly advertises your own company. Not to do that is considered bad form, and may offend both your fellow exhibitors and attendees. We do not market ourselves inside others' booths, at least not overtly. Wearing a company pin is OK. So is carrying a company bag with a discreet logo.

This does not mean that you cannot visit your competitors' booths. When you are asked where you come from, it is considered good form to be open. Frankness may give you a benefit, perhaps a chance to make new friends, or at least get a smile and break the ice that goes with being a competitor. In general we tend to think that we are always in competition, yet research shows that this mentality is not advantageous for business. Co-operation is often the best strategy for a long-term competitive advantage between competing organizations.[1] This fact is often neglected. The best competitors, like the best winners, make non-enemies (as Chinese military strategists reminded us long ago).

Others, admittedly, will prefer to be strangers when they visit competitors' booths; they will claim that they are from somewhere else, in order to avoid embarrassing questions or just in order to be left alone. This is as much a cultural as a personal question.

At social events, work to make sure that your visitors have a good time. You do not have to be selling the whole time, at least not directly. Sometimes the best way of selling a product is not to seem to be selling at all. Some of the best salespeople are those who are able to show genuine empathy and understanding, who know the art of listening. We buy from them because we like them, because we want to do them a favour, as it were. This is not an attitude or ability that can easily be faked, especially not over a period. Rather, by selling the social event, you are also selling your products. At the social event, you are showing your visitors that you are just like everyone else, that you know how to enjoy yourself and that you are a sociable and likeable person. That is a good way of building relationships. It is also a good way to do business, both in the East and in the West.

The focus on relationship building has been reinvented and theorized within what is sometimes called the Nordic school of marketing. There may be said to be two approaches to marketing, the first being the *instrumental approach*, associated with Philip Kotler and the Anglo-Saxon school of marketing. The second is the *relational approach*, associated with Evert Gummesson and the Nordic school. The first sees marketing as a function of a number of objective variables, notably product, price, place, and promotion. According to this view, a marketing initiative is a question of finding the right mix among these factors, the "Four P's". The second approach sees marketing first of all as relationship building. The logic is that by building relationships, you develop trust. Where there is trust, the product will be of good quality and the price will be competitive, because you do not want to break the trust. In other words, you are not going to sell a poor product at a high price to someone you have built a relationship with.

How, then, do we ensure good relationships at a trade show? One model, suggested by Li (2006: 168), specifies the "relationship properties", going into

---

[1] The flipside of this is formation of cartels. This term refers to cases where competitors collude to fix prices to the disadvantage of their customers, which is illegal.

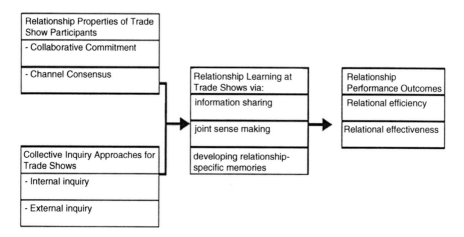

Fig. 2.1 Developing relationship learning outcomes

the show, and "relationship learning", at the show, to give the relationship learning outcomes (Fig. 2.1):

The initial properties include collaborative commitment and channel consensus. There are two approaches to information gathering at this stage: internal enquiries and external enquiries. Learning at the trade show consists of information sharing, joint sense making, and investment in the development of relationships. The final outcome can be defined in terms of relational efficiency and relational effectiveness.

At trade shows, there are a number of types of social event to choose from; at most, such as cocktail parties or buffets, participants stand rather than sit. Stand-up get-togethers enable people to circulate more easily and get to know more people. But do bear in mind that, if you have a stand-up buffet, you also need stand-up food and tableware, for instance holders for a glass that attach to a plate with a clip (and don't fall off). When you plan catering, you may need to reckon on providing staff to serve food and other staff to clear plates. The former help visitors so that they do not have to abandon a conversation in order to serve themselves more food. The latter help to keep the place tidy, and they support the logistics involved in the whole process from ordering the food to taking everything away.

If you serve elaborate food for a stand-up buffet, then your guests have to find a place to sit down to eat. The practical reality is that it can be quite difficult just to balance a plate and glass at the same time, especially late in the evening of a long day. Therefore, if you are going to have stand-up food, the best solution (if you can afford it) is to have waiters walking round serving items from separate serving-dishes. Then you need only hold whatever you are eating at the moment (and your glass, if it is not clipped to your plate). By employing waiters, you avoid breaking up interesting conversations when visitors go to fetch more to drink or eat. Of course, ultimately the solution you choose will often be dictated by budget.

You may want to hire a suite in a hotel or at a conference centre for these activities. People expect social events to be held in locations with a certain style, since they come primarily for the ambiance, rather than for the food and drink. Also remember, social events are not parties: they are less about drinking than about mingling. If you want to arrange a party, do so afterwards. Also, social events do not actually have to take place during the trade show period. They can take place earlier or later, too. Some of the more expensive social events involve cruises or trips abroad. These are best held after a show, perhaps as a prize for a competition run during the days of the show.

A word about dress code: make certain that your dress code is specific. That is, all staff should wear the same easily-recognizable clothing. It must be possible for visitors to see who is working in the booth and who is just visiting. In other words, visitors ought not to have to spend time puzzling out who the staff are. Too often during a show we hear people at a booth asking "Do you work here?", or feeling surprised when someone comes up to them saying "Can I help you?". If the staff had worn easily-recognizable clothing, these problems would be eliminated. We would have known who was who in advance. If you need to turn round and search for some identifying feature on staff clothing in order to confirm that a person is actually working for the company you are trying to contact, then you are wasting time and getting entangled in unnecessary confusion. If a visitor looks round and cannot find any staff (whether because there are none there or because they are not immediately recognizable), the chances are that he or she either will not come into the booth in the first place, or else will leave the booth after walking around for a while without getting his or her questions answered – which is even more frustrating. Many visitors will look for the booth staff first, before walking in. If they cannot see the staff, the chances are that they will walk on past. To avoid this happening, all staff should be readily identifiable – even from outside the booth, if possible (sometimes walls make it impossible). If we can see, from outside a booth, the things we want to examine and the people we could talk to about them, the likelihood is that we will enter more booths, with more determination and confidence.

You ought to look professional. That means different things in different industries. As a general rule, if you dress too formally you are likely to scare people off (unless it is a bankers' exhibition). If you dress too casually, people will probably not take you seriously (unless it is an exhibition for surfers). The specific dress code will depend on the type of exhibition and on the clothing norms in vogue at the time.

Dress according to current fashion, or simply wear classic clothes. Dressing fashionably shows people that you are up to date and understand your own generation and era, but don't overdo it. Dressing fashionably tends to inspire confidence. If you overdo it, it makes you look as if you spend more time on your clothing and appearance than on your work and your products – which will be more of a problem in some industries than others. Don't dress in a style associated with some earlier period (unless you are at an art exhibition). Exhibitions are not nostalgia parties. You are not there to draw attention to your clothing. Many people recommend a

Table 2.2 Dress codes

Location	Low profile	High profile
In booth	Shirt (and jacket)	Suit and tie
In the aisles	Casual	Formal shirt
At a social event	Shirt and jacket	Dinner jacket

two-piece suit for men and a suit or a dress for women. It is commonly said that most colours are acceptable so long as they are not too striking. On the whole people aim to wear relatively neutral or low-key colours. It goes without saying, of course, that clothing should be clean and tidy. At the same time, you may want to have something which clearly identifies you as an exhibitor while at your booth. In some cases, a clearly displayed badge will do, but you could also consider dressing alike, as discussed earlier (Table 2.2).

Dress codes at exhibitions are not a matter of individual choice, but rather a collective decision, in the same way that your booth staff are a team, which will be judged as a unit. At all sites, the principles of uniformity and simplicity should be respected.

Visitors gain their first impressions not only from your clothes, but also your facial expression. Be the first to smile. A smile is the best invitation to a conversation. When someone looks friendly, we want to walk up to that person and exchange a few words. Don't wait for the other person to make the first move, and above all, don't look unapproachable.

Eating is of course taboo within the booth. It not only looks unprofessional and messy, but it also suggests that you have more important things to do than talk to visitors.

If you sit eating in an adjacent room, close the door. All doors to private areas should be kept closed. Seeing "behind the scenes" gives a passer-by a strange peeping-tom feeling, and it is seldom positive. It is not that, as visitors, we walk round trying to peer in everywhere, but an open door is an automatic invitation to curiosity and we cannot help looking. By keeping doors closed, we help passers-by to avoid distractions. If there is a meeting behind closed doors, put something on the door to say so. A clock is also a good thing to put on the door, something to show when the meeting will be over. Or one could use, for instance, a sign with a timetable of vacant slots. That way you avoid having people knocking on doors and opening them when you are busy.

When staff are not working there is an excellent opportunity to do some *discreet marketing*. Rather than lunching behind closed doors, staff could walk around, or sit somewhere where visitors are passing, in promotional costume. If your clothing shows what booth you belong to, that will draw attention to your booth. Thus, you might have a T-shirt saying "I belong to the *XYZ* booth" and featuring a humorous design or cartoon. That way you might even get one of those rare smiles we need so badly at a place like a trade show. Don't make promotional clothing too complicated. Passers-by do not have the time, or the energy, to figure out what you are all about. Trade shows are not the place for quizzes.

Avoid filling the booth with too many company representatives and friends.[2] A show is not your own private social event. Don't tell friends that they can stop by. The same rules apply here as in the office. You don't invite friends to drop in. If necessary, you meet away from the booth, and preferably away from the conference halls. As trade shows are events which are very compressed in terms of time, you will probably have very little free time available to see friends or to walk far. It is best to think of trade shows as 24-h working days. And if they are seen in that light, then the work should be remunerated accordingly, with the appropriate number of overtime hours allocated in the budget.

The stress involved in trade-show activities can be overwhelming. That stress arises from several factors, which include working at *hyper-speed* and in an *uncontrolled area* over an extended period of time. Steve Miller (1999: xi) may have expressed this best, when he chose to start his book with the following story:

> I worked my first trade show 30 years ago. I hated it. I was surrounded by thousands of attendees, exhibit staffers, media, and guests – all of them strangers. I was out of my comfort zone and needless to say, didn't do a good job of working the show. I developed a negative attitude about the show, which, happily for me, was shared by almost every other salesperson I met.

And there is something of a paradox here. Because the environment is stressful, companies and exhibitors often present their worst side to the public when they are in the presence of their best sales opportunities. The professional approach here is not to deny the stressful situation, but to find ways of dealing with it. As the reader will have gathered by now, the solution offered in this book is planning. Planning is also, often, what separates a salesperson from a marketing professional, and it is what we expect from someone who has studied marketing at university or at a business school. Successful planning is a combination of marketing education and experience, since it will take more than one show to get it right.

Trade shows are almost always overwhelming, especially if we are there for the first time. Consequently there is a real need to understand how to cope with them. The best way to do this is to prepare ourselves in advance, by finding out as much as we can before we travel to the show and by a debriefing after the show. Part of what we gain from all this is gathering of experience and developing techniques that will stand us in good stead next time round.

One of these techniques is to find time to relax in between meetings and activities. Make sure that you find a quiet place to stay overnight, well away from traffic noise and excessive social events. Bring earplugs and a blindfold. You don't want to ruin your next day through poor sleep. One team member's failure to get a good night's sleep represents a planning failure for the entire team. To maintain mental and physical tone there need to be occasional chances to at least get some fresh air during the day, and to get out of the conference hall if only for a few minutes. If you can do some physical exercise, so much the better. Some larger

---

[2] Luckily, the number of entrance passes for staff is often rationed by the show organizers.

booths will have a small couch in the private room where staff can lie down for a few minutes. A weary exhibitor is less helpful and valuable as a conversational partner representing his or her company.

To be a valuable member of booth staff, we also need to practise how to recognize and handle the various kinds of visitor who come to our booth. This is the next topic to discuss.

2.1   Various Participants at a Trade Show

Exhibition attendees can be divided into a number of categories. Thus, we have:
- Exhibitors (sellers)
- Visitors (buyers and people of influence)
- Suppliers
- Show organizers
- People of influence (including industry analysts, representatives of industry associations, and policy makers/regulators)

The exhibitor must make sure he has the personnel to fulfil the needs of all the various expected attendees. *Visitors* are there to buy, gather information, or assess products. *Suppliers* are there to see if they can sell you something. *Show organizers* may be there to make sure everything is running properly, *industry analysts* may be there to gather information for a report, *industry associates* to see what they can do for you as a member, and *policy makers* to listen to your opinion about an issue. To approach all of them in the role of a salesperson will be directly counterproductive, and may risk offending some of them. Therefore, begin the encounter by finding out what category of person you have in front of you. Then try to understand what they need and what they may bring to your organization.

To make the picture even more complicated buyers are not all alike. There are:
- Current buyers
- Potential buyers
- Non-buyers

Each of them has his own particular motives and needs. Even more complicated: there is often not just a single buyer, but a whole group of people – sometimes referred to as the "buying centre" – whose members all have influence on the purchasing decision, though to different extents. This is particularly relevant in a business-to-business context. Identifying this group, its members, and their *relative weight* in the purchasing decision is a major challenge for the selling team. The larger and more expensive the products we are selling, the more effort should be devoted to this identification and mapping task. The problem is that the more influential members of the team will often not disclose who they are. Sometimes they will have job titles which allow you to guess their relative importance, but not always. And you cannot normally phone the company and ask. They will not tell you, because they do not want you to be aware of who decides what. Rather, they want the upper hand in negotiations, and they will be afraid that if you knew these things, you might be less than frank, or too well prepared (which in some cases may actually amount to the same thing).

So you have to guess, by listening to what the visitors say and how they react to one another's comments and behave towards each other (if they arrive as a group). Sometimes they will arrive individually, or only two at a time.

If there are many potential suppliers, a purchasing team can decide to begin by splitting up and sending a few people to their various booths, mostly to save time. Then they will consult with each other in a neutral location. If some particular supplier is interesting, they may come back to that supplier, often with different members of the same team. On the whole, the larger the size of potential orders, the larger the buying team is likely to be. If the same members of a large team come back, that may be in order to confirm details, or check information. If different members of the team come back, this can be to get a second opinion about something that the first group found interesting. This means that as a member of the booth staff it is not worth your while to speculate too much (situations like these can test your patience to a mind-blowing extent). It is normally OK to ask discreet questions about the purchasing centre. "When are they looking to make a decision, do you know?"; "When are the goods for, or to be delivered?"; "How does a purchasing process typically run in your company?". Visitors who are too secretive and do not want to answer any questions normally arouse justifiable suspicion.

During a conversation with a potential buyer – who is saying all the right things to encourage you to think he could be a strong lead – you might ask how many people from his company or organization there are at the show. What departments are they from? Who would be making the purchasing decision? As we become better acquainted, we can ask more. Sometimes we find that the person in question has just come along for the trip. That does not mean that we should treat him or her with any less politeness, but it does limit the time we can spend with that person. Note also that, even in such a case, we do not know what influence the person may have on the actual decision-maker. He may be her husband. Husbands and wives, who sometimes go along on trips like these, can have a great deal of indirect influence on purchasing decisions, if they are knowledgeable about the business. To bring the conversation to an end politely and move on to other visitors, we might say "Have a look round, if you'd like to", or "Let me know if I can be any more help".

At every trade show, there will be booths that are packed with visitors and other booths with hardly any visitors at all. If your booth is in the latter category, you do not have any problem with time scarcity. In that case, you might rather want to try to keep each visitor as long as possible, simply to make your organization or products look popular. No one likes going into an empty booth. It makes us feel a bit uncertain: "maybe there is something wrong with this booth or the people in it". Or, "this company must be a failure if there is no one there". To avoid this, we might even ask a staff member to change clothes and play the role of a visitor for a while, even though that is not an easy thing to carry off. Unfortunately, many members of booth teams fall for the temptation of using the time to talk among themselves while there are no visitors in the booth. That is a serious mistake.

Table 2.3 Types of leads

	Strong	Average
Direct	Strong direct	Average direct
Indirect	Strong indirect	Average indirect

It makes us look not just inaccessible, but unprofessional. In a well-organized booth, all important questions and discussions among staff are sorted out in advance or behind closed doors. For minor messages, booth staff can send or leave brief messages behind the main reception desk at the booth – preferably not via text message, because that again risks making us look unavailable (switch the sound off, at least). Set up a system of sticky notes or a notebook lying somewhere accessible, out of sight of visitors, but visible to the booth staff. That way, visitors are not aware of the communications at all, but the problems and issues that are bound to come up can be resolved nevertheless.

A few words on leads are needed, too. Leads are not all the same, and they must be distinguished with respect to quality. For one thing there are *non-leads*, *leads*, and *strong leads*. Secondly there are *direct leads* and *indirect leads*. An indirect lead means that the person is a member of the buying centre, but not the actual decision-maker (Table 2.3).

A strong indirect lead will guide you directly to the decision-maker. At the next stage this decision-maker may turn out to be either a strong or an ordinary lead. An *average indirect lead* will need to be worked on before you can hope to know if a sale is on the cards.

The classification of leads will help you prioritize once you are back from the show. It will also help you select who among your staff should make contact with whom. As a general rule, the one who made the initial contact should also be the one following up the lead once back from the show, but there are various exceptions to that. These include examples of situations when it became clear during the initial conversation that the personal chemistry with a particular visitor was poor, or that the staff member was not able to answer all (technical or other) questions. In these cases it would be advisable to change contact person for the follow-up.

Trade shows are not only about selling, they are also about building and maintaining networks. A large share of visitors to your booth are likely to be non-buyers. As we have seen, this does not mean that they are unimportant. As one example, *suppliers* are non-buyers who may give you a good price on future deliveries, for instance if invited to social events. *Show organizers* could be potential buyers of a number of products, and they are in a position to make your future trade-show arrangements smoother. *People of influence* may write articles or change market conditions for you in a way that enables you to increase your sales figures in the long run. A potential sponsor may walk past and decide to support your efforts. By classifying each visitor you are able to optimize all your trade-show efforts and adapt your communications accordingly.

Sales are important here and now, but good public relations will influence your sales in the future. Thus, we must distinguish between the *short-term "tactical" goals* for the trade show, and the *long-term "strategic" goals* of our company. Unfortunately, tactical goals tend to dominate our thinking as managers. As competition increases, the pressure on short-term results is also bound to increase, especially in smaller and some medium-size companies which have to struggle just to survive, but also in larger companies, particularly public ones whose management are forced to prioritize quarterly results in order to satisfy shareholders' requests for immediate or short-term return on investment. Companies that are trapped in short-term thinking rarely survive for more than a decade. They are reactive, simply running the line out, squeezing the market for maximum profit here and now. As such, they will not be able to adapt to change for long, whether changes consist of new technology (*inventions*), or just better, cleverer ways of satisfying existing needs (*innovations*).

Screening visitors is an unavoidable process at any show, in view of the limited resources and time at our disposal. At the same time, it is one of the most significant and potentially most damaging activities we carry out at the show. Ultimately, screening will depend on a combination of constraints: numbers of visitors, their relative interest in our products, the number of our staff and the size of our booth, and our capacity to handle the visitors who arrive. If we have a popular product but do not allocate the resources needed to meet our potential customers, then we are going to damage ourselves. Failure to interact with our visitors, or interacting with them poorly, will turn potential customers away.

Many salespeople believe that they can spot a customer a long way off, just by sight. For instance, some exhibitors will think that because a given person is introverted in personality, he cannot be a major decision-maker. Such prejudices are potentially very dangerous. The introverted person, especially in a B2B context, might be a leading technical engineer who has most of the say within his buying centre. Many chief executives of high-tech companies dress extra-casually, in part because this may be the norm in their industry, in part because they have nothing to prove by dressing up, and perhaps also because they enjoy the contrast as a personal trademark. Hence we would do well to allow for the few minutes of active conversation it takes to detect what a visitor's real motives are, before we jump to conclusions.

Motives can also change during the conversation, or they may be mixed or confusing; for instance, a visitor may discover that he has a need for a product he was not thinking about before he entered our booth. Thus, what was a rather uninteresting customer at first glance could turn out to be a strong lead, without any of us including the visitor himself knowing that in advance. A savvy exhibitor therefore will be one who not only knows how to classify different motives, but also how to awaken them. That is particularly true in the B2C context, where emotions play a larger role.

When we have found a strong lead, we shall want to take our visitor to a suitable quiet area in the booth so as to be able to focus better on that person and avoid interruptions. Therefore, be sure always to have a quiet corner in your booth. A noisy booth environment can lose you your customer simply because he or she does not feel comfortable. It could be that you both suppose you will be able to talk to each other later, at some other point during the show; but the opportunity may never arise a second time, since there are so many other distractions at the show and the time goes by so fast. We may also find it difficult to remember all the contacts we need to follow up, unless they were ones of which we made a special note. Or the visitor will forget about contacting us.

Simply filling the booth with experienced salespeople will not do, either. If we are a major player, we shall need people with different skill-sets in our booth at all times, so that we can answer any type of question at any time; for instance, if we have a technical product, we shall need someone who can answer technical questions. It is a sign of lack of professionalism if, as a visitor, we are told to come back later because the person we need to talk to is not present (and that is quite a common scenario). After all, this trade show is important for everyone, including the visitors. Visitors often plan what they want to see, what booths they want to visit, which people they would like to talk to. It is not just the exhibitors who plan. What could possibly be more important than to have the booth staffed with the right people? If we are a major player, we have no good excuses for failing to ensure that our booth staff have the right mix of competences. Ultimately this is a question of budget, but if money must be saved it will be better to cut down on the cost of the actual booth itself, or as a last resort you should make sure there is someone you can contact by phone or online, who will at least be able to talk to the visitor while he or she is standing in your booth.

Because staff need to take breaks and because they need to do other things, such as doing interviews, gathering marketing research, and so forth, we have to plan the staffing of the booth in such a way that on each shift we have a suitable range of people present, or at least available by phone. If you are a small or even medium-sized company, regard the advice given here more as an ideal to progress towards than as a set of absolute requirements. What is most important is that we make progress for each trade show, not that we have everything in place first time. (No one manages that.)

We need to understand the difference between an ordinary sales job, and selling at a trade show or conference. Exhibition buyers come to see sellers, not vice versa. To be turned away because no one can answer our questions, or to be overlooked or abandoned too soon during a conversation because the staff member does not see us as a good lead, will leave us with a feeling of disappointment, and in some countries and cultures possibly even of dishonour. Thus, in many Asian cultures there is a fear of losing face, that is of feeling inferior and neglected by the person we are talking to. Many Western exhibitors are not sensitive enough to such factors. With the Asian economies growing in importance, cultural factors will need to be taken more seriously. As booth staff we need to show greater sensitivity in our conversations.

The single most common mistake made by salespeople at trade shows is that they fail to appreciate the importance of the class of visitors we call *people of influence*, one subset of which can be identified as *sponsors*. People of influence may be:

• Journalists, contributors to industry publications
• Trade association members

- Trade union officials
- Representatives of independent companies who sponsor and operate trade shows
- Members of special interest groups of all kinds

These people fall into three categories. There are those who want to take up our time for free, for instance trade union officials; those who are willing to pay for it, such as sponsors; and those who want us to pay for it, as in some cases journalists who would like us to pay the costs of their trip in return for a write-up. This last is not considered ethical in all cultures, but nevertheless seems to be the way things are done in most countries. (The journalist's article will not usually mention such payment, as would be required nowadays for an article in a scientific publication, under the "conflict of interest" rubric;[3] and as readers most of us will not suspect the existence of the payment.) There are also many other journalists who are willing to come and write about our company at their own expense, but for that we need to be talking about a major trade show and a company well known to the public.

People of influence, such as trade-association members or industry-publication journalists, will operate and behave quite differently from our sales leads. If we expect to encounter only sales leads we will look surprised, even puzzled, and through our reaction we might lose an opportunity. We need to be able to identify who we have in front of us and what their interest is in attending the trade show. Only then can we begin to act in our own best interest.

People of influence will want to talk about things other than our products, such as what suppliers we use and how we organize production, or they may aim to get us to do things differently, to modify our values or opinions. This type of encounter can be quite a shock, especially if we are not prepared for it. Hence, many sales staff see people of influence as a nuisance. But steering clear of them is based on a misconception, namely that because they are not there to buy they are no use to us. We should instead consider them for what they are, people who influence others to buy.

We are in fact giving up on an opportunity to cultivate our public relations, an opportunity for co-operation, co-branding, or sponsorship. Instead, we need to develop a system allowing us rapidly to identify and channel the different types of visitor to our booth. If we do not have time to talk to a person of influence there and then, we should set up a meeting later when things are calmer. In many industries, the people of influence can be more important than the customers. One example of that is in the fashion industry. When the representatives of *Vogue*, *Elle*, or *Marie Claire* arrive, they are treated as royalty. What they write will decide what people buy. So in this industry they are much more important than the actual customers at the show, because they have such a large influence on consumers' choices.

---

[3] For the record it should be stated that the author of this book has received no financial support from any source in exchange for favouring or disfavouring particular organizations or industries. The book has been made possible through a number of standard annual Swedish government research grants to the University of Halmstad, a special grant by the Knowledge Foundation, and in particular through the patience of my family.

People of influence do not want to be treated as buyers. Most often they are there for information and want to be given facts, or they may simply want to be recognized and acknowledged as important people. In these situations we are often best advised to play along with their game of vanity. Sales pitches only risk irritating them. People of influence do not take it lightly if they feel they are being misled. Rather, give them the feeling that they are discovering the truth. If we do not have any truly new products at the show, they will want to hear about that. They do not want to hear lies, and they do not want to find out, for themselves or via others, that the information we gave was wrong or misleading: that would only destroy whatever trust we may have managed to build up. Many people of influence are rather full of themselves. If that is so, then so be it.

If we are a larger company and can afford it we should invite our *non-buying customers* to a *non-commercial night out* or to a social event. If you have a large number of different visitors attending your social event, don't make this a sales event. If potential buyers have questions they will come to you. Also remember that there is usually a working day following the party, even if it is the day for packing up. To be prepared and fit for the next day is usually more important than trawling for sales at any one social occasion, unless you are in B2B and rely on a few customers. Social events are not drinking parties, but opportunities to mingle.

All this relates to an ideal world of trade-show experts. In reality, sales forces continue to distinguish sharply between buyers and non-buyers. When non-buyers are recognized as such, they are too often given the cold shoulder. It is commonly thought that they are just wasting the time of the booth staff. That way of thinking belongs to the old school of trade-show marketing (cf. Bello 1992: 59–80; Bello and Lothia 1993). The newer approach is to classify our visitors according to their visitor type, and adjust our communication accordingly. It makes our task of analysis much more complicated, but also potentially much more rewarding. Over the past decade we have seen increasing sensitivity to these issues building up, so that staff are now trained to identify a broader selection of visitors and visitors' needs. Thus there is every reason to believe that the professionalism of booth staff will continue to improve. This is a very positive and welcome development.

Some may ask, why should I keep in contact with a non-buyer if he or she does not belong to any of the other categories of visitor on my checklist? Well, in the first place, the sales process in real life is not so black-and-white. Non-buyers may become potential buyers later on, or they may be or may become important people of influence. By allowing certain categories of visitor to become aware that we are less interested in their presence, we can generate *ill will*, the opposite of *goodwill*. Instead of that, we might prefer to see all our visitors as potential ambassadors. It is just a question of finding out where they fit in and what they can do. We find that out through a series of tactful questions.

The cold shoulder is not necessary at all; rather, it is a sign of weak character on our part. Common courtesy and a general interest in the condition of other human beings costs us nothing in terms of time or money. In that respect a trade show should be seen as no different from life in society at large, and our duty is at least to "do the right thing" (as Spike Lee reminded us in his 1989 film with that title), that is to do what is proper and courteous. Anyone who comes to our booth is a potential ambassador and should ideally be given something, even if it is only a smile or an inexpensive giveaway. For this purpose we will also need to develop a detailed, ranked selection of giveaways.

2.1.1 Product Lifecycles and Giveaways

There are two main kinds of giveaways, *reminder giveaways* and *inexpensive giveaways*. Visitors can be divided into three groups with respect to giveaways. One group are given nothing, which means that you think that their actions will have no bearing on the company. That is, they are not going to buy anything or write anything or talk to anyone who may be influenced to buy our products. Reminder giveaways, such as a baseball cap, a good-quality mug, or a T-shirt, are given to strong people of influence, potential buyers, or returning customers. Inexpensive giveaways, such as a pen, a plastic mug, or sweets with our logo on, can be given to anyone else who wants them.

We will not know in advance how many we will get of each category of visitor to our booth. Nevertheless, we have to make some estimate, in order to decide what quantities of the different types of giveaways to stock. Also, we cannot always know what category of visitor we are talking to, and it can be difficult to find out from them. So sometimes we will give a reminder giveaway to a non-buyer. When that happens it is no great disaster. We have to see what information we can obtain from the conversation, and beyond that we just have to guess. In some cases, we can even ask straight out – but politely – "Are you a potential buyer, or are just looking round?" (in a tone which gives the visitor the feeling that it is OK to be looking round, not a criticism). The answer we get may not be clear either, but normally we will at least know a little more than we did at the outset. Of course, in some cases a person who is actually a potential buyer may say he is just looking round, in which case we are in the same situation, unless we can detect something in the way the person acts that suggests differently. In any case, we are now moving into the area of rather sophisticated psychology. As human beings, we are all born psychologists, not formally of course, but by nature and through experience. In most cases that psychological ability will be good enough for the tasks we face at the show. In all cases, we shall need to rely on a whole lot of guessing about people's real intentions. But then, that is not so very different from what we do in life in general.

When we begin our training scheme, staff will need to be given some simple rules to go by. Then, when these are well-rehearsed, we can elaborate them. Ultimately a great deal will revolve round psychology. A simple set of rules for what to do, depending on visitor category, might look like this (Table 2.4):

One group that many exhibitors are surprised to find in their booth is *current buyers*, people who have already bought what we are selling, and who are not looking to make any additional purchases in the immediate future. Their visits

Table 2.4 Buyers' motives for show attendance

	Short term	Long term
Current buyer	Confirm decision	Reinforce contact
Potential buyer	Become advocate	Develop contact
Non-buyer	Receive reward	Support industry

A modified version of the table presented by Godar and O'Connor (2001: 79)

should not be surprising. Current buyers often go round to seek confirmation that they made the right decision. This is what is sometime called *buyers' remorse*. They may also be there just to gain recognition for who they are, for being good customers. When they notice your booth they will run over as if to say "Hi, I'm a buyer, make me feel important". This is all part of human nature and ought not to surprise anyone. Our response may be to say "Yes, you are", and then encourage them to leave without feeling pushed out, perhaps by giving them a small gift. We may even provide a special gift for this category of visitors, something that is understood as *existing-customer gift*.

Potential buyers go about seeking data to inform the decision they are going to make. Current and potential buyers both treat the trade show pretty much like a shopping precinct, wandering from store to store. In fact a trade show is much better than a shopping precinct. It is a *mega shopping precinct*. If you are looking for, say, a watch it is like walking through a precinct full of watchmakers. There are conferences and speeches on watches, people who represent watch organizations, and people who write about watches. In other words it is rather like an Eldorado for whatever business or industry you happen to be in. You will never find a better selection than at a trade show, and you are less likely to make impulse purchases than in a shopping precinct because the focus is principally on information, distribution, and image building.

From our first-year course on Marketing, we will remember being taught that potential buyers are diverse depending on where they are in the product lifecycle. Different visitors are located at different stages in the product lifecycle, as stated in the theory of diffusion of innovations.[4]

In phase *A*, the potential customer is unaware that our product may fulfil his company or personal needs. In phase *B*, he or she discovers this and starts gathering information about our product, maybe even assessing it at the booth. In phase *C*, he is actively engaged in discussing the conditions of sale with booth staff. Only in phase *D* does he make the actual decision to purchase the item. That means that before this point we have had only outgoings, no income, as there has been no sale. Rather, phases *A–D* (period 1) are part of the investment we as producers and sellers make in the effort to gain a future sale. This is only a model, of course, but still it

---

[4] See Everett M. Rogers (1962). His theory was built on those of German scholars like Friedrich Ratzel and Leo Frobenius. The same basic ideas in macroeconomics were used by Raymond Vernon as a response to the failure of the Heckscher–Ohlin model to describe changes in sales from international trade.

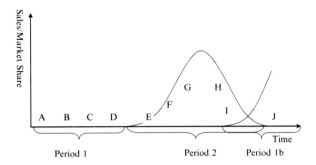

Fig. 2.2 The purchasing process in the product lifecycle

corresponds to a process which most buyers go through in one form or the other. For all the buyers as a group, economic theory suggests that aggregate sales follow a bell curve. The marketing logic is familiar: in the beginning, there will be only a few buyers. We call this group *innovators* (*E*), representing here some 2.5 % of market share in the general model. The next phase is that of *early adopters* (*F*), comprising 13.5 %. At a certain point the curve will start to rise. We call this the *early majority* (*G*), at 34 %. Then follows *late majority* (*H*) at 34 %, and the final group which we call *laggers* (*I*), comprising 16 % of total sales. Of course, all this is according to a standard model for the industry as a whole and does not reflect actual sales for an individual company. Phase *J* is defined by no sales. For any company, it is important to have another product on the market before we reach this point, represented in Fig. 2.2 by the start of a new period (period 1b). Put differently, it is the product sold in the previous period which finances the phase of non-sales in the next period. That is why the two curves are shown as overlapping. If they overlap, this means that we have no period without income. For most companies, that will not be feasible in reality. New models and innovations cannot be sequenced in this exact fashion. In reality, most companies will rather have a range of different products selling at the same time. What is lost on one product is financed by profits made on another, and so forth. The same *evolutionary model* is used to explain the rise and decline of different technologies and of whole industries.

There may be numerous people involved in phases *A* and *B*. It is only in phase *C* that we discover who has a genuine purchasing intention. Phase *D* may be conducted by the same person as phase *C*, but this is not necessarily so. The purchasing company or customer may well have a special negotiator and someone else who is the purchasing decision-maker. That is, it may send one person to the trade show to look and ask questions, and another, often more senior person to negotiate the deal.[5] This largely depends on the size and organization of the potential buyer and the size of the order. In general, the more expensive the product, the longer the *buying decision process* takes and the more resources are allocated to it.

---

[5] This book does not contain chapters on negotiation techniques, beyond some simple advice about the actual face-to-face meeting, since they are considered a separate area of study with their own expertise and corresponding literature.

Most companies focus on the actual sales history of a product – the sales period (period 2). They pay less attention to the processes of the pre-sales period (period 1). The sales history of a product starts at the moment when the product is released and the first potential customers are becoming aware of it. This often occurs at or just before a trade show. Thus very often the trade show will be the first chance for a customer (or a competitor) to see the new product. The trade show then corresponds to period 1. As a company, we want to come up with something that is brand new or just about to be launched on the market, in order to create a buzz in the mass media or at least in trade journals. At the same time, we also want to show products that are already selling well (period 2).

In period 1, the focus is on information gathering. In period 2, the focus is on negotiations. That does not mean, of course, that we cannot purchase and negotiate in period 1. In many cases it will be convenient to do that, but it is not our primary intention. Period 1 is an excellent opportunity for the whole membership of the purchasing centre to go around and shift from one phase of the purchasing process to another with a minimum of resources. We may, for example, conduct phase B over the first 2 days of the trade show and phases C and D at the end of the show. The actual purchase decision will sometimes occur immediately after the trade show. The customer needs to move quickly, but also needs some time to think and evaluate different options. Normally there is too little time for that during the show. It may also be that all members of the purchasing centre are not present at the trade show.

Booth staff need to be trained in the complexity of purchase decisions. If they suppose that every visit is a sale/non-sale situation, they are not going to perform effectively, maybe jeopardizing a future sale though their behaviour at the booth. A phase-B visit needs to be recognized and respected as such. Salespeople must acknowledge the need for potential customers to gather information before making any decision. A phase A or B visitor should be met with the same service and goodwill as an actual buyer.

If we as a company are giving out a lot of information in phase B, but are not able to get a sufficient percentage of people to return in phase C, that could mean that our product fills a genuine need but that our particular version is not competitive enough. It is an indication that serious marketing research is needed to identify our shortcomings. The same goes if we are able to attract many visitors in phase C, but not in phase D. This is an indication that our product fulfils the company's needs, but that our price and/or conditions for delivery and service are not sufficiently competitive. This is less of a problem than the first one, since it does not require any modification of the actual product, but it is serious enough, since the consequence will still be no sales.

Depending on what phase of the purchasing process a visitor has reached, he will have different needs which may be fulfilled by different people in your booth or by different forms of technology. A person at phase B, who requires specific and detailed information, may be best served by meeting staff who are technically trained. Sometimes the person is just looking for a brochure or a QR code. In phase D the need may be more for a salesperson who can negotiate a price.

International visitors deserve special attention. A visitor who flies across continents to see our product or negotiate with us will normally be serious. His costs for attending the show will be much higher than those for other visitors. That means that he is investing more, and stands to lose more if he cannot find a product that fulfils his needs. In general, the greater the distance that a potential buyer has travelled, the more serious his or her interest is likely to be – though this rule is not without exceptions. The long-distance visitor is also more likely to be a bigger customer, placing larger orders. Someone from the same region may just be there because he or she is curious – maybe he or she just happened to be in town, and saw the show chiefly as an amusement.

2.1.2 Technological Aids

Nowadays, most exhibitions provide colour-coded badges to allow for immediate role-recognition: exhibitors in one colour, suppliers in another, "international" in a third, etc. Many companies have access to computer systems allowing immediate scanning of badges, so-called *Lead Retrieval Systems* (LRS). This does not mean that business cards are no longer used. They are still standard, and an engraved card on high-quality paper is still appreciated in many circles, especially in relation to luxury goods and among high earners and highly-educated visitors.

Manual systems require more time for analysis before a contact is made. Some companies enter data from badges directly into their own *customer relationship management* (CRM) applications with space for additional comments. That allows the company to contact potential customers the same week (cf. Tynan 2004: 27). Their system also enables them to add quotations from the actual conversation – possibly even a sound bite, with the visitor's approval. LRSs are frequently hired out by show organizers. The critics of these systems often complain that they are difficult to personalize and that data is often erroneous or scarce. Consequently, until you know for sure just how good such a system is, use your own PC-based solutions, preferably with a smart phone for easier mobile use. Beyond this, it is difficult to give long-lasting advice on technology in this area, since the pace of change is so rapid. As an example, a company called iZettle was thought to be a sure thing with the service it offered for paying via credit or debit card over a mobile phone, using a small device attached to the smartphone. A few months later came SEQR, which allows one to pay with a QR code. Also, many banks are now collaborating to build their own systems based on mobile-phone apps, thus disinter-mediating the card companies. All these developments are affecting the trade-show industry on an ongoing basis.

QR codes are becoming popular in more than one respect. Many visitors will have a QR application on their smartphones and will expect to be able to scan different codes at your booth rather than picking up brochures, which they would have to lug along with them all day. Thus you may want to provide QR codes at your booth to cover different kinds of information. QR codes can also make up for time wasted in a booth which is crowded. Rather than waiting their turn for personal attention, many visitors will just scan your code and move on to the next booth. As well as written documentation you can also link to sound files and video material. It is therefore important that the codes are easily visible and that they actually work. Do not link directly to websites from your QR codes, but make sure that the information is clearly and easily visible and readable on a smartphone. Technology that does not work is a common problem, but its frequency does not make it any more excusable at a trade show.

Mobile apps are now rapidly changing the opportunities for information exchange in society, including at trade shows. Many shows already have their own apps developed by the organizers, and the functionality of these apps will be increasing significantly in the years to come. With new apps visitors can not merely acquire information about the show, the participants, hotels, flights, and so forth, but they can also make purchases, and see where other people they want to meet are located and exchange information with them. With a built-in GPS function you can even find the way to the toilet all by yourself without having to ask anyone.

As the importance of internet solutions increases the demand for free, or at least straightforward, access, Wi-Fi is becoming ever more important. There are no excuses for poor internet connections at trade shows any longer. As a trade-show organizer you will need to test your internet infrastructure and plan for eventualities. As an exhibitor you will want to check the internet speed at the place where your booth is located. To ensure that the technology works we need to include *technical support* personnel among our staff. Categorizing staff by groups of roles may make this easier (Table 2.5):

In the model above, the exhibitor staff are classified into three main groups: *administrative personnel*, *sales*, and *technical support*. Administrative personnel and sales are divided into *junior* and *senior* levels. They are used not only in contacts with the exhibition organizers, but also to inform visitors about the product. They also have the special role of handling complaints.

2.1.3 Complaints and Stress at Trade Shows

Complaints are a delicate matter, for several reasons. First, the matter is delicate because you are dealing with a dissatisfied customer who may already be showing signs of anger or at least frustration. Second, it is delicate because of the location. The last thing you want in your booth is a customer loudly venting his anger. Third, it is delicate because of the restricted space and the limited time you have available to solve the problem.

First, you do not want the complaining customer to get any more upset or angry than he or she already is. Showing understanding and listening take special training, which few sales or technical staff tend to have. Hence these situations may be better handled by administrative personnel or by a specially designated person, as are often used when customers complain to companies in general. Whatever your view may be of the merits of the complaint, you need to show respect for the person standing before you. In order to achieve this, it is necessary to make a distinction

Table 2.5 Exhibitor response by buyer motive type (From Godar and O'Connor 2001: 84)

Visitor's motive	Exhibitor responses		
	Personnel	Location at booth	Promotional mix
Seek information:			
Actively	Sales + technical support	Inside	Information kit, commercial social event
Passively	Technical support	Inside	Inexpensive giveaway, commercial social event
Purchase	Sales, senior	Inside, seated	Commercial social event
Receive reward (old customer)	Any	By aisles	Reminder giveaway, commercial social event
Support	Any	By aisles	Inexpensive giveaway
Complain	Administrative	Inside, standing, isolate from others	Inexpensive giveaway
Inform	Administrative, senior	Inside, seated/standing, isolate from others	Inexpensive giveaway, non-commercial social

between the person and his or her complaint. Secondly, however bad the situation may be with regard to the specifics of the complaint, you can always try to build a better relationship with the complainant than what you started with. In other words it is not an either/or situation. If you cannot see any immediate solution, or if further information is required, suggest that you meet at a later date, after the trade show is over. Assure the person that you take his complaint seriously. The faster you can come to a mutual agreement the better – preferably without the visitor feeling that he has been chased out of the booth. Of course, sometimes the demands will be utterly unreasonable and no mutual agreement can be found. Sometimes complaints are about finding a solution; sometimes they are more about limiting damage.

With the exception of complaints, which are preferably handled in the administrative room away from other visitors, all other *short-term contacts* are handled close to the aisles. *Lengthy contacts* are handled inside the booth. If it is practical, you might consider two locations for assessing the product, one close to the aisles for short-term contacts, and one inside for longer contacts. As a rule, all contact by the aisles should be made standing. Contact inside may be seated. Remember that visitors who come to you are often weary – their legs will be tired, naturally, but they will also very likely be mentally weary, depending how much time they had already spent walking around the trade-show halls before they reached you. The further away from the exits you are located, the more likely your visitors are to be weary. Weary people are glad of a chance to rest and will appreciate a glass of water. A place to sit down is then often preferred. Certainly our booth is not a nursing home, but if our leads are given a seat and a drink of water then we will already have made some progress in building a relationship.

Putting it differently, when people walk into your booth they are going to have several needs, and these may or may not be linked to your products. By easing the needs that are not related to the actual purchase – rest, thirst – we increase the likelihood of a successful visit, always assuming that they are interested in what we have to offer.

The point is so easy to understand, and yet it is so often ignored: people at trade shows are weary.

Here is a brief example to illustrate this theme:

Minicase 1: Booths That Make Vistors Even More Weary

Company: Samsung, South Korea
Trade show: CES, Central Hall

Samsung is the world's largest conglomerate by revenue and the single most important South Korean company. Their exports account for more than 20 % of that country's total exports. Even though the Samsung Group is involved in a large variety of industries, in heavy machinery, in construction, in chemicals, financial, and entertainment, it is Samsung Electronics (SEC), started in 1967, which is best known. In the 1990s SEC became a truly international company. Today it is among other things the world's largest manufacturer of dynamic random access memory, refrigerators, flash memory, and DVD players.

Samsung usually takes one of the largest booth spaces of any participant when it attends trade shows today, reflecting who they are and how they want to be perceived. At the CES the booth was divided into a number of departments spread over a large area. The booth had TV screens everywhere, outer walls were well used, and so was the height below the ceiling of the hall. One part of the booth area was made to look like a high-class jewellery store (for mobile phones).

On the downside, the booth made a rather confusing impression with too many different colours, and despite the large booth area there was no place to rest (visitors were resting in the booth next door). A thick carpet made the visiting experience even more tiring. When you are dragging tired feet along, you do not want to have to make extra effort to lift your feet. Moreover, there was no clear tour or track to follow once inside the booth. That is very tiring in itself, because you are then forcing people to use additional energy to work out which is the best path to take round the booth. Indeed, many visitors will not enter a booth if they cannot see from outside where to go once they are inside. For larger booths, like the Samsung booth, this was difficult. You simply could not see where the path was taking you before you went in. If you are going to have a large and complex stand, you might have an overview map by the entrance (making sure not to place it in the middle of the entrance, since that will hinder the free flow of pedestrian traffic).

When you consider how much money is spent on these booths, it is surprising that the solutions adopted are not thought through better than they are.

> *Conclusion: less effective use of resources than might be expected from this large company; on a scale of 1–10, score 6.*

When we walk through rows and rows of booths, they all seem to look more or less the same. In fact the more of them we see, the more similar they look. In addition to which, after a while we get tired of walking round. It is astonishing how few exhibitors think about the state their visitors are in after a few hectic hours in the exhibition hall. The chances are that he or she will be more interested in sitting down than in examining your products. Here are some suggestions for a trade show that takes place in an environment which is both warm and hectic:

- A bench to sit on (tired feet)
- A glass of water (thirst)
- A complimentary neck message in one corner of your booth (stiff muscles)
- A jar filled with sweets, or some inexpensive food (hunger, energy)
- A fan or air conditioner (heat, stale air, lack of oxygen)
- A darker corner (against the intense lightening)

The value of such facilities can be enormous at certain trade shows and for certain visitors subject to deprivation of a series of *physiological needs*. This all matches Maslow's "hierarchy of needs". Your booth should not be seen a division of the Red Cross, certainly, that would attract the wrong kind of visitors; but you can make things easier for those visitors who are actually interested in what you have to offer once they have reached you. Who knows, if a visitor is only slightly interested in your product initially, he may feel compelled to become more interested just because of the supportive facilities you offer. Thus the facilities can be seen as resembling sales arguments in a negotiation.

Another problem at booths is stress. Trade shows are highly stressful environments. And research tells us that perceived time pressure leads to fewer purchases (Tafesse and Korneliussen 2012). This makes the trade-show environment a paradoxical one. It is an environment that people have made a stressful one, yet where we know that people under stress will be less inclined to buy. One of your concerns as a staff member should therefore be to know how to adapt to and reduce the visitor's *stress level*, in the first place by your manner of speaking and your body language. The best way to relieve a visitor's stress can be to let him or her talk. If you are stressed yourself as a staff member, the chances are that this will be transmitted to everyone who walks into your booth. Another way to reduce stress among your visitors might be by playing calming music, or no music at all (trade show halls tend to be too noisy anyway).

What is it, then, that causes all this stress? There are a number of factors. One is the awkward way we walk at a show, not in a straight line and at a steady pace as we do when outdoors, but twisting round while we are walking and standing still. (You might recall encountering the same kind of weariness when walking round a museum.) Another is the heat. A third is the poor air quality. Then there are the harsh lighting; the noise, including loud music; the limited time available; and the thought of everything you need to get done or to see before everything closes down (*mental stress*). Add to these the company's expectations for sales, and all the unresolved problems you left at home. Most likely several of these factors will come into play together, creating a mixture of physical and mental stress. And we could probably think of many further stress factors. The point is that they all emerge here together at the trade show, as a consequence of the very nature of this environment, so compressed and intense.

It sometimes makes you wonder why they set things up in this way. Would it not be better if everything were quiet and people moved around slowly? Perhaps so, but bazaars are by their nature hectic, and they always have been. If we move around slowly everything will take longer and we will probably get less done. If we speak slowly and quietly we are afraid of being perceived as passive, non-salesman like, unengaged. This last fear is not justified; confidence is often won through being calm and not too talkative. We are not selling our products at a fish market, where those who scream loudest sell most. Indeed, many individual booths even succeed in keeping their sound levels down; but the halls are filled with loud voices nevertheless. To some extent this is inevitable. There are just too many people under the same roof talking at the same time. Ultimately this is in the very nature of trade shows.

We occasionally see people at trade shows sitting with their head in their hands. You can imagine what this means: how much stress and how many failures it takes to lead someone to act like that in public. Yet it is not uncommon. When a few things start to go wrong at the show, it does not take long before we feel like complete failures. Expectations are often too high, so the fall is all the harder.

We are just bombarded with too many impressions at trade shows, without sufficient time to digest them. Besides, we do not act naturally at a show. Too often we are not truly ourselves. There is too much pressure. We may also be affected by more complex psychological problems, like existential questions, the one-dimensional nature of it all; the monotonous landscape, a feeling (especially after Day 3) that we are losing touch with reality and normal life outside. Trade shows can feel so unnatural as an environment. The problem may largely be the lack of any real personal contacts; that is, it may arise because we have too many business contacts there and too few contacts with people we would choose to have around us. While at the show we do not see our families and perhaps do not see any people we truly care about. At work, at least we can go home at the end of the day to recharge our batteries. In short, all this may leave us with a feeling of emptiness: a feeling of lack of real purpose and general fatigue. Mankind is not made for trade shows; they do not suit our nature or conform to what we consider a normal environment. This may be the underlying reason why we tend to become so stressed. On the other hand, there are those, especially among the younger generation, who seldom get stressed and think that trade shows are great fun. In any case, we cannot do much to change this environment, so it is important that we prepare ourselves for it, physically and mentally. Preparing for it doesn't have to be a big deal. It might be enough to arrange a few sessions where we sit in a circle and discuss these issues. That ought to be part of the pre-show training. Then when we encounter the negative feelings, we are better prepared to deal with them.

It is important to know about all of these problems. A truly competent exhibition manager will know how to lead a dialogue with his staff about these topics. The way exhibition managers react is very different. One common point of view is that staff who are stressed just do not have the stomach for it, so that they would probably be better off working somewhere else. In reality we react differently to the same stress symptoms regardless of how good we are as salespeople or employees. Our first concern should not be to fill the booth with people who can "stand the pressure". On the other hand, these issues should not be overlooked, simply because they are real problems.

If you have time during the show, do some anti-stress activities, for instance give one another shoulder massages when you are together in the evening. Set up an *anti-stress discussion circle*, a follow-up to the one you started in the pre-show period. Or go for long silent walks together in the evenings. You could also phone home and talk to your loved ones. Tell them about your day, what your good and bad experiences were, as a means of relieving stress and exchanging empathy. This form of *conversation therapy* can be a great help to lift weight from your shoulders. During the day, you should drink plenty of fresh water, and you should eat well at breakfast and lunch. If you have two teams of people, you should consider going outside the premises, leaving the trade show area for lunch, just in order to get away from it all for an hour.

Do not try carrying out any kind of anti-stress activities while you are in the booth. It might look as though you were trying to sell yoga lessons or some other alternative therapy. Such activities will only draw attention away from your products and core activities – away from the reasons why you are there. What you can do, if you like, is to offer your visitors complimentary massages at another location. Sometimes such services are provided inside the trade-show arena, alongside the popular shoe-shine stands.

In general, trade shows have large unexploited possibilities for other services, catering to our physiological and more basic, practical needs while there: places to eat, drink, lie down for a few minutes, take a shower, a place to change or repair our clothes, or get a haircut. It is surprising that more organizers are not bundling these service facilities into their shows. Most trade shows display a lack of overall analysis on the part of the organizers and owners. Instead, we frequently see too many food stands together in one place, with no places to sit down. Or the toilets will be too far away from the food stands. There is also often a problem of toilet capacity. In this respect trade shows have much to learn from rock festivals, another form of event with its own particular features.[6] (Trade shows and concerts are both studied under the heading of event marketing.) Food areas, restaurants, and stands are often arranged in an uninspiring fashion at most exhibition halls. At most sites

---

[6] The author was a consultant for the Sweden Rock Festival at a time when it was still relatively unknown outside of Sweden. Much of the success of the festival came after the organizers decided to take event marketing more seriously, continuously improving their logistics, studying traffic flows, and developing new catering facilities and larger-scale toilet capacity.

they are just somewhere you go when you need to eat. These are missed opportunities for trade-show organizers. But there are also admirable exceptions. At the Gothenburg Book Fair a restaurant was sited on a higher level than the exhibitions, so that it could serve as a sightseeing platform. Visitors could go up there not only to eat and relax, but to plan what to see next. As an *easily-visible landmark* it also becomes a natural *rendezvous point*.

Some marketing experts seem to think there are few limits to how much entertainment and fun there should be within their booths. Others think that all people want is a lifestyle, and that their main task is to link their products to a particular concept by deploying entertainment or associated products. These lines of thinking lead to the creation of quite different types of booth. Some will be all about products; others will hardly contain any products at all. On the question as to the value of such diverse *exhibition strategies*, opinions differ. There are no major empirical studies from which to draw conclusions as yet, but personally I believe that the *concept-booths* overplay the attraction of lifestyles. Opinions about this will also differ greatly depending on what industry and what consumer segments we are dealing with. It is clear that entertainment-oriented booths are a current trend, in other words we are doing much more with our booths nowadays that is not directly related to displaying our products. Disagreements relate more to the extent of entertainment at the booth, rather than to whether it should exist at all.

Younger people tend to want more entertainment, in the same way that young professionals are more interested in lifestyle. An exhibition strategy which tries to adapt to these wants can be very successful or a complete failure, depending on how the strategy is executed. But we must at least say that it is a risky strategy, as illustrated in the Motorola case below:

Minicase 2: How Too Much Lifestyle Diverts Attention Away from Your Products

Company: Motorola, USA
Trade show: CES, Central Hall

Motorola, Inc. was an American telecommunications company based in Illinois. It was a provider of analogue and digital two-way voice and data radio products and systems for wireless and broadband communications. The company was best known for its mobile phones. After failing to keep up with competition in the consumer market for mobile phones, the company was split in two: today, Motorola Mobility is owned by Google, and the rest is now Motorola Solutions.

At the CES the company had a well-ordered display of its products in a line along the central wall, easy to see and get at. Amphitheatre seating offered an opportunity to rest, and plenty of staff were on hand.

On the downside, they were trying to do too much. Colours were too many and unclear – orange, blue, green. The company logo was not clearly displayed, but tended to be lost in the midst of all the other graphic messages. From a distance it looked as though they were selling glasses/eyewear (because of an advertising campaign involving fancy spectacles and associated products). The specs were a part of their lifestyle strategy, evidently aiming to look cool. This diverted attention away from the company's core business and away from its products.

Also, too many exhibition staff were talking to one another, without paying attention to passers-by. Their uniforms were cold-looking and hard to identify.

A large dividing wall in the middle of the exhibition created a confusing impression, as if the booth contained two different exhibitions. There was a high chance of visitors to one side missing what was on the other side. The passage between the two booth areas was too narrow for visitors to pass one another.

On top of that, Motorola had fallen for the most obvious trend-gadgets of that year, such as the Hummer car. Everyone wanted a car in the exhibition, but unfortunately the link with Motorola products was vague and unclear, to the point of amounting to a form of involuntary co-branding.

The complexity of messages in their booth made it unclear what the company was actually selling. The company was trying to do and to be too many things to different visitors. This lack of clarity was reflected in the slogans displayed in the booth.

Conclusion: far less effective use of resources than might be expected from this company, low visibility of core products: score 3 out of 10.

2.1.4   International Boothmanship

Boothmanship at the larger shows today is the same thing as *international boothmanship*, since business has become truly global. This means that cultures are becoming similar to one another; but each culture is still individual enough to require special attention. Trade shows are organized all over the world, and it is expected that company representatives will travel to wherever the best and most popular trade shows are held. That means that our booth staff are going to encounter increasing numbers of visitors from other countries and cultures, and they themselves must be willing to travel to trade shows in other countries and on other continents. These cultural encounters impose specific demands on us.

A good way to begin confronting cultural differences in marketing is to use whatever is common to us all. Thus, if we have an advertisement for chocolate and it could work in another country, we will not create an entirely new advert. Instead, we might just change the text. The reason for that is that culture for the most part means difference, and differences in business normally mean increased costs. Ideally we would like to broadcast the same commercials in all countries, since that would be the least expensive alternative, but doing that seldom works. What is funny or popular in one culture can be unfunny and unpopular in another. When it comes to advertising, it is important to be spot on. Anything else looks at best odd, and odd is not a good basis for advertising. Television is full of such examples, of dubbed commercials from other countries. Only seldom will they be any great success, and frequently they will do more harm than good. To know why, we need culturally-specific competence: meaning that if we are selling our products in Sweden, we need to know enough about the culture to know what Swedes like. This is often a problem even as between neighbouring countries. For example, German humour, as represented in commercials, seldom works in Sweden. Still, some German companies will go on broadcasting the commercials they have made for their home market, simply because that is less expensive, and they see it as better than nothing. Well, sometimes nothing is better. We see the same logic at trade shows. The reason we start with what is common to everyone is because those elements do not cost anything extra, in training and planning. International marketing, hence also international boothmanship, is largely about how to change what we are doing at home so that it will succeed in the other country. Changing nothing will be very risky; changing too much will be expensive.

So what do we have that is universally shared? The first rule is to be polite. Politeness is appreciated in all cultures. The second rule is to use plain English; preferably no dialects, metaphors, sports analogies, slang, or the like (cf. Hill 1996). The third rule is to try to adapt to what the other person is saying, which often means trying to imitate their style. This is of course a difficult task, and can go frightfully wrong. So, if you do not know how to connect to a particular culture, you should avoid trying to do so.

To speak several languages is an advantage for successful trade-show staff. When attending international trade shows, mastery of more than English is greatly appreciated. For example, if you are in France you will know that the French prefer to speak their own language. A German or Japanese will appreciate it if you can say a few words in their language, as they too regard themselves as leading nations. The Chinese are thrilled if you can say just a few words in Chinese, in part because they do not expect it even though they are become increasingly aware of their new role as a rising superpower.

Learn at least the most basic words in the country you are visiting, such as "thank you", "good morning", and "how are you?" Attempting to use these phrases correctly is seen as a sign of general politeness in most cultures. It is true that the international business language is English – just as the international language for scholars in the Middle Ages was Latin, and just as diplomats used to use French – but English-speaking visitors are also sometimes seen as arrogant when they insist that everyone should speak their language while refusing to learn those of others. If you are attending an international trade show and speak a less-used language – such as Norwegian, in my own case – keep it to yourself while you are at the trade show unless it should happen to be useful in some special circumstance (such as when there is someone else who speaks it). We do not make our visitors listen in to us and guess where we come from if we speak a minority language. If they hear an accent when we speak English and ask where we are from, that is a different thing. Talking about nationality can then become a way into a good conversation: "Ah, you went to see the Norwegian fjords . . .", and so the conversation gets off to a good start.

If you are an exhibitor and hear another language, do not go on about your visits to that person's country unless you are invited to engage with such a topic. Do not say "I love your country" just because you have been there or know where it is on the map. Comments like that often sound superficial. Another thing to bear in mind is that it is our voices, the way we say things, that build relationships, often more than the actual words we use. So, speak from the heart.

The third rule is to respect a certain *comfort distance* between you and your visitor. Let the visitor decide what that will be. In some cultures the atmosphere becomes uncomfortable if you try to reach a hand out to the other person or if you move too close to them. A fourth rule, which applies to Asian countries in particular, is to think about how to build a relationship before attempting any sales pitch. Westerners often think they have to be pushy to get a sale. In most cases the visitor already knows what you want to sell; and he certainly knows *that* you want to sell. To be too eager can be seen as a sign of desperation. If we like a seller very much it may in fact be us who eventually feel we have to say "So, you probably want to sell me this item . . .?" If the visitor gets to that point, you have probably already made your sale.

According to Gesteland (2005: 17–18), there are two iron laws to follow in the relationship between different cultures at trade shows, or in any other selling situation: first, the seller adapts to the buyer, and secondly, the visitor is expected to observe local customs. Most people prefer to do business with people they know. This means that they will take time to get to know you as a human being first, before deciding to enter into any business transactions. The only exception is the Western culture, which accepts doing business with strangers. Another way to say this is that Westerners are *transaction focused*, whereas Asians are *relationship focused*. This difference can hardly be overstated. Westerners in Asia will be taken out to dinner and invited on various outings, asking themselves all the while when things are going to get started – when you will be getting down to business, as the saying goes. Well, by then they probably already have started. All this does not imply that the other party will necessarily like you and end up doing business with you. Sometimes things will end with a series of mutual thank-yous, and that will be that.

At the end of each day, there should be a short staff debriefing. What went right during the day, and what went wrong or less well? How can we change what worked less well? This part of the staff training may be built around some sort of reward system, whereby the best staff member gets something, if only a pat on the back in the presence of his or her colleagues. A reward can also be linked to future trade shows. It might, for instance, be a guarantee of a place among the booth staff for the next trade show. It could also be a new set of responsibilities within the booth staff, perhaps as trainer for certain aspects at the next pre-show seminar. It might also be a trip together with spouse and children to participate in an external booth staff training seminar at some pleasant holiday resort; but the reward does not need to cost much. Often it is the recognition that really counts. Appraisals can cost so little that it is a wonder that they are so seldom given.

In the following sections, we will go into more detail on the functions of each category of trade-show participant. We begin with the exhibitor.

2.2   The Exhibitor

An exhibition is a salesman's microcosm. Within this microcosm he has little time to work out who the valuable customers and visitors are and what to do next. It is rather like playing chess against a clock: in order not to lose on time penalties, you need to know a set of good moves in advance. Thus success is something that comes over time, through having attended many shows.

The exhibitor is there to meet as many hard prospects as possible. To know who is just floating by and who is out to buy your product takes training. Until we have learned the basics and developed that skill and instinct, we should avoid taking a chance by showing less interest in particular groups of visitors. The initial trick is often to find the right balance. An exhibitor should not spend too much or too little time with any one group of visitors before knowing better how to distinguish among them. The rules of communication are pretty straightforward. Be polite, speak to the point, but do not talk too much, especially not about things other than what we are all there for. Doing that takes up too much time which we have not got, and it is considered unprofessional. Note also that this is more true in certain cultures than in others, for instance silence and pauses are more appreciated in Europe than in the USA.

The exhibition or booth staff is headed by an *exhibition manager,* the company's or the organization's representative at the trade show. It is his responsibility to see to it that all marketing activities are carried out as described in the exhibition plan, and to report back about the outcome of the exhibition to *senior management,* if it is a larger company. In smaller companies, the owners or chief executives often go to the trade show themselves. They will also be working in the booth. That makes reporting unnecessary, but it does not mean that we have nothing to gain by jotting down notes about our experiences for the day, or for the show. How well did we do, relative to what we expected before coming to the show? What was different or unexpected, and what can we do about it next time? Unless we pose these questions clearly to ourselves on the way home, they will probably be forgotten. They will not completely evaporate, of course, and we will accumulate experiences even if we do not write things down; but, unless we have a remarkable memory, we will forget many important lessons, and in consequence our future performance will be less efficient than it might be.

There are a number of initial questions to be answered before a trade show:
1. How many people should I employ in the booth?
2. How big should my booth be?
3. How many people or visitors should it be able to hold?

Many of these decisions may already have been made for us by the rules and regulations laid down for the show. Booth sizes may be limited to a small range of options, say small, medium, and large. The average size of booths organized by AUMA members is between 50 and 100 m^2. The average size of a booth in Europe in 2010 was 36 m^2, according to UFI. If there are no restrictions and we are free to choose, as a rule of thumb our booth should reflect the economic size of our company and our aspirations. Another answer is to say that it should be large enough to enable us and our staff to fulfil our marketing objectives. So we need to ask ourselves what we will be doing in our booth? How many visitors do we expect at a time?

You do not need a *mega-booth* for your products to be noticed, even if you are a multinational; but on the other hand it is somewhat expected. There is a great deal of psychology about this. If your booth is smaller and less expensive this year than last year, some industry experts and people of influence may infer that your company is facing difficulties. "Ah, so they have a smaller booth this year, well that is interesting . . ." If you have a marvellous booth 1 year, visitors will remember that. If your booth is less spectacular, less inventive or creative or what have you, in the following year, then some people will notice and comment on that – probably the experts, the people of influence, those writing for trade magazines. They will say "Yes, they had a great booth 3 years ago, I don't know what happened after that", and some of these reflections will end up in print, but in another tone. Thus, to demonstrate that you are doing well it is often thought wise to make each new booth somewhat bigger or better, or at least no smaller than last year's – but not too different, either, because that will only create greater expectations in future. It is a little like when people buy new sailing boats. There is something called the three-foot disease among enthusiasts: many of them want a boat that is 3 ft longer than the old one. There is a certain parallel in the logic of trade shows, though I cannot tell you just how many square feet or how much larger the budget would need to be. There is no research demonstrating a specific relationship between booth size and number of visitors, but people tend to gather around the larger booths, as they become landmarks in the exhibition halls. Surveys have tended to confirm this (Table 2.6).

Thus, according to a survey in the *Trade Show Marketing Manual* (2006), a 200 sq. ft (18.5 m^2) space will average 280 % more responses than a 100 sq. ft space, and a 300 sq. ft space will average 360 % more responses than a 100 sq. ft (9.3 m^2) space. By the same token, a 400 sq. ft (37 m^2) space will average 832 % more responses than a 100 sq. ft space.

To exploit the ability of a large booth to function as a landmark, it is important to build it as high as possible also (within the limits set by the show organizers), so as to be clearly visible from a distance. Larger booths tend to offer more entertainment too, since they can afford the space, and that again draws more people. In general larger booths give greater opportunities to use colour and design, and these things again make a booth better remembered by visitors.

Once we have determined the floorspace area and the heights, we should staff the booth with enough people to cover all parts of it. Some prefer as a rule of thumb to assign 1 person per 9 m^2, depending how many products and obstacles you have in the booth. Others work on a basis of 5 m^2 per staff member. With 1 person per 9 m^2, if each person covers a reach of 3 m in any direction then that will be enough to meet visitors over the entire area of the booth.

In our pre-show training we ought to have the staff practise moving around within 9-m^2 patches, without intruding on one another's patches unless a customer's demands require that. This exercise may feel a bit odd at first – like a

Table 2.6 Increase in
response with different sized
booths[7]

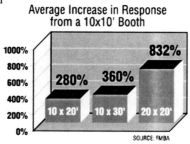

Average Increase in Response
from a 10x10' Booth

stiff, robot-like game – but it is well worth undertaking. It helps us learn how to
move around in relation to one another. It teaches us to cover all open spots and to
co-ordinate movements. Have one set of people play staff and another set take the
role of visitors. The visitors should stand in difficult locations in the booth, such as
close to other visitors, so that the staff member will need to move them to one side
without disrupting the conversation. If you are spread out at fixed stations, perhaps
represented by tall round standing tables, then you could simply say "Let me show
you an example over here" and the problem might be solved.

Many of the tips and advice given here really depend on just how much effort
you want to put into the trade show. For some, it will be enough to lay out a basic
plan, show up, and hope that all goes well. You might also use the tips in this book
to guide a series of small incremental developments year by year. You do not need
to undertake everything at once. You may also have other well-founded ideas about
what works best for you. In many situations there will be more than one correct
answer.

Being more professional does not mean being more mechanical, stiffer or more
robot-like. But that often is the first result of implementing too many rules and
regulations at a single time. We should never forget to be fellow human beings. We
ought to know the basics of the trade-show profession sufficiently well to stop
having to think about all the plans and rules and to focus rather on the people we are
meeting. But that often means learning the basics well enough before we can
concentrate on other issues. Research shows that the best salespeople are those
who can show most empathy – real empathy, not the fake version of a stiff smile,
which is so often the outcome of too much pressure. To have that confidence means
that we not only need to have basic trade-show knowledge, but also need to have
resolved our own personal problems so as to be able to give the other person our full
attention. Full attention does not mean that we are looking the other person in the
face the whole time – that is often perceived as too aggressive, especially in many
Asian cultures – but it does mean that we listen to everything he says, and that we

---

[7] *Trade Show Marketing Manual*, 2006, MFV Expositions.

react quickly when there are matters that need to be clarified. Empathy in conversations means that we follow and try to tune our emotions to what is being said, feeling what the other person is feeling. It is not, of course, the same as flirting, which can be rather dangerous at trade shows. Flirting not only risks taking your mind off what you are supposed to be doing at the show, but also wastes too much of your time and distorts your judgments about visitors' intentions. If you happen to meet the love of your life at a trade show, ask him to phone you when you get home. He will understand. If he does not, then you will have avoided wasting time.

Remember that your staff need a break every 3–4 h to function effectively. Without it they will under-perform, no matter how much training they have received.

Minicase 3: Excellent Boothmanship

Company: Case DirecTV, USA
Trade show: CES, South Hall

DirecTV offers a direct broadcast satellite (DBS) service. The company, controlled by Liberty Media, reports that it has 20 million subscribers in 2011. Its major competitors are dish and cable providers.

The booth was well thought out and designed in white. The main entrance was formed as a thick white arch which visitors could walk under. Products were well placed, and well spread out over the entire booth area, with a clear separation between different products. Information was placed in large letters high up on the wall for all to see. The company made excellent use of the height with square white cubes hanging from the ceiling. These hanging cubes matched the square cubes that weary visitors could sit on. The company had also provided comfortable areas for groups to sit together, these also in a squared white design.

The exhibitor staff were evenly spread out across the booth area, and all were busy talking to visitors. Exhibitor staff never got near to one another, other than at the counter. The company showed some of the best boothmanship at the trade show. It all looked so simple, but everyone who works on this knows that it takes a great deal of planning. There are very few companies who succeed at this level.

On the downside, white carpets easily become dirty. A different floor covering would have been better. Besides, it is questionable whether the choice of white makes a suitable association for television. For many visitors it will be associated with the pharmaceutical industry and with laboratories, not consumer electronics. The feeling was rather like walking into a dentist's office.

Conclusion: Effective use of resources by this company, a well-prepared staff: score 8 out of 10.

Professional staff is key. If you can afford it, have two teams, one on and one off the set. The *off-set team* can be used to carry out a number of crucial tasks, as well as eating and resting; their assignments can include:

1. Exhibition intelligence
2. Market surveys
3. Attending talks

We have more on exhibition intelligence towards the end of this book. Market surveys, or marketing research, is a topic well covered in other literature, but we shall say a few words here nevertheless.

Many conferences at trade shows leave a great deal to be desired. For example, it can often look as though a show has been organized just because it is expected of the companies to be there. Speakers are often poorly selected and poorly remunerated, two factors which no doubt are linked. It is rather like the case of trade-show food. Because this is not the main attraction at a trade show, the quality tends to be a secondary consideration. It should not have to be that way, but that is how it goes. Having said that, there are usually some talks that are worth attending at any show. Pick them out, have at least one person attend, and make sure that the others are briefed about the content of the conference or the convention.

In the box below we explain the difference between conferences and conventions.

Special Topic 1: Marketing of Conferences and Conventions

▶ We talk about a *conference* when the focus of the *event* is on the talks and the speakers. Exhibitions and trade shows sometimes overlap with *conferences* and *conventions* as forms of events. Conferences are normally of two kinds, or a combination of two kinds: they are either *academic* or *professional*. Academic conferences are normally peer-reviewed, meaning that participants have submitted a scientific paper and had it accepted before attending. These papers can be anything from *full-length scientific papers* to *poster papers*, which are more like sketches of papers covering a few pages.

Professional conferences are normally without any commitment on the part of participants, after they have paid their fees for attending. Both conferences and conventions are places where we listen to experts and mingle. A *convention* may not be all that different from a conference in reality. However, they are often intended for a particular profession, and admission to them is often free but by invitation only, for delegates; they will be organized by a common-interest organization. Examples are a *medical convention* and a *political convention*, for a particular party. Nowadays there are also *fan conventions*, bringing together people with the same hobbies. Examples are *science fiction conventions* and *gaming conventions*. These normally cost money to attend and are designed more as social events for people sharing the same interests.

The marketing of conferences and conventions is quite different from the marketing of exhibitions, and indeed there are differences between conference marketing and convention marketing. Accordingly this topic merits a separate book, under its own title, as another aspect of *event marketing*. Our decision to say a few words here is based simply on the fact that trade shows often have a conference component built in.

The key to the marketing of international professional conferences today, what we call *key success factors* (KSF), can be summed up as follows:

1. Inviting well-known speakers. The speakers are the main attraction. Speakers from well-known companies or speakers who have written successful books are preferred. To attract them you will either have to pay handsomely, or convince them that the conference will attract a large crowd so that they will sell more books or other services through you.

2. Well-targeted marketing to company employees. For example, if it is a marketing conference we want to contact staff in marketing departments and top management interested in marketing.

3. Holding the meeting in an attractive location. People go to conferences when they are held in attractive towns or resorts. The idea is often that family and even friends can come along. Sometimes companies will even cover their expenses. Frequently-used places in Europe include, in the case of France for example, Cannes, Nice, and Deauville.

KSFs for marketing of international academic conferences are somewhat different:

1. Organizers need scientific credibility to attract visitors, meaning that they need to be established and recognized in their field.

2. Visitors need a minimum of 3–6 months' notice, to plan for articles/research and financing.

3. The conference should be held in an attractive location, because academics too like to use these occasions to take a few days off for sightseeing. For the same reason, it can be a good idea to time the conference immediately before or after a weekend.

4. The conference needs to be able to attract major researchers in the field. There is often a sort of "wait and see who comes first" attitude at conferences. Consequently the bulk of attendees often register for the conference at the last moment. For the same reason it may be a good idea to have *early bird prices*, that is discounts during an initial period long before the date for the start of the conference.

There are a number of ways for booth staff to attend conferences during a trade show. The person designated to go to the conference can take notes and present a summary to the rest of the staff: this will be a few pages only – title, speaker's name, and the main points and arguments. Perhaps also a short critique of what was said, for others to respond to and to be used as a background for further discussion. Such discussions can be held later in the evening or after we come home, as part of the follow-up process. You might also want to consider printing the critique in a company newsletter, for your customers and potential customers to read.

Newsletters can be a stroke of marketing genius for companies. Instead of pushing products and too much information about your own company, in a newsletter you have a chance to cover a broader range of topics, to show that you are on top of what is happening in your industry. This can potentially give your company much credibility if it is done right, that is if you are able to select truly interesting stories and can write well and to the point. With today's internet technology you can even publish the story soon after the presentation is given, noting down your ideas on a laptop or electronic notebook as you listen in. If you are allowed to record the whole conference on audio tape, the chances are that more people will hear the content. Podcasts are still popular. If you can get permission to film the event, then even better.

Summaries from conferences can also be e-mailed to potential readers after the trade show is over for the day (together with all the other things you have to do before you can go to bed). Mentioning a talk by a well-respected specialist during a conversation with booth visitors will produce a professional and informed impression when done correctly. "I see you are interested in distance learning tools, did you by any chance get to hear the presentation by *N* yesterday in conference room *XYZ*? No? Well, there will be another chance to hear him tonight at *PQR*, or you can visit our website and download a summary". Trade shows, ultimately, are largely about confidence and trust, and trust is largely about information and communication. Showing that you know what is going on among experts is another great opportunity to demonstrate to visitors and to the world that you are well-informed, that you are up to date in what you are doing and can be a source of useful information. All employees know their own company, far fewer know what is going on in their industry more widely.

Filling the timetables of your staff with various activities which are not all about being at the company booth is seen by the staff concerned as a positive thing, a chance to break free and enjoy a change of pace. Often it will not even be seen as work at all. When well orchestrated, it will sometimes be seen as fun, enriching the trade-show experience and making booth staff better prepared to meet visitors during the day. These are opportunities to build the company's *knowledge management abilities*.

One reason why staff often find trade shows boring is because they have nothing to do during their free time. Another is that there are no visitors to their booth. The latter is normally more annoying than having too much to do. What companies should realize is that dead time is a *knowledge opportunity*. The problem is that these ideas will seldom come from the booth staff themselves. They are opportunities which need to be recognized by top management and planned by middle management. The company should set up an *exhibition schedule* assigning each staff member specific tasks for the entire period of the show, making the experience less dull for staff and more effective for the company.

This does not mean that everyone should be running around outside the booth whenever there are no visitors to it. Sometimes, doing nothing is the best behaviour in the booth, since it invites people to come in and talk to us. It makes us look available. If booth staff are engaged in various other activities or there is no one there to talk to, passers-by will not walk into our booth. They will think we are too busy with other things to answer their questions, and at worst they will see us as unprofessional. It is worth bearing in mind that trade shows are also a place where one can unintentionally create *bad publicity*. That is, it is quite possible for a company to generate more negative than *positive publicity*. In such a case, it would have been better not to have attended at all, but of course that is difficult to foresee in advance. No one plans their own bad publicity. There are some decisions to be made, though. At a certain point in the post-show planning phase, we have to ask ourselves whether we are well enough organized to carry off all the activities. If not, we should consider lowering our sights, perhaps cutting back on some activities, maybe even planning to leave it a while before we are ready to take part in another show.

There are seldom any opportunities to repair things that have broken in the booth during the day, because we will be too busy meeting people, unless the repair is absolutely vital for other and more important activities we have planned. Whatever repair is needed, say laying down more cables to set up extra lighting, or changing wording on the wall of the booth, we should see to it before the show opens or after it closes for the day. Anything else would look unprepared. At every show there will be some booths where alterations or construction are being undertaken during opening hours, and where exhibitors begin by excusing themselves for all the mess. Make sure you do not belong to that group.

Being prepared to talk to visitors means being ready both physically and mentally. You are *physically ready* by standing facing them in a place where they can see you and where they can walk up to you. You are *mentally ready* by showing that you want to talk to them. Moreover, the readiness will often show in your facial expression. As human beings we are specialists in reading people's faces, even though we are not usually conscious of the fact. In consequence, we also disclose much more information about ourselves and what we are thinking than we would sometimes like. This is part of what it means to be human. As we stand facing each other we are delivering ourselves to the other person, communicating before we even get an opportunity to speak.

When we need to talk to a colleague in the booth, we should be discreet about it. If your need to contact a fellow staff member arises from a visitor's question, say to the visitor that you should both go over and ask your colleague. Don't leave your visitor alone or turn your back on him or her. Use the opportunity to introduce the visitor to your colleague formally. "This is Mr So-and-so, he is *PQR* for the *ABC* company and he has some questions about *X*". When done correctly, this verbal interaction can introduce into the relationship some much-needed participation and confidence. What we are doing is raising the degree of commitment in a professional way, by being polite and a little formal. It is not about being excessively courteous, but simply polite. Situations should not feel awkward, but should reflect normal behaviour.

At international trade shows Westerners, in general, should bear in mind that Asians are often more polite in their behaviour, and accordingly they also expect to be treated in a more polite way. When dealing with people of different nationalities, you are therefore recommended to set the standard of politeness and respect not at the lowest common denominator, or at your own norm, but at the higher level of the culture you are in.

If you get a question from a colleague, consider using a notepad instead of talking, if that risks disturbing visitors. Write your questions on a slip of paper or an electronic device and leave it by the counter. For each question, write "From staff member X to Y at time T1", and then the question. When Y comes past, he can write his reply and the time T2. This enables questions to be sorted out in a discreet way without visitors being aware. Bear in mind that texting – grabbing the phone and staring at it at all times – gives the impression that you are busy and unreachable for visitors. Thus the mobile phone, too, should be used very discreetly. The notepad at the desk is not somewhere to spend your time head down for long periods either (think of the irritating experiences you will doubtless have had at hotel reception desks), but rather something for staff to check at regular intervals while coming and going. Don't use the front desk as a place to hang out, where you gaze towards the horizon looking for customers. With respect to inviting visitors in, the desk is a barrier between you. You should only go to the desk when you need to, as a place to demonstrate products, exchange certain kinds of information, or check messages.

Apart from that, there is no strong need for a reception desk at a trade-show booth. Dialogues with visitors more usually nowadays happen face-to-face with nothing in between, either standing in a free area or, if need be, sitting down. In certain cases we may need some kind of station we can take the visitors to, say to look something up on a computer screen. But the station should not be used as a place where we wait to initiate conversations with visitors, let alone a place to hang around or lean on wearily. If we are acting as we should, our movements in the booth support the dynamic of our company, reflecting who we are as people: open, keen, and professional.

Some remarks on *voice volume control*: speak clearly so that the visitor can hear and follow what you are saying, but not so loud that you drown your colleagues' voices. Practice voice volume control during the pre-show training. Have all staff engage in separate conversations simultaneously. Add noise to the exercise using a radio or suchlike, so as to simulate some of the noise which will really be occurring at the show. Walk around and measure the volume at different points in the booth. Can everyone communicate comfortably? What can be done to reduce noise, in terms of where we stand, but also of the way we construct our stands? You will be amazed how basic problems at trade shows can be. Once they have arisen, there is often little we can do about them.

If someone will be using a microphone as a part of a special presentation, that demands extra and special care. If you can discover what kind of booth set-up your neighbour has, that will be helpful. Are they using microphones? Some booths will play loud music even though it is prohibited. You should immediately make a complaint to the exhibition organizers if you suspect or notice this. If music is allowed, a rock group next to your own booth can wreck your whole exhibit, rendering any kind of conversation impossible. In the worst case this can even fill your booth with non-buying music fans. (Yes, that does happen.) If you use microphones yourself, try to design your booth so that the sound is confined within a limited area, or hire an additional facility at another location.

In addition to good music, good-looking staff, male or female, are another way to attract attention at trade shows. Unfortunately trade shows tend to attract more men than women, though this trend has been shifting over the last 20 years. Male dominance can make the environment a bit too one-sided at times, especially at the more technically-oriented fairs. Because trade shows are seen as a male-dominated environment, exhibitors have always been tempted to bring in so-called *booth babes*: women who attract attention primarily because of their good looks. To be even-handed, we could also talk about male *booth gigolos*. Many disapprove of the idea of choosing booth staff for their looks. Where it continues to be done, that is because it often works, meaning that it does attract more people to your booth. However, whether it attracts the right kind of people is another question. That should be a concern for staff managers. It may very well be that the wrong type of visitors are attracted, those who are not interested in our products but merely in meeting someone of the opposite sex, and who can carry on a conversation simulating interest in our products for half an hour just to fit in. There is also a cultural dimension to consider. Some cultures, especially in the Middle East, will be sensitive about booth staff showing too much flesh. That is often seen as inappropriate in the Scandinavian countries too, even at consumer shows, but for political reasons. Half-naked women in trade-show booths are, to many people, a symbol of the inferior value of the female sex. For others it is a matter of social class. In the worst case you might even find a demonstration mounted outside your booth. In Eastern European countries they tend to overdo the use of booth babes at trade shows, which may have something to do with Cold War suppression, economic difficulties, or institutional weaknesses. In Germany it is seen as a less serious matter. In the USA it should be done with tact, but is still a popular gimmick.

It also depends on the particular industry. Motor shows have always featured booth babes and this is still more or less expected for certain types of motor show, while in technically-oriented industries it is a more sensitive issue. In general, we can say that it is much more common in the B2C than in the B2B context.

So, before you run out and pick a bunch of good-looking staff for your booth, consider some of the counter-arguments:
- It may draw attention away from your products
- It may fill your booth with non-buyers, or lead to overcrowding
- It may be offensive to some potential buyers, particularly women buyers
- If you overdo it, it may make your company look less serious

Booth babes tend not to know much about the products and the company, as they have been recruited on other criteria. If asked a question by a visitor they may not be able to give an appropriate answer. If you are going to use booth babes (or gigolos) at all, it should be a question of how you use them. To station a handsome man or a beautiful woman at the entrance to the booth is better than putting him or her on the inside. At the entrance he or she can serve as a come-on, as a way to draw the attention of passers-by to your booth. They can also be used to distribute information or draw attention in the aisles. As the minicase shows, there are even creative ways to use booth babes, even though I do not approve of the term personally. "Models" is probably a better term, also because it is sex-neutral.

Minicase 4: Booth Babes Used with a Twist of Humour

Company: Boynq, The Netherlands
Trade Show: CES, Central Hall

Boynq is a designer of USB gadgets and USB toys, such as travel speakers and stereo iPod speakers with integrated docking stations. The distinctive Boynq design can be described as a clean techno look featuring a narrow orange horizontal. It is this narrow orange line which makes these products immediately recognizable.

The booth at the CES was elegantly integrated with their product design. At the entrance of the booth the company had placed a booth babe, dressed in a white dress, with a shocking orange hair tint. The orange hair colour created a playful association with the company's design. The company succeeded in twisting the typical bimbo association, making it look funny and joky instead. This would probably also have worked with a good-looking male.

The design of the booth as a whole was oval in shape, with counters all along the sides to display the products clearly. It was a pity that the overall size of the booth was small; that made it practically impossible to pass anyone once inside. The claustrophobic feeling made you want to leave the booth sooner than you might have liked, given the interesting miniature products there were to look at.

Conclusion: an effective use of resources by this company, a well-executed design planned down to the smallest details, booth babes mixed with humour, score 7 out of 10.

2.3   The External Co-worker: Exhibitor-Appointed Contractors (EAC)

Exhibitor-appointed contractors (EAC) must in most case be approved by show management. *Co-workers* are here defined as anyone contracted to come in and work on your exhibition for a limited period. The period in question may stretch over the whole duration of the show, and may go beyond that. For example, *booth furniture suppliers* may be consulted on an ongoing basis during the pre-show planning phase.

External co-workers can help with any of various tasks you have outsourced; they may include booth designers, booth builders, hauliers, the person you hire booth furniture from, or the person who comes to clean your carpets once you are finished. In some cases, all these tasks are performed by one company. In other cases, you may want to split them up. Normally, the larger your booth set the more external co-workers you will need to include in your trade-show plan. Hotel personnel, and any activities arranged through the hotel, do not normally count as

EACs since they are not attached directly to the exhibition and are not affected by exhibition rules and regulations. Likewise, the person from whom you buy air tickets is also not included under this heading. Instead we may consider these as *exhibition-related services outsourced.*

Make sure you know all the individuals who are going to be involved in your trade show, preferably face to face. If possible, let everyone meet, so as to see if they can work together happily and to make sure that each individual knows what is required of him or her in relation to everyone else. Once out there you need to work as a team, as a single organism. For most exhibitions, this will feel like a luxury given the limited time available for planning the event, but normally it is well worth while. You may think that you have a good relationship with a carpenter who has agreed to come and install an extra wall for your booth, whether it is wooden or a simple "pipe and drape" (tubing draped with fabric). In reality, he may have made a dozen similar agreements with your competitors, and you may not be the preferred customer when time runs short. If you can, invite them all out for an evening, including the external co-workers. That raises the level of commitment and involvement in the team. Staff and co-workers will see that they are part of a larger effort and feel contractually bound to succeed as a team.

The exhibition or *floor manager* not only has to co-ordinate his own booth staff, but is also in charge of a number of people who perform support roles. You may have the world's best booth staff, but that will not make your computers or lighting work when you encounter a problem about electric supply. Delivering electricity to your booth is the responsibility of the exhibition organizers, but distributing it among your electrical devices and making them all work when they should is your own responsibility. Exhibition staff are often not suitably qualified or prepared to deal with electrical problems. And with other kinds of problem it may be that any small repair will require a carpenter.

You may also need to engage an external co-worker for your transport needs once at the show. Getting to and from airports, hotels, restaurants, and between trade shows at different sites in a town can be a nightmare. Often the nearby car parks will be full, taxis difficult to obtain, and buses overcrowded. You do not have time to queue. Few things are more demoralizing than finding yourself stuck in a traffic jam and watching a clock as time slips past, without being able to do anything to solve the problem. Sometimes you will even see people leaving their taxis and running the last mile. So, try to work out in advance what your transport needs will be. If you comprise a team including guests and so forth, you may want to hire a dedicated driver for the duration of the trade show. If a good customer or a person of influence needs a ride, offer him your services for free. That is guaranteed to give you real brownie points. Your customers will often feel that knowing the trade show means that you know your industry, despite the fact that the one thing does not in fact entail the other.

As travel costs are often the second largest category of costs for a company at a trade show, many companies will try to develop a good relationship with a *travel agency* or similar consultant. Internet technology makes it easier for exhibitors to find prices by themselves, but it can still be worthwhile to hire expertise in this area, especially when travel becomes more complex, including many overnight stays for many people in many locations over a year. Changing rooms and unbooking flights is often seen as a hassle, better left to those who have the patience to do it efficiently. Ultimately this will often be a matter of the level of the agent's fees.

Few things bring more delight to a trade show or an evening reception than a flower arrangement. Flowers are also a good thing to give away, and should be considered along with other giveaways, for example as gifts for special customers. So you might want to make contact well in advance with a *florist* as part of the show arrangements, unless this service is offered by others, such as the hotel. Depending on the size of the trade show and the host city, florists will often be the first services to be fully booked in the run-up to a show. So we need to make contact early.

Sometimes flowers are that final human touch which your booth lacks. Ask yourself which would you rather have: a pen with a logo on it, or a flower with a small company card attached? Admittedly, a flower is difficult to carry around, but it is hard to refuse and throw away. In general we might say that the value of flowers is underestimated at trade shows, and indeed in marketing generally, possibly because the idea is just too simple.

Above all, make sure that you understand exactly where the organizer's responsibility ends and yours begin. Only then will you start to get a true perspective on your overall responsibilities at the trade show.

2.4   The Co-exhibitors

Co-exhibitors may be divided into (i) *direct competitors*, (ii) *indirect competitors*, and (iii) *non-competitors*. Of these, we are most interested in our direct competitors. That is not to say that non-competitors are uninteresting. On the contrary, it may be easier for us to go and spend time at a non-competing booth, especially with a show or industry where most people know one another.

There are not only the products to consider at the show. We can learn a lot from an exhibitor's booth design and booth behaviour. We may pick up an idea for a way to run an event with a speaker, or for how to construct a booth using the third dimension (i.e. height – very often neglected). Somewhere else, we might come across an interesting promotional gadget or giveaway, or we will see clothing which we think looks particularly suitable for the event and which we would like to copy or borrow. Larger booths always have something useful to contribute to our fund of experience. If nothing else, when a booth we visit seems poorly executed, we might learn how to avoid wasting money. In short, trade shows are full of lessons like these, for anyone curious enough to make notes.

Indirect competitors are often easier to make contact with than direct competitors. Many of the same advantages apply here with respect to lessons we can learn. And who is to say that it is not possible to have a close relationship with one's direct competitors? It very much depends on what industry and culture we are in. In the B2B domain, there are often very close relationships between competitors, especially in markets with only a few major players. For instance, in the pharmaceutical industry it is not only common to know the competitor well, many of one's employees will have worked there too. Quite often the companies will even know about one another's research programmes. Thus there is already a shared experience and understanding of the business. In consequence, many booth staff will go to meet ex-colleagues in other booths. In an industry with a few big players, you do not want to play too ruthlessly, simply because if you do it will eventually backfire on you. Your employees will talk when they go to work for your competitor. Better, then, to go about competing in a fair and professional manner. Your competitors will know about it and respect you for it.

Always bring a small notepad with you when you walk round the fair site, like one of those authors used to bring with them when they travelled in to deserted places before, made of moleskin. Or, if you are quick on the keyboard, use a smartphone. Whenever you see something good or bad, make a note of it, turn it into a lesson. Get your staff to do the same. Or better, do a SWOT analysis: make a note of opportunities and threats too. Then, after the trade show is over and you are gathering ideas for next year's show, discuss your findings with colleagues. Or, discuss them over a lunch or at a dinner with your co-exhibitors and with people of influence you know at the trade show. What could have been done differently? "Did you see the . . ..?" "What if we did something like. . .?" Little things can make a difference.

By now there may be one or two readers who feel that all this planning is getting a bit too heavy-handed. Well, is that really so? If you take into account the share of marketing expenses devoted to trade shows, in most cases the answer will be that it isn't so. On the whole the opposite is true: companies do not take trade shows seriously enough. We are walking round the show anyway, so we might as well take notes about things we see that could help improve our performance.

All of this is fairly simple and straightforward. There are no elaborate theories in this profession, but a 1,000 experiences and an ever-changing environment. What is it then that makes trade shows so difficult, leading many companies to underperform or to downright fail? The short answer is that we are happy to do a certain amount of planning, but we don't like spending as much time on planning as trade shows require nowadays. We don't enjoy training to that extent, either. Companies and managers talk a great deal about strategy and planning, but actually doing it, and doing it for weeks on end, is something quite different. That is what makes trade shows difficult.

Much of it is not rocket science either; sometimes the solution can be simple almost to the point of banality. One company was worried about the low numbers of visitors they were receiving in their booth. Then one of them noticed how a competitor had placed a bowl of sweets close to their entrance. The sweets seemed to attract a large number of visitors, and once they were there they also checked out the products. Perhaps that was merely to justify having taken a sweet, and perhaps they were not serious potential customers at all, but then again who knows. In markets where products are very similar, little things can make a big difference. We are not always as rational as we suppose.

There are a number of things to learn from experienced co-exhibitors. Observing them and listening to them is always worthwhile. The very fact that they are there and have not gone bankrupt speaks for itself. Don't treat your competition as enemies; they are also potential partners. Above all, they too are sources of experience. Just as we gather experience about our own performance and try to learn from it, so we can also gather others' experience.

2.5   The Visitors or Attendees

The term "visitor" is a misleading one, since all those who attend an exhibition are visitors by definition. In terms of motives there are (i) *buyers*, (ii) *potential buyers*, and (iii) *people of influence*. People of influence can be media or university or educational staff. There can also be (iv) *non-buying public*, who go to some (consumer) exhibitions more as a form of entertainment, just because they happen to live not too far away or because they think trade shows are fun, which they often are. As an example, many Milanese visit the fairground (Fiera) in the spirit of a Sunday outing.

We can also categorize visitors according to psychological type. Thus, visitors may be divided into (Table 2.7):[8]

The people who come to our booth will be very diverse. Most of us are unsure about how to act when we encounter behaviour that we are not familiar with or which is unexpected. The golden rule is to approach visitors with the same behaviour that we see. That way, we make it easier for us and them to connect. If they are shy, then we will be shy. If they are eager, then we should be eager. Otherwise we risk scaring them away. This *theory of reciprocity* has been observed in nature and in human behaviour, e.g. by Robert Axelrod. It is also a winning strategy in business and shows just to what extent evolutionary theory and biology is the better paradigm for the study of economics and management, not physics.[9]

The exception is aggressive visitors. You will of course not be aggressive in return, but you are allowed to be short in your remarks, and find a way to end the conversation quickly. There is another golden rule and that is to be yourself: that is, you should not put up too much of an act. Doing that, you just risk looking fake. Sincere, natural reactions and conversation have tremendous value in their own right; they promote sympathy and create empathy. Likewise, most of us can be shy or eager, without losing our true self. It is difficult to get away with putting on an act, and it will make us feel out of place. As human beings, we are good at knowing when someone is for real and when not. When we meet people we like personally, we tend to want to do business with them, perhaps believing subconsciously that we

---

[8] Modified version of Center for Exhibition Industry Research (CEIR) (2003). The role and value of face-to-face interaction, Chicago, Ill.: CEIR. CEIR has now merged with the International Association of Exhibition Management; see http://www.iaem.org/

[9] For a longer explanation of the evolutionary approach to the study of economics and management, see my previous book entitled "geoeconomics", available for free on the internet, cf. Solberg Søilen (2012).

Table 2.7 Psychological profiles of visitors

Type	Behaviour	Exhibitor response
Enthusiastic	Truly interested in the products; come into the booth eagerly and expectantly	Engage directly in communication
Curious	Stay on the edge of the carpet, but appear interested	Make room for them to enter the booth
Passive	Aisle walkers, stop and look	A friendly professional greeting/smile

will also be helping them. Some biologists would say that we want to help people who resemble us, because they remind us of ourselves so that we think we are helping our own kind; but that is a topic too deep to delve further into here. Let's just say that there are many theories from the evolutionary sciences which can be applied to economic life.[10]

What makes a good salesperson? As already said, empathy is key. Some years ago I observed a number of car salesmen. I found that the individuals who sold most were those who showed that they truly liked the customers. Research shows that the most successful salespeople are those who are also excellent negotiators and knowledgeable about their company's products and various offers. In sum, the most successful salespeople are those who are patient, caring, responsive, good listeners, and honest. This is often quite opposite to the salespeople we encounter on the phone today, or in the streets. Most of them seem to belong to the school of push marketing. Push marketing may have been a good strategy when products were new, advertising related to established products, and demand was seemingly end-less. This is not the case any longer. Instead we have gone back to basics now when it comes to selling, at least in the Western world. Possibly in another generation it will be different again. People today have experienced or are experiencing an economic crisis. Such periods tend to change people, making them more sceptical, but also humbler. Hence, now, you have to try to make a sale by building trust. Customers are not so easily fooled. They have seen most of the tricks. (And that is probably a good thing.)

Salespeople are motivated by three basic factors: the *organizational climate*, the *setting of sales quotas*, and *incentives*. The problem for salespeoples' effectiveness is that they spend too much time not selling. The biggest thieves of selling time are the general downtime in between activities and travels, and administrative time. Unfortunately, trade shows are associated with both of these. But trade shows must be seen and assessed as moments of extraordinary sales activity. They cannot be evaluated on the same basis as ordinary sales activities in one's home territory. The atmosphere is extraordinary, the setting of sales quotas bears no comparison with

---

[10] In fact, many economists think nowadays that it was a mistake for the study of economics to part company with evolutionary science and biology after the Second World War in order to follow the model of physics (equilibrium theories, neoclassical economics, the marginalist school), but a new superpower was demanding a new social-science paradigm. (Please bear with my digressions!)

other non-trade show activities, and incentives do not really play any role in a normal sense since one is selling more as a team. To have staff compete for sales while participating in a trade show is usually a sign of collective and organizational failure. Companies can and should set norms, but it is best to make results from other trade shows the basis for comparison.

Much of salespeople's time is spent making sure customers and potential customers are enjoying themselves. That is particularly true of B2B shows. Many companies will have a special VIP lounge or room for this purpose at a trade show. The VIP customer is given everything from a hotel reservation, transport, surprise giveaways, access to social events, to a special reception at the show by the CEO or other executives. Some companies give VIP customers special treatment because they believe it will make other categories of customers aspire to the same status, when they see what they could be having. However, there is no research to confirm this; rather the contrary. It may be that other customers, or indeed even the VIPs themselves, will feel that it is all a bit over the top sometimes, that the gifts are undeserved and hence receiving them is uncomfortable. Most people prefer sincerity over a hyped circus. Gifts are fine, but they should be carefully calibrated to the value of the individual customer, so that both buyers and sellers are left with a feeling of fairness.

Furthermore, we do not engage in conversations for the fun of it, but rather in order to gather data and make decisions accordingly. We want to find out why the visitor is there, what her needs are, and then work out whether the person is a potential customer and a decision-maker. In other words, is the visitor (i) a *decision-maker*, (ii) a *person of influence*, (iii) a *specifier* (someone who brings home information, most often technical data, with a view to drafting specs), or (iv) an *initiator*?

To find these things out, we need to take time at the outset to listen, rather than talking ourselves. It is amazing how difficult this can be, but it must nevertheless be attempted. It is probably difficult because we never really learn to do it. Instead we learn to talk. When we can answer the question above by placing the visitor in the correct category, we should return the ball, so to speak, into the visitor's court: "How would you like us to proceed with this?", "What do you want me to do?", "Where do we go from here?"

If a customer needs a lot of time and traffic to the booth is high, timetable a meeting. Most exhibitions today offer conference rooms as an additional service; use them if necessary.

Above all, remember to get all sales representatives at your booth to write their names on name tags in large clear letters. You must have seen the visitor who peers at your tag, trying to work out what it says. And one doesn't want to ask a person one is talking to come closer so that one can read his or her name. It feels a bit silly to have to ask for the name when there is a tag there. All this risks making the visitor feel foolish before the conversation has even begun. These are unnecessary confusions, which only get in the way of communication.

High admission fees at trade shows tend to improve the quality of visitors to the exhibition. If you are just going to look round without buying anything, you are not likely to pay a high entrance fee. If you are going to buy something, the entrance fee is seen as an investment. You then typically think that you will save the entrance fee and more by attending. Psychologically, the entrance fee should not be so high that you risk scaring potential customers away. In that case the admission-fee strategy is counterproductive. On the other hand, you do not want to set it so low that the exhibitions are crowded with *trade-show tourists*.

Analysts, journalists, and people of influence are a specially demanding type of visitor. In their minds they want there to be a clear reason for meeting. When talking to them, booth staff must be frank. If they have something new, then that is good, they should demonstrate it and be up front about it. But if not, then they should be up front about that too. Don't pretend you have a new product if you have just added a few extra buttons to a gadget; they will know this, and they will say so. If you irritate a journalist, receiving no publicity is the best outcome you can hope for. Unfortunately, that is seldom an option on the menu. If you feel that your meeting with the journalist went badly, ask him what his deadline is and try to book a second visit to see if you can convince him to write a different story. Be better prepared on the second visit.

Trade shows provide an excellent opportunity to test new products out on a critical segment of your market. A product which is a success at trade shows often turn into a success in the ordinary market. When done properly the show will function as the big boost that sets the ball rolling, that gets the product off the ground. Consequently we can also say that a trade show may serve as an *indicator of future sales*. It can also be a great opportunity to test out different colour-schemes and new designs. If visitors do not like them, perhaps it is not too late to change some features. Potentially this might give the company a chance to correct any mismatches between the new products and the preferences of potential customers. (In most cases, though, especially with physical objects, it will be too late for that year.)

When I worked for the Twentieth Century Fox marketing department in Beverly Hills as a student intern, I spent most of my time at cinemas in the Greater Los Angeles area listening to people's comments during trailers. If the audience did not like a product, there was time to change parts of it before the film was eventually launched. The logic was much the same as when other companies make prototypes and test them on potential customers. When a film is ready to be launched, this is sometimes done in connection with film festivals or similar events, i.e. as a part of a glamorous party. For most products, trade shows can be the equivalent of those glamorous parties. Once you have shown your product here, there is no turning back. You will be observed by the world and publicized. This is make or break time.

Analysts, journalists, and people of influence see themselves as almost a cut above trade-show activities and the other participants. As a company you need to recognize this and play along. Try to offer them something special, let them in on some secrets; tell them something that may be of value to them. Analysts are looking for more facts and data, journalists are looking for stories, and people of influence are looking for an opportunity to take up some of your time. For analysts and journalists you can tailor-make bespoke kits. For people of influence you can arrange an after-hours invitation where they can be given some of your time in private.

There is a third way to categorize your visitors, namely according to the generation to which they belong. Identifying the generation to which our customers belong is an important aspect of our work with respect to market segmentation. Each new generation grows up with a different range of technology and slightly different values. As companies we need to understand this, and adapt our marketing accordingly. In marketing theory we can see this as another aspect of *market segmentation*. Right now a new generation is appearing as customers at trade shows, named *generation Z* (born in the 1990s). Then there is *generation Y* (born between 1981 and 1989, but sometimes also including those born in the 1990s and later). It sometimes includes and overlaps with the *MTV generation* (1975–1985) and the *internet generation* (1986–1999), referring to a generation who grew up with MTV and cannot remember how the world was before we had the internet. The point is that this variable has a direct effect on the way some people want material to be presented, among other differences. For them, the focus is no longer just on entertainment, but on new media (internet, texting, multimedia messaging). Thus, generation Z and Y customers do not enter competitions using e-mail any more, they send text messages. So you should consider sending texts to your target customers falling into these generations, if you want to attract their interest. If you send them ordinary snail mail, they might assume it is an invoice or some sort of contract. Generation Y is also a highly competitive and pragmatic generation. As such they are less appreciative of wordy phrases and formal language. All these differences will play a role in an effective marketing plan.

Another example: *baby boomers* are often less used to the idea of intensive competition. Their focus is often more on production than on marketing. They are often engineers, whereas generation X (born in the 1960s–1970s) are often economists or marketing people. It was the type of education promoted by society at large when they were young which often decided what the members of a given generation chose to study. We are all to some extent products of our times (Table 2.8).

The more refined a market segmentation we can make, the better our chances will be of adapting our communications appropriately at the trade show. As a rule of thumb, it is often said that 80 % of visitors to a booth fall outside the relevant market segment. Of the remaining 20 %, some are more interesting as customers than others, either because they are likely to place bigger orders or because they may become good repeat customers. It may be useful to define a number of *customer profiles* within the segment. These profiles may be defined according to the expected sales they might generate (Table 2.9).

All these estimates will be guesses until they are confirmed or refuted. It may be that a person who has been seen as a profile 2 actually becomes a 4, or does not become a customer at all.

A booth may be open to all comers, or it may be closed to the general public and open only to selected guests. For some businesses which depend on exclusivity, creating a distinction based on high-quality sales leads may generate higher sales

Table 2.8 Generations

Generation	Period of birth	Characteristics/influenced by
Baby boomers	1946–1964	Economic prosperity
Generation X	1961–1981	Pop culture
Generation Y	1977–2003	New media
Generation Z	1990s	Highly connected

Table 2.9 Detailed market segmentation

Profile market segment	Type	Sales volume
Profile 1	Large orders, repeat customer	Very high
Profile 2	Large order	High
Profile 3	Repeat customer	Fair
Profile 4	Smaller order	Small

than if the booth were thrown open to all. Most examples of this technique of creating exclusivity are found in B2B trade shows, with expensive products, but it can also be relevant with B2C, e.g. for certain clubs and luxury goods. If you sell private jets you will know who your customers are, and you may even know who they are not. Having your booth crowded with members of the general public who have only come to see things they dream about or who are there purely for educational purposes may be a luxury your company cannot afford. It creates a risk of crowding out those who really would like to buy your product. Thus certain restrictions on the types of visitors allowed into the booth may be justified.

2.5.1 The Psychology of Waiting and Meeting in the Booth

Exhibition marketing is a kind of *face-to-face marketing* or *relationship marketing*, and probably the most effective kind you will ever be involved with. Each second while you are at the show is a moment of truth. Much of what we are doing is to create trust, and trust requires personal contact (cf. Tanner 1996: 80).

By the *psychology of waiting*, we refer to the mental processes connected to time, place, and activity within the physical booth before a customer meeting takes place. The reader may wonder why it is even worth mentioning the psychology of waiting. There are two reasons: first, the way you prepare yourself mentally before meeting a visitor affects your chances of gaining his or her attention. In other words, the better prepared you are psychologically for the meeting, the better meeting you are likely to have. Secondly, waiting is a large and often tiresome part of attending an exhibition – particularly if your exhibit is not attracting too many visitors, whether by your choice as mentioned above, or because of your mistakes or unpopularity. In any case, learning to cope with time is essential for your wellbeing and your performance.

So, while waiting, don't let you mind wander off into all sorts of questions and problems, and especially not your private affairs. A worried or daydreaming expression may arouse sympathy from a bystander, but it is not going to create interest on the part of passers-by in visiting your booth. On the contrary, you probably look as though you don't want to be disturbed. How we are feeling shows; it is part of our communication. That does not mean that we should act as a form of *thought police* for our staff. That would only add stress to a situation which is stressful enough as it is. But we can discuss the issue with them. How can we try to keep our focus on the people who may come in at any moment, but are not there yet, so as to be mentally ready for them? After all, this readiness will be apparent at a distance, and it will make the communication much smoother, especially at the outset, as we will be better prepared.

2.5.2 Conversation at the Booth (Face-to-Face Marketing)

There is a great deal of psychology in communication, hence we may also say with confidence that there is a great deal of psychology in marketing.[11] Here are some basic points to bear in mind when preparing for face-to-face communication at a trade show:
- The purpose of meeting the visitor is to learn enough about him to be able to contact him again after the show is over and convince him to buy our products
- For that we must gather detailed information about his needs and preferences (getting his name and contact details is *not* enough)
- Focus on what the visitor says, not on what you would like to be said
- Adapt your own messages to his or hers
- A standard selling phrase or formula will be recognized as such and only shows lack of interest. Avoid clichés and stereotypes in your conversation.
- Do not interrupt
- Show interest
- Ask whether something is unclear, if you have reason to think it might be
- Keep the balance and the harmony of the conversation in mind while speaking
- Inject some energy into the conversation when you can, e.g. by displaying a touch of humour. It is too easy to become stale, on both sides. Look at it this way: by adding humour, you are supporting both sides in what is often otherwise an unnatural and difficult communicative situation
- Do not "badmouth" your competitors in talking to visitors. Many people will take this as representing a poor attitude. If a competitor's name comes up in the

---

[11] Marketing as it developed after the Second World War, especially after Wroe Alderson, has been lacking in relation to the study of psychology, which has been quite unfortunate for the former discipline. The tendency towards specialization has in this case led marketing further away from the very reality it aims to discover and describe. This is particularly apparent in connection with trade shows.

conversation, acknowledge the fact, and go back to what you have to offer as soon as it feels natural to change the subject again.

The *AID* formula is a good way to start thinking about the actual conversation. *AID* stands for Attention, Interest, and Desire. First we try to gain the visitor's attention. Then we try to get him interested in what we have to offer. Finally we try to leave him with a desire to learn, to come back and ask for more.

When starting the actual conversation, begin with active phrases to which the visitor can give a clear positive response:

- What are you using for . . .
- What do you do when . . .
- Have you used/are you familiar with . . .
- Have you seen our new . . .
- Can I show you . . .
  Do not say:
- Have you got a minute . . .
- I guess you are the kind of person . . .
- This is a great show, isn't it?
- How important are profits/efficiency/good sales (etc.) to your company?

These questions smack of cheap sales training and a mechanical approach to conversation, which is often the same thing. Don't engage in any verbal marathons, either. Don't treat the visitor like a fool. He will only be annoyed. The people who are sent to trade shows to represent their company or to buy a product are usually the abler ones, intellectually and in other respects. Show that you understand that.

Also, remember why you as a member of booth staff are there: to sell. It is expected that the question of buying will come up: not only your employer expect this, but the visitor too expects this of you. We do not bring the point up too quickly and we do it in a subtle way, but we do not leave it too long, either. One suggestion would be to bring it up at the first moment when you can bring it into the conversation naturally and without being pushy about it, making it fit into the conversation more as an enquiry how you can help, a request for a piece of useful information.

Good conversation is an art form. Not many of us master it, and for most of us it takes years of practice. Even then, few can claim to fully master the art. We academics seem to be particularly clueless in this respect, perhaps because we have learned to distance ourselves and reflect on issues like these objectively, rather than simply engaging in them and learning by doing. Some good advice for anyone who wants to excel in this art is to listen well, answer questions, show some empathy, and not be afraid of periods of silence. A well-placed silence, as actors know, can render communication more effective and positive.

Eye contact is very important. If you lose eye contact for too long it may look as though you have lost interest in the person standing in front of you. If you stare at him for too long he will start to feel uncomfortable. As with any form of communication, you try to adjust your behaviour to the reactions you are receiving, and you try to find a good balance of looking at the other person while not staring at him or intimidating him. These are skills most of us have acquired through decades of socialization, but which we rarely think about consciously.

When we are talking to more than one person at a time, we try to look at each person for similar amounts of time, so that each of them feels included. If after a while you look always at one person, the others will see you as having decided that this is the most important person in connection with the purchasing decision. That may be correct, but it is not very polite. Besides, you may be wrong. If one of the people feels offended, he will say so when they leave your booth, and that could well be the factor that decides them not to come back. It is not uncommon to hear comments like "I thought the lady was arrogant, she had an attitude". In a case like that, even if someone else at the booth was nice that may not help or compensate for the negative perception. This may sound silly or irrational as a reason to decide not to return, but that is how we human beings sometimes are. So, being aware of this, we try to pay due attention to all visitors, acknowledging each of them through our participation in the conversation.

Be constantly alert for signs of interest or lack of interest. Look also for decision symptoms. The visitor might shift the subject of conversation towards the product and prices. Or he may talk about the specific requirements of his company. If communication is not going smoothly, try passing the person on to someone else on the pretext that he knows more about X. As already mentioned, introduce the person by name, title, and job title (if possible), and recap on your conversation to avoid repetition of questions.

Allow the visitor to get warm and comfortable before you press on with any further questions. Once you have established a good rapport, you can ask more detailed questions about the visitor's business and business needs.

A good way to break off an unwanted conversation can be by saying you have an appointment (and looking as though you mean it). At trade shows there are always a series of legitimate excuses to choose from. With some unwanted visitors it may be that the other person is talking too much, so that you cannot get a word in. If that happens, it will even be difficult to explain that you are needed elsewhere. In that case, a good way to get someone's attention when they are in full flow is to say the person's name. Most of us tend to take that as a cue to stop talking. If that does not help, you are indeed faced with a difficult case. If this happens, you are allowed to say "excuse me" and leave.

Paying attention to psychological aspects of conversations should not lead to what is called *psychologization*, where we use most of our energy to analyse the other person's thoughts. We are not there to pretend to be Sigmund Freud. In reality there should be a fine balance between trying to meet expectations by listening to and understanding the other person, and at the same time trying to engage in a warm and constructive conversation. People who spend more time analysing the person they are talking to than engaging in the conversation freeze up in their posture and look as though they are staring, or they get that sceptical look on their face which speaks of a certain distance and disengagement, and will quickly torpedo the conversation.

There are many kinds of distance between sellers and buyers. Two types which have been identified are *social distance* and *technological distance*. Some buyers feel threatened by the fact that the other person is a seller. Suggestions about how to reduce these two kinds of distance have been given by Davis Ford (1980): give the buyer an impression of the ways the seller works. By displaying what you are, you make the encounter feel less scary. This also shows that you are able to distance yourself to an extent from what you do: you are not just a seller.

To reduce the second kind of distance, technological distance, give the buyer an opportunity to inspect the products and grasp how they fulfil the buyer's needs (Ford 1980: 339–353). It is a very simple point, but one which is still often forgotten: have your actual products in the booth. If your product is too big or heavy for the booth, make a model of it, so that you can focus a constructive and informative conversation around it. It should be unnecessary for exhibitors to jot down little sketches of the things they are selling, once the potential customer is there. He expects to see the actual product, and to try it out if appropriate. Photos and brochures are not good enough by themselves, and will not do for this purpose. Even a video may feel a bit amateurish or inadequate in these circumstances. Brochures and flyers are often best treated as reminders of conversations; they should not be seen as an alternative to showcasing the products. In many cases a business card giving a website and an e-mail address will be preferred to literature on paper. In these days of QR codes people are becoming less willing to carry several kilos of brochures along with them in a bag. And paper is also undesirable in connection with the threat of climate change, too, a factor which is gradually coming to concern people.

Feeling welcome is an important issue for visitors entering your booth. Far too few exhibitors welcome their visitors properly, in part because younger generations are more informal in their communication, in part because they have never learned how to do it. At trade shows it is important that each person entering your booth is clearly acknowledged, to the extent that is possible. The easiest way to do this is by some sort of greeting. When we say "Welcome to *XYZ*", and mean it, the visitor automatically feels involved and ready to engage in conversation with us. We do not say "Welcome to *XYZ*, how may I help you?", because that is often considered slightly offensive. Many visitors walk into your booth simply because they are curious. By being too direct you might scare them off. Sometimes we need time to look around. We may discover products that we did not know about. Visitors must be given time to explore these options by themselves before we begin to ask them about themselves.

For all our expertise and training, most exhibitors are inaccessible to visitors in one way or another. It may be in the way we stand, facing away from where people are passing. It may be in our body language, transmitting a "don't bother me" look, or it may be in what we say, as just discussed. If you are not comfortable about meeting people, they are going to notice. If we are not the social type, perhaps we should have let someone else in our company take our place. Here are some tips for how to look more accessible in the booth:

1. Stand where visitors can see you
2. Stand where visitors can come to you
3. Stand where you can be private enough to exchange meaningful information as required (but not so private as to create doubts about your professional motives)
4. Stand on your own

Meeting two exhibitors at the same time is seldom successful. First, it makes you wonder as a visitor why there need to be two. Second, it looks as though they have not got much to do. Third, it gives the impression that they would prefer to be talking to each other rather than talking to you. Fourth, it is often more difficult to meet and talk to two people simultaneously, in part because you always have to think about the other person who is not immediately involved in the discussion. This mistake is often made by important companies occupying large booths, where there are plenty of young staff. At worst these situations can look more like teenage parties than serious business encounters, which represents a misunderstanding of the role of entertainment at trade shows. The mistake is also made in smaller booths containing just one standing table. As that is the sole focal point, all booth staff tend to congregate there; in the worst case they may perch on the corner of the table, looking like a flock of ravens ready to attack. It would be much easier for visitors to walk up to that table if there were only one person at it.

After a face-to-face meeting with staff, the visitor will take away an impression of the encounter. This impression will be either positive or negative. Naturally, we want to make sure it is positive, or as positive as possible, but that is not always easy to ensure. This issue raises a series of questions, including "what is a positive meeting?" and "how can I try to ensure that the meeting is positive?"

First, there will be many different kinds of positive meetings. There will not be one guaranteed route to arrive at any one of these different sorts of meeting, but many. The general recommendations, such as being positive, alert, and polite, can serve as a basis, a set of necessary conditions. However, they are not enough to crack the problem. For that we need something more.

If we dig deeper into the question, we find that building trust is a key concept for a positive meeting. It is in fact the single most important concept in all business transactions, especially for service businesses. This in turn raises another question, how does one build trust? Two rules to follow here are to be well-informed about one's subject and to be focused, which means answering visitors' questions as accurately as we can. We do not oversell or take unnecessary risks by being too clever. If we are selling holiday homes in Spain, say, we do not assure the buyer that prices will not go down next year. We do not know; no one knows. Knowledgeable visitors will be aware of that. Most visitors react negatively to pretentious and "wrong" answers. It may be that they like the houses you are selling, and that they are even comfortable with the price. But, without trust, they will not proceed. Often there will be many sellers of a product. What matters most is not necessarily the best product, or even the best price, but the best relationship. Another way to look at this is to think of the relationship as part of the product.

It is not always easy to leave a visitor with a positive impression of our products and services. Some visitors are downright difficult and rude. Some love to hear themselves talk and will carry on forever. Others keep repeating the same questions.

As a golden rule, stay with the visitor for as long as you are needed, provided there are no other visitors in the booth currently. If other visitors require your attention, make sure you do not simply walk away without some sort of polite leavetaking. Every meeting should have a clear beginning and a clear end. Say "Would you excuse me for a moment?" or something similar. If there are no other visitors in the booth and you are on duty, there are not really any good excuses for ending the conversation prematurely. Bear in mind that it will look quite strange and rather comical if you end the conversation and the visitor remains in the booth with you standing silently in another corner. So long as you are engaging in conversation with visitors, it looks as though you are popular. That will attract more visitors. When another person walks in, we try to wrap up the conversation we are already engaged in.

For many practical reasons we are not allowed to get bored with our visitors. That is a great sin (but one often committed), and although it may be understandable it is unforgivable. It is an indication that the member of staff in question is not the right person for the job. If you enjoy your work and you like talking to people, you should not need to get into this situation. There should always be things to talk about. That does not mean that we have to behave like clowns or crack jokes the whole time. To adopt the role of entertainer is seldom a good conversational strategy. Be, rather, a rational but polite individual. Try to make an effort to understand everything that is said, and answer as accurately as possible.

That is all very well (you may say), but what about those really annoying visitors who refuse to leave the booth? Well, if you cannot encourage the person to go elsewhere, plan a set of agreed signals with your booth colleagues. For example:

- Arms crossed could be "Help me get rid of this visitor", for instance, tell me I am needed on the phone
- Arms on hips could be "Could you take over this visitor?"

Some conversations simply do not work because of bad chemistry, as we say nowadays, that is the fact of having very different personalities. Sometimes that can be enough to wreck a conversation. That is all right, if it happens occasionally. We do not connect with everyone. No one does. Try not to overanalyse these situations. If we do, we only risk distancing ourselves further from the conversation. When we are in a conversation we should focus on what is being said and nothing else. Don't be afraid to say "Excuse me, what did you say?" or the like. If you are being a good listener, not only are you entitled to ask such a question, it actually demonstrates that you are listening well. Thus it becomes a positive element in the conversation, and helps build the relationship.

Some exhibitors, through error or sheer bad luck, take up the position of a guard at the aisle, making a barrier between the company and its potential visitors. It may be that they are tired of being inside the booth and would like to look around, but cannot leave the premises. There should be no need for people to stand at the entrance of your booth like security guards. This only tends to scare potential visitors off. Your booth is supposed to be a welcoming place. The barriers to entry become unnecessarily high if you place your staff at the entrance. People will feel that they are being a nuisance by edging you back inside. And another impression this creates is that the contents of the booth cannot be all that interesting, since the staff are distancing themselves from it.

This does not mean, though, that you should not assign someone among your staff to take responsibility for security at the booth. Whoever is given responsibility for security should plan and co-ordinate efforts with the show organizers' security people. He should also draw up a range of likely scenarios, and involve all staff in training for them, so that everyone knows what to do in each case. It may be anything from a visitor who faints in your booth as a consequence of dehydration or stress, to someone who starts yelling at you and refuses to leave. In the first case, at least one member of your staff should have cardiopulmonary resuscitation (CPR) skills. In the second case, you need to get someone to practise how to escort a person away through a crowd without getting too physical. In most cases it is enough to wear an item of clothing labelled "Security" and to lead the person away with clearly directed words and a hand showing the way: "Please sir [it is almost always a man], leave the booth at once". Once in the aisles, stand with the person until he leaves the area. If he does not leave right away, call the organizer's security detail. They should be able to lead the person outside the hall. Luckily, these situations rarely happen at the average trade show.

Make sure also that the flow of people along your aisle is free enough for people to walk to and fro at their own pace. You do not want anyone in the aisle slowing down the traffic. If that happens, try to sort it out in a friendly way before it causes a problem. It may be anything from a food seller to a few people talking on mobile phones and blocking the flow of traffic into our booth. Whatever you do, never use *exaggerated violence*, that is more than is absolutely necessary. Just the idea of something like this being recorded will be enough to keep your chief executive awake at night, and will certainly not earn you a promotion.

Try to avoid having your entrance diagonally across from the entrance to your neighbour's booth. A blockage outside his entrance will tend to lead to blockage outside yours also. We are not permitted to police the aisles, but we can make simple requests to passers-by.

If there is a real hold-up in the aisles, contact the organizer straight away.

2.5.3 Body Language in the Booth

As we have seen, we communicate with more than the words we utter (their meaning and the way we say them). We also communicate with the way we dress and the way we move our bodies in the booth, including our facial expressions. We should pay attention to our body language. We do not make sudden movements or anything that could make a visitor uneasy. In a booth there is very limited space to move around, so doing so can be really problematic.

Booths are very often overcrowded, at least at certain times in the day. If that happens, we might consider asking people to queue to enter the booth. We would then only let new visitors in as others leave. When done properly this can be perceived as a positive sign of exclusiveness rather than a restraint and a consequence of poor planning (which is what it sometimes is, for instance if too small a booth size was chosen initially). Overcrowded booths are no use to anyone. They quickly become chaotic and stressful. As visitors we cannot see the products or talk to any of the exhibitors. Our visit risks becoming uninteresting. When the booth is beginning to get crowded, it is recommended that staff try to remain at their stations, spread evenly across the floorspace in order to handle as many requests as possible.

If on the other hand the booth is empty, we do not under any circumstances leave it unattended. For all practical purposes, an unattended booth is worse than not being present at the show at all. At best it looks odd, but more often the passer-by will take it to reflect some crisis, as if everyone inside had to rush out to solve a big problem. Nevertheless it always happens from time to time, usually because the booth was short-staffed and the only remaining staff member had to go somewhere, even if only to the toilet. This situation simply says "unprofessional", or "poor planning" – which is much the same thing.

In general, while one is moving round in the booth one's arms should be kept down and by one's sides, as when making a speech (though this is less applicable if you are at a trade show in the Mediterranean region or in South America, where gesticulations are part of communication). Your body should be held straight, facing the person you are talking to. If you stand a little twisted and turned away from the person, it looks as though you are trying to get away, or as though you do not want to engage fully in the communicative situation because you feel sceptical and are looking for a way out. At any rate it certainly does not look good. When a group of visitors arrive, try to create a circle by stepping back. If you do not try to include everyone in the conversation, you will appear excluding. Those excluded will want to leave, and will look irritated. Consequently those you are talking to will want to leave too, because they look on one another as one big group. Having a conversation with a group of people is more challenging in various respects. In general the discussion will become broader, and humour will play a more important role in easing the extra tension.

Avoid any kind of tic, such as tapping your finger or your foot, flicking your fingers, or the like: these are perceived as nervous movements. (This might not apply if you are at a trade show for the music industry, but in that case the tapping should at least be rhythmical.)

Some readers might want to see the topic of facial expressions covered in more detail. After all, they seem so important for making a sale. But, in my view, too much training in this area will often lead to unnatural and stiff behaviour, as when we hear that people are "going to smiling school". Who has not seen a staff member sitting on a bench with a cold smile which slowly turns into a grimace? The cold smile becomes even worse than no smile. The problem is psychological. If we think too hard about natural behaviour, it tends to become less natural. Some basic ideas about body language are worth teaching and bearing in mind, but this can quickly become excessive. The same applies in the case of facial expressions.

People who focus too much on how they look tend to focus less on what they say, that is, they pay less attention to the actual conversation while their attention is elsewhere. When communicating it is important to listen, to be able to respond quickly to what the other person is saying. Our minds should not be wandering. Again, most staff do not need to "work" much on these issues. It is important not to turn this into psychologization. While we are generally content with our lives, this shows in our face and we do not have to worry about it. Our communication and body language will follow. With some general politeness we should be all set to meet any visitor, no matter how awkward.

To make the conversation successful, we offer a smile at a convenient moment and try to show real interest in what the visitor has to say. In most cases he will repay us in the same coin. Now we have a good basis for productive communication. Good, positive energy is an upward spiral of giving and receiving. We should give of our best and wait for this to be returned. Then we give some more; and so forth. It normally works. If anyone needs a theoretical reason for accepting this, presumably we could apply *the theory of reciprocity*, already mentioned. And that also gives us the golden rule "Do unto others as you would have them do unto you". If you smile all the time, you run the risk of looking like an idiot. Try instead to be in tune with the person you are talking to.

During the pre-show training, comment on one another's behaviour. You might also consider videotaping body language in the booth while training. Get the participants to comment on their own body language, too. What worked and what did not, and why?

Most of us do not need to be told about all this; we know how to act, how to be natural. However, most of us can do with some gentle reminders occasionally. It is very easy to show a less attractive side to ourselves at times, and we do not always give a conversation the attention it deserves.

2.5.4 Booth Tidiness and Organization

All objects lying around the booth which do not contribute to attaining the company's goals can be seen as "noise"[12] and should if possible be removed or put away. These items merely divert attention away from what we want said and done, and within an environment that is very restricted in space and in time, at that.

Untidiness can stem from small and seemingly unimportant things. For instance, if you leave a few used plastic cups on a table, visitors will notice them and find them out of place. This is not about the cups in themselves. The likelihood is that some visitors will associate them with mess in general and this may reflect by association adversely on your company. If there are many cups lying around, visitors will think the booth looks messy, untidy, or at worst, say if the cups are half-full, even disgusting. The next step may be that they start to wonder if the

---

[12] "Noise" in communication is anything distorting the original message. At a trade show the message is defined in the strategy. Anything which does not contribute to attaining that goal is classified as noise.

sloppiness they have seen is typical of other parts of the organization's activities or of their products. Having some mess in your booth may not be such a big deal if you are selling motorcycle parts, but it will certainly be an issue if you are a pharmaceutical company. And there is another point about plastic cups: they look cheap. You might want to invest a few dollars more in mugs with your company logo on. And if so, you can also use them as valuable giveaways.

Does all this sound too harsh, verging on over-policing? Well, everything we place in that booth is going to impinge on our product and our company – everything from the things we leave lying about to the shoes we are wearing and the perfume we chose to wear. This is not a thing about trade shows in particular, it is just that at trade shows everything is compressed and put to the test before such a large audience. That is, the effects of our behaviour and the impression people get from our booth become much more striking, since we are exposing ourselves to the whole world over just a few days.

Untidiness can arise from items such as:
- Cups and drinking glasses
- Cigarettes, lighters
- Sunglasses
- Newspapers
- Printed material from other exhibitors
- Luggage
- Garments, shoes
- Completed and half-completed inquiry forms
- Cheap pens spread across a table
- Kettles and vacuum flasks
- Waste paper
- Cardboard boxes
- Pieces of unfinished booth decor or structure

It can be a good idea to put one of the exhibition staff in charge of tidiness in the booth each day, and to ask everyone to pick up after themselves and their latest visitors. By rotating responsibility for tidiness you avoid making one staff member look like a policeman or rubbish collector. If the booth is small, you will probably not want a cleaning lady running round it. There are already enough different roles to keep track of and enough people to deal with as it is. Furthermore, such a person could seem rather out of place in this environment. She might get questions from visitors. And that would also send a signal that our staff cannot pick up after themselves – which might be true, but this is not the place to show it.

If there are tidiness problems, issues that cannot be resolved quickly, or issues which keep recurring, they should be reported to the booth manager/team captain for the trade show straight away, not left till the end of the show. Ultimately, tidiness is a major concern for our joint marketing effort at trade shows, because it reflects on our image.

2.6   Organizers, Show Management, Show Owners, Show Promoters, and General Service Contractors (GSC)

Trade show organizers or hosts are usually either an association (that is the norm in Germany, for instance), or a company owned by a private individual. These alternatives correspond to considerable differences in the way a trade show is run. With an association, the focus is on the interests of its owners. That will usually imply maintaining certain standards, and often involves a strong educational aspect. When a show is run by a private individual, the focus is often on profits and the short term. Find out who is behind the show you are participating in. That will help you understand what kind of show you can expect. For instance, *privately-owned trade shows* are not always known for inviting the best speakers, because they usually charge high fees. That does not mean that privately-run, for-profit trade shows are necessarily less good, but it changes the way participants see the show and what you can expect. Then there are also mixed forms of trade show, part-association, part-private company.

Sometimes, the owners of a show will contract with *show promoters* to run the trade show for them. In all cases, the show will be run by a *show manager* or someone with a similar title.

The sites of most conferences are fixed and long-established. Organizers who want to develop a new conference will be looking for interesting destinations and exhibition spaces. Organizers nowadays are more likely to think in terms of entertainment and tourism, as people are often looking for an excuse to go away somewhere nice. That could be a major city, of course, but it might alternatively be a resort, such as Las Vegas or, today, the even larger casino city of Macao.

A trade show is an excellent way for an *industry association* to achieve many of its objectives, as Table 2.10 suggests. We may categorize the various functions of an association in terms of their relevance to the trade show:

We see, for example, that providing greater purchasing power through group discounts is a major function of the association which is highly relevant to trade shows. We also see that trade shows are excellent opportunities for disseminating general information, creating and maintaining social relationships, and developing statistical data and research. But we also see that trade shows are not a place where associations improve employee–employer relations or handle industry/professional legal affairs. For those things, the environment is too noisy, too turbulent, and too much oriented to other activities. Such things are better handled in direct, private conversations with the parties when they are calm and at home and can focus on activities that are not part of the trade show.

Another class of associations are *trade show and event associations,* which work for the improvement of the trade-show industry itself, primarily to enhance the trade-show experience and performance for exhibitors. Here are some examples, predominantly from the USA (Table 2.11):

These associations work to help members become better at what they are doing at the trade show, which includes basic training, best practices, insights, business intelligence, and seminars.

Table 2.10 The functions of an industry association (See also Hoyle (2002: 10–11))

Functions	Relevance to trade shows
Providing greater purchasing power through group discounts	High
Disseminating general information	High
Creating and maintaining social relationships	High
Developing statistical data and research	High
Promoting members' professional development	High
Offering education and training	High
Providing group travel opportunities	High
Creating positive public relations	High
Introducing opportunities for entertainment, networking, and peer interaction	High
Establishing industry standards	Medium
Influencing legislative/political affairs	Medium
Building a body of knowledge through publications	Medium
Defining the industry/profession though demographics	Medium
Performing public service activities	Medium
Identifying and defining common causes	Medium
Improving employee/employer relations	Low
Handling industry/professional legal affairs	Low

Returning to the organizers: we often forget that trade shows are very much like shops which we can rent for a short term from someone who has in turn rented the site for a longer term. This can be a profitable business. Behind these shows we find companies like Canon Communications, Reed Elsevier, ROC Exhibitions, etc. These companies take tenancies of exhibition sites, trade-show centres, convention centres, and hotels in order to rent individual booths out to exhibitors. This business is very much marketing- and sales-driven.

Trade shows are big business, often bringing great benefits to a city. That was how they started, and that is how they are often seen and judged today. In many cases host cities will turn the trade show into an important component of their own self-promotion. Many cities will try to benefit from their trade show by channeling visitors and exhibitors into other activities as well. For instance, it is no accident that Las Vegas has become the host to many of the world's largest trade shows. It is a showbiz city. If places like this are able to persuade so many industry experts to travel so far in the name of work, that is because they offer leisure activities. Once at a trade show, exhibitors and visitors will find time for other activities besides work. From a company's perspective, that may be seen as interference, stealing attention away from the trade show itself and reducing its effectiveness. On the other hand, companies want to be where everyone else is, meaning of course first of all their customers. And customers like going to casinos too.

The leading trade-show cities continue to be established commercial centres such as Hanover, Milan, Frankfurt-am-Main, and Düsseldorf. Of course, these

Table 2.11 Trade show and event associations (See http://www.all-about-trade-show-exhibits. com/associations-resources-and-publications-49/(2012-09-20). Some changes have been made to update the information on this site afterwards. EACA is now E2MA)

Association	Website	Aim and services
Center for Exhibition Industry Research	www.ceir.org	For 30 years, CEIR has been highlighting the importance of exhibitions in today's business environment. Its goal is to promote the image, value, and growth of exhibitions. This is accomplished through producing primary research studies that demonstrate the effectiveness and efficiency of exhibitions as a marketing medium. CEIR then incorporates those findings into a targeted, continuing promotional campaign
Exhibition Services and Contractors Association	www.esca.org	ESCA is dedicated to the advancement of the exhibition, meeting, and special events industries. Through the education, information exchange, and level of professionalism shared by members and their customers, ESCA promotes co-operation among all areas of the exhibition industry
Exhibit & Event Marketers Association (E2MA)	www.e2ma.org	The Exhibit & Event Marketers Association (E2MA) is the trade-show industry's newest association, formed by a merger between the Tradeshow Exhibitors' Association (TSEA) and the Exhibitor Appointed Contractors Association (EACA). The mission of the E2MA is to enhance the expertise of exhibition and event-planner professionals in exhibition and event marketing, and to raise the level of service excellence on the show floor
Exhibit Designers and Producers Association	www.edpa.com	The Exhibit Designers and Producers Association (EDPA), founded in 1954, is an internationally recognized national trade association with more than 400 corporate members from eighteen countries which are engaged in the design, manufacture, transport, installation, and service of displays and exhibitions primarily for the exhibition and event industry. Its purpose is to provide education, leadership, and networking for the advancement of its members and the exhibition industry
Healthcare Convention Exhibitors Association	www.hcea.org	The Healthcare Convention & Exhibitors Association (HCEA) is a trade association representing organizations united by their common desire to increase the effectiveness and quality of healthcare conventions and exhibitions as an educational and marketing medium HCEA promotes the value of exhibitions as an integral part of healthcare meetings

(continued)

Table 2.11 (continued)

Association	Website	Aim and services
		Since 1930, HCEA has provided healthcare exhibitors, medical associations, and suppliers with a forum for the exchange of mutually beneficial information and ideas
International Association of Exhibitions and Events	www.iaee.com	IAEE promotes the unique value of exhibitions and other events which bring buyers and sellers together, such as road shows, conferences with an exhibition component, and proprietary corporate exhibitions. IAEE is the principal resource for those who plan, produce and service the industry
Canadian Association of Exposition Management	www.caem.ca	CAEM is the Canadian Association of Exposition Management. It is Canada's national association of professional individuals involved in managing, planning, and producing trade, consumer, and professional expositions and similar specialized events, as well as companies providing products and services to these events. Together it works to ensure the industry is heading in a direction that will benefit everyone. It provides valuable industry-specific services, programmes, and products, including a newsletter, unique publications, employment referral, seminars, an annual conference, professional certification, and industry research
Event Marketing Institute	www. eventmarketing. com	The Event Marketing Institute is a think-tank, educator, and global professional resource dedicated to the advancement and development of best practices, insights, and business intelligence for individuals and companies using live marketing as a strategic marketing initiative. EMI serves as a catalyst for innovative thinking in event-marketing strategies, tactics, and measurement

cities, like all major cities, also offer a wide variety of leisure activities. Visitors to the Fiera di Milano may also want to find time to see the Duomo or go to an opera at La Scala, if they can get tickets. Knowing that, exhibitors can use these attractions to their advantage, for example by buying tickets well in advance, organizing visits, and integrating all this into their marketing activities while in the city.

General service contractors (GSC) are companies which the organizers contract to provide all the labour and services required by the exhibitors. If everything works well, you should need no further contact with the organizers themselves once you have registered for the show and know how things work. Still, in case something does crop up, you ought to know who the organizers are and how you can get hold of them. Know who to contact for different problems that might arise at all hours. The information may be crucial when something goes wrong, and sooner or later something always does. It might be anything from a noisy co-exhibitor to malfunctioning electricity supply. When time is scarce we do not want to waste it finding out who is who and what they do. Instead we just want a list of functions, names, and phone numbers.

Having a good relationship with the organizers may turn out to be an advantage for you if you should need some special favour. It might also influence your chances of securing a specially desirable location at the trade show, or of getting first access to suppliers for external services needed around your booth – say, a bench along the aisle, some extra plants in the odd corner, or perhaps even a food stand close by. Trade shows are about face-to-face meetings. Organizers are just one of the categories of people you want to meet in this way. Good personal relations with the organizers are likely to take you further towards achieving your marketing goals.

Find out what kind of insurance the organizers have, and in particular whether it will reimburse your costs in case of fire or other damage. Study the whole range of issues related to liability law: who is responsible for what if something goes wrong? Who pays? This should be a part of your *overall risk assessment*. If the documentation is not clear, ask straight questions. If you are a major player, set conditions specifying your own requirements.

Start by reading the contract and the rules and regulations section of the show manual. Show organizers can help in a number of ways apart from their role as sellers of trade-show space. They can provide statistics on previous shows, directories of exhibitors and press, a good deal of material which will help you become better prepared. You can also ask them for advice.

2.7   Trade Shows and Trades Unions

It is always a good idea to read the exhibitor manual when you can get hold of it. It will help you to prepare and tell you what you can do and what you cannot do. Many trade shows are heavily regulated, not least with respect to the people you take on for the work of constructing and dismantling your booth. Many trade shows have a *union-only set-up* policy, intended to avoid high insurance costs if exhibitors were to do it themselves. That is standard in the USA, for example. Union-only policies are usually non-negotiable. This means that things can take time.

What kinds of services are provided by unionized labour? These will include (cf. Levinson et al. 1997: 154–156) the work of:

- Carpenters
- Decorators
- Electricians
- Plumbers
- Projectionists (required at some shows)
- Riggers (handle all machinery)
- Lorry drivers (handle material in and out of shows)

At some trade shows you will be allowed to set up your own booth, provided you can do it in less than 30 min. If it takes longer, the union may have the right to come in and take over. Of course, that will cost more, so make sure to include these costs in your total trade-show budget. In many countries, tips are given for excellent service, but if a bribe is suggested you should contact the show manager.

The above has covered the "software" side of trade shows. In the next chapter, we shall look more closely at the "hardware" side.

Booth Design and Marketing Materials

3

A booth at a trade show is like a *pop-up store*, a temporary shopfront to attract special attention over a short time period. We can divide the booth market into *standard* or *budget booths,* and *custom booths.* Most of what we shall discuss in this chapter relates to the latter.

When someone walks past your booth, you have about 3 s to get their attention. That is much less than the time it takes to read a sentence explaining what your booth is all about. A person walking for just 10 min without entering any booth may have passed 50 booths before he reaches you. It goes without saying that he will become weary and lose more and more of his concentration. He also becomes less easily impressed. Eventually, all he will see is legs and green carpet as his head keeps tilting towards the floor. Then he passes your booth. Now, how are you going to grab his attention?

Most of what is written on the walls of the booth he cannot read even while walking in an upright posture, since what you have to say will be either too distant or written too small. The focus should therefore be on design: form, colour, and material. Copy should be kept to a minimum. Where text is used, and is intended to be read by passers-by, it should be written in very large lettering. Preferably you should use only a few words, hence short sentences. In an environment where everyone is screaming for attention, you have a very short time to make an impression.

Once people are inside the booth, they have no time to waste. Most visitors (58 %) wait 60 s or less for help before they leave. Forty-two percent are willing to wait 3–5 min. Eleven percent are willing to wait half a minute, and 6 % are not willing to wait at all. That is the hard reality of trade show conditions. Those are the conditions in which we in marketing must work (Fig. 3.1).

To grab our visitors' attention, we have very little time to make a good impression. If they do not see anything they like straight away they are going to walk away promptly (unless they were looking for us in the first place, that is).

The *golden rules of booth design* are uniqueness, uniformity, and simplicity. In addition, we can define a number of *guidelines*, thus it has often been found that rounded shapes lead to better and more positive reactions than booths constructed

K. Solberg Søilen, *Exhibit Marketing and Trade Show Intelligence,*
Management for Professionals, DOI 10.1007/978-3-642-36793-9_3,
© Springer-Verlag Berlin Heidelberg 2013

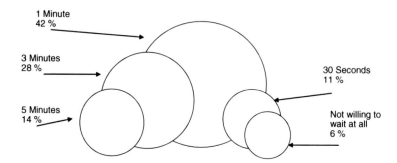

Fig. 3.1 Visitor willingness to wait for a staff member's attention once in the booth (From Friedman 1999)

with straight lines. This may be because they are perceived as softer, friendlier, and more appealing to the eye. Straight lines on the other hand tend to terminate eye movements abruptly.

Your booth needs to be unique in order to stand out and grab the attention of passers-by. Everything you include in it should be consistent, that is, it should complement what is already there rather than conflict with it; so for instance your clothing should fit the overall design of the booth. You would not want to have a modernistically designed booth filled with staff in conservative clothing. Instead you ensure that styles and colours harmonize. Simplicity is necessary because complex design and complex messages are not absorbed in this kind of environment, where so much design of so many kinds are competing for visitors' attention. You might think that this would lead to booths that are unique, uniform, and simple. In practice, it does not. Rather, small and medium-sized booths tend to look much the same as one another. This is of course largely a matter of budgets and time constraints, but that is not the whole explanation. It is also due to the relatively low priority placed on booth design, and a lack of understanding about the complexity of the environment. When we plan our booth, we typically approach the task as if we were going to be the only exhibitors, without considering what other exhibitors will be doing with their booths. We scan new technology on roll-ups and floor designs, and glance through trendy designer magazines. The result of this is that too many exhibitors end up with similar plans. What they think is original will turn out not to be so; at best it will look trendy. In an environment where everyone is trendy, no one is special, so no one stands out. Thus everything risks looking flat, or even foolish.

Even the larger booths often tend to look alike. The total statement they make can be summed up as "I am big and solid". It all looked so good on the drawing board. Of course, at that point you were only considering your own booth. When you place five to ten of these booths next to one another, you get a whole wall of them and you can hardly pick any one of them out. Sometimes it is as if they are not there at all, as if the booths were all part of the permanent structure of the exhibition hall. This may be acceptable (at best) if you are a bank, or a volume car manufacturer, but it is not even acceptable if you are any kind of innovative company and need to communicate that message to visitors.

There is another way to look at this situation. The fact that other exhibitors do poorly in this area means that you have a better chance of succeeding. Focus instead on being different. Different is more noticeable than trendy.

As already mentioned, many visitors will have planned in advance to visit certain booths because they are interested in the company and/or its products. For them the design of the booth has no influence on their decision to walk in. But the design will influence their perception of the company. Depending on your design they will be more or less impressed with what they see. It is also true that a large proportion of the passers-by who are attracted to your design or your booth will not purchase anything from you. They will just walk in because that seems like a good idea. On the other hand, some will actually purchase from you, so if you have the capacity to welcome them you gain more than you lose by planning an interesting booth.

From a wider perspective, there are only so many ways for a company to gain competitive advantage. These can be summed up as: the need fulfilled by the product, the offer, and the design. Design is not confined to the product; it applies to the booth too. You want to use the opportunity offered by the trade show to stand out and do better than your competitors. This is ultimately just another dimension on which you can compete. That is a good way of looking at it.

When it comes to booth design, we are not free to construct just whatever we might think of. Booth design is *externally constrained* by the rules and regulations for each trade show. The major constraints are size (width, depth, and often height) and a prohibition on various kinds of potential interference with co-exhibitors (activities that block the aisles, loud music, etc.). If your stand is particularly tall, you might want to make early contact with the organizers to negotiate a suitable location for it. The trade-show manual should also specify types of booths permitted, information about evacuation routes, fire regulations, all the things you are not allowed to do (such making holes in the floor), etc.

Having studied the exhibition plan, make a note of what the traffic flow is likely to be, that is, how you think people will walk around given the layout of the halls. What size are the aisles, and what is the capacity of the staircases and lifts that will bring visitors to you? Where are the bottlenecks? Based on this analysis you can provide a better route description for your visitors. Publish your location and the route to it on your website. That should increase the number of visitors you attract.

Beside the external constraints discussed above, we can also define a number of internal constraints. *Internal constraints* come in the form of budgets and our own company's specific user requirements. These will typically be in the form of explicit objectives relating to product distribution and availability, and they ought to be in line with company strategy.

Then there are a certain number of rules of thumb about construction and how to attract visitors to your booth. You want to build a booth where there are:

- No obstacles to entry, no counters blocking the way.
- A natural path to follow, into the booth as well as out (*flow-through*).

Table 3.1 Trade show constraints

Internal constraints	External constraints
Objectives	Target groups
Product availability	Traffic flow
Exhibition theme (if any)	Location of other stands
Strategies	Previous year's stand
Budgets	Visitors' access to stand

- An opportunity for visitors to view a map of your booth from the outside so that they know where to go. The map will typically feature a green or red "you are here" spot large enough to see straight away. If some visitors cannot see this spot from outside they will hesitate to walk in, for fear that they will waste too much time finding their way round and out again. Mark each interesting product or activity in your booth with a spot in a different colour.
- Room for a display demo: expect and plan to manage a queue of people.
- Places for people to meet and talk, perhaps round freestanding tables.

The trade show constraints can be summoned up as in Table 3.1.

Given the constraints and rules of thumb, the goal of the booth designer is to attract as many customers to your booth as possible, or as many as you would like to have. This is done in several different ways. First, we need to ask ourselves how many customers are likely to come. We want to distinguish between visitors and customers. If our answer is that we expect a large number, then we should build a booth that can receive as many as we can handle without turning the whole place into chaos (in which case it would do nobody any good). If our answer is a smaller number, then we might build the booth with more assumptions about usage patterns: more groups of seats than standing room. In either case, the booth needs to be a well-functioning working area. It should also illustrate and reflect our company values. We need to be clear about what these are, then. What two or three words best describe who we want to be? For example, is the company tech-savvy, conservative, trendy, innovative, creative, inexpensive, exclusive, fashionable, or reliable? For each set of values, there will be a corresponding palette of designs, in the shape of appropriate forms, colours, and materials in any given year. For those companies which have already chosen and defined their design, it is merely a question of applying it to the booth. For others, it may be a question of modifying an existing design to fit new trends.

As a starting point, we would like to build a more attractive booth than all the other companies have. The problem or challenge is that everyone else is trying to do the same. Another problem is that we do not know what the competing booths are going to look like. That is usually something we discover only when we actually arrive at the show. If a competitor shows up at several trade shows during the year, we might assume that he will be reusing the same booth at least for a while, which allows us to come better prepared. Booths are expensive, so they are reused, in some cases over many years. They have to be replaced sooner than most other equipment, though, because of the extensive wear and tear stemming from heavy use, transport, and frequent erection and dismantling. In most cases, companies will at least try to reuse parts of a previous version just to save money. These are all reasons why booths do not last long. In any case, we need to find out what our competitors' booths look like. For one thing, it will give us an idea of the kind of resources we would have to deploy to make something better.

For a booth designer there are two kinds of competition: competition with companies which offer similar or competing products, and competition with nearby booths. The booths of competing products are important because they will attract the same people. These visitors will consciously or unconsciously compare our booth with theirs. The neighbouring booth matters because it determines how good we need to be if we are going to succeed in winning attention in our corner of the trade show. Being next to a carefully-designed booth tends to diminish the impression visitors get of your booth. But on the other hand, if you are a small fish, it could be an advantage to be sited next to a bigger, better-known company. Small booths grouped together in a particular aisle can easily become a desert area where no one goes. Large companies draw a great deal of attention to their booths, including attention from people of influence. To avoid being "swallowed" by the large-company booths, design something simple that will make you stand out from your neighbour. If he paints his booth white, make yours black. If they use square shapes, make yours rounded; and so forth. The organizers will often place companies of the same size and in the same industry together, in order to avoid too much mixing up of odd-sized companies in different industries. Location will also depend on fees paid, so that many of the larger companies will be sited in the same area of the show anyway. Studying the nearby booths before you design your own is at any rate never a mistake, if you have any means of finding out about them in advance.

To give an example of what it means to be "swallowed up by your neighbour": even if you have a nicely-polished four-wheeled truck in your booth, no one is going to notice it if the next-door exhibitor has a massive lorry in his. His monster lorry will steal everyone's attention. What seemed like a good idea at first, to spend money on a nice four-wheeled truck, becomes a poor idea in the event. Examples of similar failures are found not only at car stereo exhibitions, but in all kinds of consumer shows. If everyone is using the same effects, their value will be reduced. For example, at CES'06 too many companies had installed a Hummer car in their booth. After you had seen about ten of these, you realized that the value of having one had dropped significantly. In the end, you did not even notice them. And as for those who used other, less prestigious off-road vehicles, it made them look even less attractive. Difficult to know in advance, you say. Well, not really: doing some market research before the show would have given you an indication of what gadgets and effects were considered hot that year. Sometimes it is enough to talk to a few booth designers. They can tell you, because they talk to others who also build booths, to customers, and to competitors.

When the show is over and people are back at work, the chances are that they are only going to remember what was "hot". Anything that was just "professionally done", that was "OK", or even "nice" – all that will often be forgotten. How many stands do you remember seeing at your last trade show? The chances are that you will only remember those which truly stood out in one way or another, or those of your competitors. Ask yourself the same question 2 years later, and you will remember very few. We need to learn from this, and try to make an impression by being innovative when designing our booth.

You might want to choose a theme for your booth. Provided it is well integrated, this can be an effective strategy: say, if you are a TV company and your people are all dressed as "Pirates of the Caribbean". But it can also be a risky endeavour to embark on. Many potential themes would simply be too much at odds with the corporate image (say, if you are a bank and dress as "Pirates of the Caribbean"). This will at best only leave visitors confused, or make them smile but for the wrong (or unintended) reasons (for instance, because of the association with dishonest bankers). Whatever you do in terms of design, make sure it is consistent with your company profile and company values. The theme should underline the company values, not contradict them. Some people think that a mix of messages will be seen as "fun", but that seldom works out in practice. It will get you noticed, but that is not the kind of attention you are looking for.

Use smell and sound effects if appropriate. An outboard-motor manufacturer played a pleasant background sound of a cruising motorboat in its trade-show booth; you could hear people having fun on the beach, and even seagulls. It was all very well done.

Perhaps the company could even have used a carefully-chosen salty scent and gentle fans to increase the seaside atmosphere, if the organizers allowed that.[1] The more messages you send out to be detected by the various senses, the greater the chance that visitors will remember you. The use of scents in what we call *scent marketing* is yet to be developed as a multidisciplinary discipline. It remains undervalued at present.

When planning our exhibit we should play on all *five senses*: sight, smell, touch, taste, and sound. Often, much of this will be beyond our influence, for example we cannot control the sounds coming from other areas of the exhibition hall. At the same time, most sense-impressions are under our control when we are inside our booth. As we stand in front of the finished exhibit, we should do an audit with our senses. What does our booth look like? How does it smell? Is the smell intended? What kind of sounds can be heard? Are they ours? Were they intended? Do the booth and its staff deliver the intended results in terms of what impinges on our senses? If not, is there something we can change at this show, on this occasion?

Arrange some sort of competition, if your products can be associated with it. For example, if you are selling basketballs, arrange a shooting competition. Tailor your booth to accommodate such activity, for instance by marking out a mini-court, or at least by installing a basketball board on the wall. If possible, design your booth in such a way that you can use it for different activities – what we call a *transformer*

---

[1] There are special scent machines, if you do not want to use bottles of scent.

booth. Activities tend to attract visitors to your booth. Just make sure that the visitors are also potential customers. If you are selling luxury cars, don't set up a go-kart competition on your stand, because that will only risk attracting people who might like to own one of your cars but will never be able to afford one. At the risk of sounding a bit cynical (which is not my intention), it is better to sell the "wannabes" some publicity item, say a cap with your logo or suchlike. In that way, you get them to pay you in order to advertise you. However, if the booth visitors really are potential customers, then don't hesitate to show them your product. Don't play hard to get. If you are going to ignore some visitors because they do not have the money to buy your products, as many luxury brands do, be very sure you know how to spot those who do have the money. In most cases, you cannot know just by looking at a visitor, without talking to them briefly. The outward difference in appearance as between a sports star making millions of dollars a year and an ordinary student can be minimal. They may in fact both be wearing the same jeans, trainers, and T-shirt.

Increasingly, booths are designed with the idea of enabling visitors to try out or assess the companies' products. This hands-on experience has been shown to be an important marketing mechanism, which leads to higher sales, especially among women and children.[2] As decision-makers, we are most comfortable when we can try the product out before we buy it. Just reading about it is not enough. After all, this is one of the advantages of participating in a trade show, as compared with compiling a brochure or making a television commercial. A trade show is a place where we can bring our products with us. And if we have them there, they can be tried out.

With new simulator technology, there are ways to present even large products like boats or larger-sized machinery without needing to install the actual products themselves in the booth. Booth designers ought to work closely with users and booth staff to work out how best to display products so that they can be tested out as well as viewed.

Don't forget the basics. People should be able to see what you are selling straight away as they pass your booth. Don't make them guess what your company is about. If they cannot see what you are doing, they are unlikely to walk in. It is easy to forget this simple point in all the talk about booth design, themes, and booth staff behaviour.

People are always looking for something new, not only in terms of products, but also in the design of the booth. The first thing they notice will not be the products inside, but the outside of the booth. If your booth looks boring from the outside, then the chances are that passers-by will miss what is new on the inside.

In general, to be successful in attracting visitors you need to come up with new and exciting ideas. Using the same booth year by year may look good in your budget, but you risk falling behind in the market. You may be perceived as an established, solid player, but outdated, a company whose time has passed, at best a

---

[2] Research by Jack Morten Worldwide and Sponsorhip Research Intenational (SRI), quoted in Friedman (2006a: 26–28).

cash cow in the Boston Consulting Group matrix. Changing your trade routines is part of the game (cf. Friedman 2006a: 28).

You cannot plan for all eventualities, and at an exhibition everything can happen. For this reason you may want to keep some flexibility in your budget. *Unforeseen costs* are a part of reality. You may end up needing a new pair of loudspeakers, an extra microphone, some chairs, or additional food. Overtime, express postage, extra fees for phone and computer may be hard to plan for. It may be a good idea to look quickly over your outgoings every day to see how you are doing, for instance checking any extras that have been added to the hotel bill. If you are renting many bedrooms and meeting rooms in the hotel, then negotiate on any extra items, such as loudspeakers, technical help, or staff. You should also make sure that you have *cancellation clauses* built into your contracts to cover cases where a speaker cannot make it or a room is not needed for some other reason.

Once you have completed the design and installation of the booth, you may still find yourself wanting to make modifications. You may discover that there are too many seats, or too few, or that some colours do not match. After you have finished, it is a good idea to get a fresh pair of eyes to look at your booth. When we work on something for a long time, we tend to become blind to such points. We get so used to seeing a booth or a design that we accept it as good just because we are too familiar with it, or we disapprove of it because we have grown bored with it. Get someone from another department, who has not been part of the project, to come and have a look at the booth. If this is possible, you might also want to show it to a few of your customers or potential customers in advance. Don't make things too complicated, but just ask "What do they like and dislike about the booth? Why?" If there are any significant negative remarks, test it on a larger audience, and get it changed if there is time. In practice, most companies will already be stressed about the whole show, so that they will choose to go with what they have. "Let's do that next year instead" is the sort of thing one tends to hear when faced with this kind of critique. If that happens, then let's at any rate make sure that we do indeed remember to make the changes next time round.

When the show has opened, study *traffic patterns* in and around your booth. How do people move? Do they encounter any obstacles – if so, where? A CCTV camera in the booth may help to identify these. There will not be time to watch the entire tape, but you shouldn't need to. If there is a bottleneck at the booth, it will soon show up as the booth fills with visitors. We might also want to fast-forward the tape to get answers quicker. Make sure first that the organizers, and your own company, allow you to use CCTV. Some staff members will react negatively to being watched in this way, even if the purpose is to analyse traffic flow. If there is something amiss in your booth, try to change it discreetly, or do so after opening hours are over for the day.

Sometimes you can solve traffic-flow problems straightforwardly via new instructions to your staff, or by simple manoeuvres like turning a screen round so that people can see it better. Those are good solutions, which do not entail extra costs. Don't look on modifications as failures. They are improvements.

At the end of the show, dismantling the stand is as important as erecting it was. Be sure to follow the rules: dismantle in time, leaving the floor clean. If you fail to do that, there are likely to be *penalties*.

3.1   Booth Location

Examine the exhibition plan. There is normally a *main walk* and then there are the *aisles*. Aisles can be classified as *side aisles*, *main aisles*, and *cross aisles* (an aisle at a right angle to a main aisle). Obviously, you want to be sited where there are people passing by, and that will largely depend on where the trade show entrances and exits are. That said, opinions differ about where it is best to be located. Some main walks are too crowded, too noisy, or too expensive. You may want to be where your competitors are, since that is the place where most of your customers will be.

To complicate the picture still further, opinions differ about where the largest numbers will be found, and although there will be figures (which are audited) on the number of entrants to a show, there will never or hardly ever be figures for specific areas of the show. Some people claim that since most visitors walk through the entire show, anywhere is best. That is often the organizers' view, since it allows them to keep site fees high everywhere. Others say it is always best to be close to the entrance, since people seldom walk far, especially as the show days pass by. Many visitors will wander all over the show the first day and then tell themselves that they will come back to places they notice and find interesting later on, another day, but actually they often do not do this. What seemed at first like a good plan turns out to be unrealistic; the show is just too big and the hours too few to do all the things we wanted to do. Therefore, assume that people will not find time to revisit you, even if they say they will. Very often that is not their fault, and not a sign of ill will on their part.

Some exhibitors may want to be sited close to somewhere where food and drink is available, assuming that queues and crowds will not disturb our booth environment. Others may want to be not too far away from toilets, but also not right next to them, because that tends to draw the wrong kind of visitors. It can be a great advantage to be sited close to one of the main entrances, of course. That will make it easier for your visitors to find you once they have entered the show, and it saves you a lot of time when going to and from the show. At certain older trade shows that can make a great deal of difference; that would apply, for instance, to the Fiera di Milano, where getting to the right location is a journey in its own right.[3]

If you have a better, stronger booth than your competitors, you might want to be sited right next to them. When people find you there, it is as if you are saying "This reflects how the industry is, and we are the obvious choice". A site on a side aisle not only is in most cases ineffective, but can easily by association become a

---

[3] A new and more accessible exhibition site has now been built in the Rho-Pero area.

metaphor for your entire business. Some visitors will interpret this as suggesting that your products are not in the premier league – your company is a bit off-trend. Associations can be merciless.

There is a kind of visitors' logic according to which the best products are expected to be found along the main aisles, even though in reality that may not be true. It is like visiting a new city: visitors want to keep to the main roads, they do not want to get lost down some little alley. We bring this kind of city-logic with us when we visit a trade show. Sometimes we decide at an early stage to concentrate on the main walks first, to give ourselves time to visit all the halls. Then, the thinking goes, we can come back again and see what we have missed in the aisles later on. Of course, we often overestimate the time we have available, and our physical stamina. After a few hours, we tend to get weary, and particularly footweary. One thing we do not want to do at this point is to go back and check out those minor aisles, and the booths we missed in them. We will just have to forget those. Other options have now become more attractive, such as going outside, going to eat at a restaurant, going to the beach (if there is one nearby), or going shopping, just to get a break. The idea of a bench or somewhere to sit down becomes more and more attractive as we walk around, and we soon reach the point where we would rather sit down than see one more exhibit or booth. All these considerations speak in favour of a central booth location.

A landmark site is important when giving directions. Telling someone you are at location A-325 is not going to help, especially not for analysts, journalists, and people of influence. "If you are behind the Google booth, say so" (Briere 2006: 41). In many cases, the landmark makes an even better reference point than the name of the hall you are in. In consequence, it may also be a good strategy for selecting your booth site.

Upgrading your booth location is often possible, either through good personal contacts with the organizers or because of cancellations. Ask show management before you set up your booth if there are any last-minute cancellations. Of course, you can only do this provided you have not already included your site in your marketing material. If you have done that, then people will walk to the wrong location.

3.2   Booth Design and Construction

By booth design we mean the spatial form and colour of the booth. As such the design will be both aesthetic and functional. Under this heading we must first draw a distinction between design and decoration. The latter refers to details, for example a flower arrangement. What is important is that design and decoration, or anything else in the booth for that matter, go hand in hand aesthetically. Everything that represents the company should be co-ordinated, as it will all ultimately be an expression of the company's image.

When it comes to the structure of your booth, begin by asking yourself some questions:

1. How many people should fit comfortably in your booth at the same time?
2. Will it be possible to pass one another when walking around without jostling each other?
3. Does the booth offer a natural path for visitors to follow as they walk round?
4. What are the most convenient sizes for each module, making it easy for visitors to walk through the doors/entrances?
5. What constraints on booth design have been set by the organizers?

The actual stand typically covers about 30 % of the booth space. This means that you are left with about 70 % to walk around in. A large empty space round your booth may look impressive, but few visitors will appreciate it. Large spaces to walk around in risk looking like no booth at all, as if you left your booth or some part of it back at home. So, we are not looking for a football field, but something three-dimensional which will help us achieve our marketing objectives.

Booth designers are seldom part of *in-house staff*. Because they are brought in to do a very specific job, it is important that the exhibit manager knows what he can require from his designer(s). At their worst, these designers are like architects who are only interested in building what they themselves find new, creative, and exciting, not what you or the customer wants. The artistic aspect of the booth should not be neglected, but an exhibit manager will be wise to avoid the bigger egos. These structures are not going to be seminal works of art. On the other hand we do not want just average booth construction either. Preferably we want to find a designer who is confident enough to have good ideas, but who can also tune in to our specific needs, of which there will be many. For each competence required by the exhibit manager there is a corresponding design need. Based on these correspondences, you can decide which designers are suitable and who could contribute what (Table 3.2).

This is much like working with an advertising agency. We want to try to find out what the designer knows and what they can do for us. Get him or her to show you what they have done before (the *portfolio*), before you commit yourself. Make that the basis for discussion. "How much will it cost to do this?", etc. Once you have decided to go with a specific booth designer, you must accord that person sufficient trust and headroom to do his or her job. When the job is done, take the same table and check your expectations against the outcome of the work done. Did the designer meet (or perhaps even exceed) expectations? What, if anything, needs to be done differently?

A good way to start working with a designer is to explain what type of location we have. There are a number of different kinds of booth. *Standard/linear booths* are open on one side, with the exception of a *corner booth* which has exposures on two sides. Standard booths are generally arranged in a straight line, so are sometimes called *"in-line" booths*. Here is a list of different kinds of booths:

- Standard booth (area from 10′ by 10′ upwards)
- Corner booth: open on two sides
- Perimeter wall booth: same as standard booth, but backs onto an outside wall
- Peninsula booth: open to the aisles on three sides
- Island booth: open on four sides

Table 3.2 Competences required of exhibit managers and designers ([a]After Thoburn H. Stiles, in Konikow (1984: 9))

	Exhibit manager	Designer
1	Knowledge of company identity and what image the company wants to portray in the exhibit	An open, creative mind
2	Integration of existing assets with new construction	Understanding of materials and how they are best used
3	Suggestions about materials and appropriate lighting	An ability to communicate ideas clearly in a professional presentation
4	Floor plans that make difficult space viable with proper traffic flow	An understanding of structure
5	Sensitive colour co-ordination of all design elements	An understanding of the limitations of his or her company
6	Outstanding co-ordination of graphics and copy layout	An understanding of graphic techniques, including typography and photography
7	An ability to spot where modularization will reduce installation costs and make for flexible regional show participation	An awareness of all media and interactive methods of product presentation
8	Proper layout of new construction designs so as to highlight new products and downplay older ones	An awareness of cost factors in order to keep within budget limitations
9		An understanding of the special characteristics of specific shows
10		An awareness of marketing trends and their relations to client's objectives

- Split-island booth: like peninsula, but shares back wall with that of another split-island booth
- Two-storey booth[4]
- Mobile booth

Mobile booths often come in the form of specially made trucks or buses built for trade-show purposes. Most trade shows will have external space for these kinds of vehicle. Mobile booths are practical if you have many destinations, little time between shows, and a sizeable exhibition budget.

Most smaller exhibitors choose a standard booth. These are offered by numerous companies internationally, and can be had from about US$1,500 upwards. They usually include a wall and a counter in a consistent design.

There is no recognized classification of booth designs. The following list of categories builds on a synthesis of a number of product presentations by vendors:

1. The *banner stand*. This consists of a poster which may be fixed to poles to stand by itself, or may be drawn out of a cartridge. It is used for free-standing booths with eight to ten feet of space. The simplest way to fill a booth at a trade show is

---

[4] With these booths you must often notify show management and the local fire service in advance by sending plans for approval (a sealed engineering drawing signed by a licensed engineer is often required). Similar rules may apply to covered exhibits.

with a *roll-down banner* and a desk with a drape. This should cost no more than a few hundred dollars.

2. The *pop-up display*. This covers a larger surface. The best can be fitted into a large suitcase and set up, taken down, and rolled away by one person.

3. The *space frame displays* (walls + counter)/space station; come as straight walls or as curves. The design can also extend to the floor.

4. The *modular display*, or *modular exhibition system*, comes with a number of structural elements: pole panel booths, stackables, and table tops. *Small panel systems* are often foldable.

5. *Video and audio displays.*

6. *Custom booths*, as mentioned above. Custom booths are made using all kinds of structural technique: everything from hand-made carpeting, to a display built on the *truss system*.[5]

Then there are a number of special effects, like lightboxes (an easy way to attract attention at darker trade shows).

You do not need to buy a booth in order to participate in trade shows, it is quite common nowadays to rent them. Booth designers also offer help with graphics. You can either send them a file with your design, or they will create a new design for you, or incorporate your existing ideas into a new design.

To save money, an exhibitor can also use various special design techniques, such as constructing towers at the entrance, which look impressive but do not need to cost much. We could also construct a simple two-storey booth with a viewing platform on top. Again, this looks impressive, but does not need to be very expensive.

Many trade shows offer *complete packages for booths* at different sizes. Some packages include a wardrobe, carpet, a number of chairs, spotlights, tables, refrigerator, electricity, a board to carry your company name and logo, free parking, and daily cleaning. Find out exactly what your show includes and compare that with your to-do list.

The maximum height for a standard single-storey booth might be 8′ 4″ (2.5 m). Two-storey booths will often be 16′ (4.88 m). Maximum heights for ceilings vary a lot, depending on the show. If you are in a large hall and the opportunity is available, there is nothing more spectacular than a tall booth. It will make you an instant landmark. Find out what rules apply here.

Apart from that, there are a number of *basic booth design elements* to consider in your planning:

• Towers: free-standing components

• One or two storeys

---

[5] According to Wikipedia under "architecture" and "structural engineering", a *truss* is a static structure consisting of straight slender members (interconnected at joints into triangular units). Most truss systems at trade shows are made of aluminium and are relatively easy to dismantle and carry away. Dismantling usually takes about half the time it takes to set up. Try to use the same team to save time. For a truss to function and be rigid, it must be composed entirely of triangles.

- Canopies: false ceiling
- Walls
- Wallpaper and paint
- Electricity
- Lighting
- Carpet or flooring
- Furniture
- Safety precautions
  Make sure you know all the *booth design and location constraints*:
- Differences in height between booths
- Pillars standing in the way
- Whether there are other nearby facilities diverting or attracting attention, such as a food stand, a toilet, or some odd corner
  When you do your design planning, keep a number of simple rules of thumb in mind:
- The layout of your booth should make it easy and unthreatening for visitors to enter.
- Display products at eye level. This really attracts visitors and makes effective visual aids for the staff.
- Have idle computer monitors default to a company advertisement or company logo. Better look alive than dead!
- Make sure a company sign is placed high up so that visitors can find your booth. Place another at eye level so that visitors walking past know who you are. Also site one at the front of your reception counter as a gentle reminder.
- Make the booth's graphics informative, eye-catching, and useful.

Spend some time reflecting on the major elements for your booth design. There are only so many ways of making a difference to your booth: colour, size, shape, and material (constraint: it should be non-flammable).

For a start, make sure you are using all surfaces. It is common to encounter blank walls – large empty spaces which tell us nothing. These are lost marketing opportunities, and they shout what they are: not completed, unfinished, missed opportunities, and sloppy. These spaces could have been used to display a logo, or to say something about what is on the other side of the wall. Putting up a simple message which might create curiosity does not cost a lot, and does not take much time to do. Deploying low-key, universal humour can be a good means of making contact with people who are passing by. "Wonder what is on the other side of this wall?" "Tired feet? . . . can't help you there, but if you are looking for a new pair of loudspeakers . . ." (well, you get the idea).

More than ever it has become necessary in marketing to be human. People have seen all the tricks there are. They are not so easily impressed any more, especially not in Europe, where the notion of selling is still sometimes frowned on. Try to be human instead, to touch someone as a human being. Copywriting is all about this. Most copy leaves us uninterested, disengaged. Most of it is wasted, often because it tries to be clever. It all seems so interesting to the people producing it, as they dream it up and draft it; but so uninteresting for those who read it. That is because copywriters usually underestimate their audience. We see the same tendency in the glossy magazines companies distribute so proudly. Few people bother to read them. Commonly they are just a waste of time and money.

About colour: stick to the ones included in your company profile, the colours of your logo and your commercial material. A trade show is not the place to introduce a new colour, it is a place where we enhance what we already have. Trade shows are not a good place to introduce a new corporate look, either. We do that better via mass media, at least initially. Customers are very sensitive towards colours as vehicles of communication. We have already seen how important it is to use precisely the same corporate colour everywhere in the booth. If the shade of colour we use in the booth is slightly different from our logo colour, there will be people who notice this immediately. They will wonder why we failed.

Sometimes companies want to change their corporate colours. For example, when I worked for KPMG the company wanted to move from a lighter blue to a darker blue. The general idea was that the lighter blue belonged to the past, and that more recently it had awaked relatively feminine associations. The darker blue was more businesslike, reflecting the values of the 1990s.[6] So they wanted to change, but did not want to appear to be changing, because change is in itself risky and raises questions. Consequently, instead of shifting directly from one colour to the other, they did it in stages. The problem with this, though, was that not everything changed simultaneously. You would have the flag outside in one blue, your business card in a second, and the latest television commercial in a third. *Co-ordination of image changes* is very difficult to achieve. In this area, even the better companies can fail. But it must be attempted nevertheless. Over recent years KPMG have come to realize that their deep blue is now often associated with the economic collapse of 2007–2008, with too-clever bankers and with Wall Street. In consequence they have wanted to appear more human, more socially responsible. To reflect this mood they have wanted to be associated with brighter, gayer colours, like those we see in the Google logo. But this time, rather than changing their deep blue, they have used extra colours in their material as additions, not as substitutes. This is an example of how companies use colours to reflect changing public moods. It is all part of a process of association.

Another way to change colours is to be totally explicit about it. Some years ago Vodaphone in Sweden was bought up by the Norwegian company Telenor. Vodaphone's colour was red, Telenor's was blue. The difference in colours was seen as an issue that could be turned into a communication opportunity. In their advertising after the deal was made, Telenor used the slogan "Everything red has just become blue". They even made a jingle for it. Consumers care little about who owns whom, where the company is located, who works for them, and so forth

---

[6] More recently the company has also been using colourful, floating capitals in its advertising, rather like Google. The idea there is to build on values that are human, fun, and caring, as a counterpoise to the various corporate scandals we have witnessed among large multinationals over the past 15 years.

(questions which are highly important for the Competitive Advantage of Nations), but they do notice any change in the name of a company, and especially in the design of the products they care about.

As a general rule, avoid fashionable colours (those are better left to clothing). You only risk having to change them in a year or two (KPMG's light blue was an example of that). A poorly chosen colour can be a very costly experiment in the long run. If you choose more than two colours, things will begin to look untidy and vague. Colours carry intrinsic messages and should be selected with care. Red, blue, yellow, black, and white are less risky options; even some shades of brown are safe. As anyone who has some experience with colour knows, there are many shades and degrees of each colour. If you put a tinge of red in a white, the white will be warmer and blend better with other colours. Green has a clear environmental association, and should not be chosen if you are associated with that kind of work. Yellow involves an element of fun, sometimes even anonymity, as in the Yellow Pages. Avoid pastel colours on the one hand, and anything that suggests alarm (normally, strong traffic-light colours) on the other – unless of course you are in that line of work, for instance you are a security company.

Colour is important, and so are smell and temperature. Most exhibition halls tend to get too hot. See whether the organizers guarantee to keep the temperature within a certain interval. If so, make sure that they honour that promise. If they don't, complain. Ask them to install extra fans if needed. How does your booth smell? Some booths smell of paint, others smell of carpet-cleaning products. Anything like that is unpleasant and will divert attention away from your products. Talk about odours with your staff and the whole team. Try to come up with a clear plan for what you want the place to smell like. It would only take everyone in the booth wearing different strong perfumes to wreck that plan. Some sort of moderation and uniformity in the use of perfume is normally desirable, even though it is clearly impossible to control smell at the booth completely.

The people who staff your stand will of course be impeccable in their personal hygiene. That, one hopes, is one of the few things that goes without saying in exhibition marketing, in what may otherwise seem like a too rigidly controlled environment. It may be too much to ask that everyone smell the same. People are individuals and should be allowed to remain so, to a certain degree. That is also how we as visitors tend to appreciate them; we don't want the people we interact with to be robots. This lesson goes for most of what we do at the show. We don't expect to meet machines, but we don't want to meet "buddies" either. Rather, we expect to find the booth staff consisting of professional individuals.

Many people working in the service sector find it hard to make a clear distinction between the "friend" and the "professional". There are those who will often talk to you about anything that happens to be on their mind, job-related or not. Others, though, will try to direct the conversation more towards your particular needs, and will bear in mind the reason why you are both there. The friend is personal, the professional is goal-oriented and rational. Both are polite and pleasant.

It is not the best idea to make the booth as elegant and refined as possible. If we make our booth feel too exclusive, we will scare potential visitors away. Using the metaphor of a house, some people's houses are so soigné and elegant that we are afraid to sit down in them. The antique, upright chairs will make it difficult for us to relax and will affect the things we say. The same logic holds true for booths. Our booth may be elegant and very clean, but it must also be inviting. If we want people to sit down, we need chairs that are comfortable. If we want people to relax and feel at home, then likewise; the same logic follows. Most booths will have to answer many different needs at the same time. Hence we should organize the booth so as to serve diverse purposes at any one time, or at least at different times.

There should be an area reserved for buyers, active information seekers, and important information providers/people of influence. In most cases this will be a *sitting area*. There should also be a relatively isolated place further inside the structure where delicate matters can be handled, whether with staff or with visitors. This place may have a chair where we hope that the visitor will be fully relaxed. On the other hand we may not want any seats by the entrance, as they will attract people who are just weary, but not necessarily interested in what we have to offer. Products should be displayed along the aisles for *fast-flow visitors* and inside for *slow-flow visitors*.

Don't design your booth in a way that makes it difficult to enter. When people walk past they will try to see whether it is possible to stand in the booth comfortably before they go in. If the booth is too crowded, with furniture and other materials or products all over the place, that will turn off some potential visitors. If they enter your booth and find that it is overcrowded, they are likely to back out of it again. The safest approach is to make it obvious to the visitor which way to walk, so that he feels confident of a route enabling him to walk round and eventually exit.

In general, these are some of the concerns to bear in mind when planning the construction of the booth:

1. Booth regulations are very different. Check the details with the show management. You don't want your display or your entire booth to be rejected because you did not check the regulations at the outset.
2. Decorations involving paper, foliage, or trees are often forbidden for safety reasons.
3. Prepare orders for material handling, electrical, cleaning, floral, etc.
4. As a courtesy to neighbouring booths, find out whether you need to keep to a set height in the booth.
5. Booth materials must be non-combustible or treated to be flame-retardant.
6. Some trade shows object to sound, including even videos, unless shown in a soundproof room. Check this out too before you start building your booth.

Normally, the larger the company, the better-planned its booth will be. However, this is not always the case. Sometimes larger companies get it frightfully wrong.

Minicase 1: A Big Budget Is Not Enough

Company: Clarion, Japan
Trade Show: CES'06, North Hall

clarion®

Clarion is a Japanese world-leading manufacturer of car audio speaker systems, CD changers, mobile audio/video components, and amplifiers. During the past few years the company has sought to extend its area of activities from traditional "in-car" products to total "mobile environment".

The booth at the CES made effective use of the total available square footage. The booth was a *two-storey peninsula booth*. It was manned by sufficient exhibitor staff to be of service to different kinds of visitors. Staff also were diligent about making themselves available. The booth was well placed on the main walk, and was sited close to a food stand and to benches provided by the organizers where visitors could sit down and relax.

What was more surprising was that there were also many points to criticize. It was a pity that, seen from two sides, the booth was closed, and almost blank. This probably came about because it had originally been made for another location. The company logo was displayed in too small a format. Colours in the booth lacked contrast. Both of these factors made it hard to spot the booth at a distance. There is too much grey in the company's colours, and the colours are too monotonous: grey, silver, blue. Furthermore, old posters were displayed in the booth that showed another, different colour identity.

(It may be relevant that the Japanese have strikingly different colour associations from Westerners. Thus, Amazon controls the colour schemes of its various national websites rather rigorously, but it had to deviate considerably from its usual norms for amazon.co.jp.)

The cars used to show products were OK (old American beauties), but OK is not enough at this trade show, and especially not for a company of this size. The bar stools and round tables placed inside the crowded booth were uncomfortable, and thick carpets made the tables unstable, creating a sense that they might fall over at any time.

Worse, the company showed no truly new products – not enough future technology.

Conclusion: the company showed a less effective use of resources than would be expected from a firm of its standing – score 5 out of 10.

Companies often argue that they could have done better if they had had more resources, that their staff could have performed better if there had been more of them, and so forth. Sometimes these points are fair, but often it is more a question of lack of knowledge and inadequate planning. Planning is as much a question of competence and knowledge as it is about man-hours and dollars.

Some marketing men plead in defence that planning for trade shows is too difficult, and they do it too infrequently. There are just too many different things to take into account, or so they say. This may be true to some extent, nevertheless we expect more professionalism from companies today in terms of exhibition marketing than we did only a decade ago. Now that more research and experience about trade shows has been assembled and exchanged, there are fewer excuses than there used to be for getting them wrong. The key is to set the ambitions of the booth staff in line with your budget and resources. Apart from that, it is all a little like sailing: it is best to start with a small boat first, then get a slightly bigger one as you get better at it.

3.3   Booth Furniture

By *booth furniture* we mean the objects you fill your booth with once it is set up. As *standard booth furniture* we usually think of objects like:

* Carpeting
* Counter
* (Round) table
* Chairs
* Wastebasket
* Shelving
* Electric sockets
* Curtains

Remember that you also need to consider the actual setting-up and dismantling of the exhibit, booth furnishings/decorations, and other related services (electrical, signage, etc.). Then there is the *transport* of your exhibit. To make things easier you might also want to consider rental exhibits, or *exhibit furnishing rental*, as it is called. Further down the line you need to decide what material to use, whether metal, coated metal, powder-coated metal, or wood. These are the basic or initial *booth furnishing decisions*.

If you have a lot of materials for the show you should think of *freight storage* and handling in and out of the exhibition. Graphics production needs to be planned well in advance and you may want to do some *exhibit photography* while at the show for future shows.

In a custom-made booth it may be more difficult to distinguish between the booth itself and its furnishing, since the two are often integrated and seen as one entity. Some facilities will typically be built in, for instance special displays for goods. A custom-made booth will include various tailor-made solutions specially designed to facilitate the display of a company's products. Carpets or special flooring may also be included, together with specially-designed furniture, etc. By comparison, for standard booths it is more of a two-step process: first the booth, then its contents.

Chairs and sofas should be comfortable to sit in, but not so comfortable that they tempt visitors to sit longer than they need to (or to fall asleep). A comfortable sofa is just asking to be filled with weary visitors. A large arena-like structure of benches risks turning into a meeting-place for all kinds of visitors who are not the least interested in your products. It could even become a favourite lunch spot. Unless your business is soft drinks or some other broad-segment product, you do not want your booth to be a general place for hanging out at. To avoid problems like that, many booths will simply not have any chairs or sofas.

The furniture should fit in with the rest of the booth design. We should pay careful attention to colour and form. When arranging the booth, we should not fix chairs close to one another, but give each chair an appropriate surrounding space. We are not a kind of conference hall. Some exhibitors place bar-stools so close to one another that you wonder how anyone can get up from one of them without pushing the next one away. To eliminate this sort of problem, try each seat out yourself. Does it fulfil its function? Remember that furniture is a vital component of the total booth experience. It is there to support your other activities, to make it easier for you to display your products and make sales.

The horizontal dimension is the primary element of booth furnishing. Floors are most often either kept bare, covered with carpeting, or they are the object of some special design, like a *floorshow*. In a floorshow, the design from the walls of the booths continues, or overflows, across the floor. Also, some exhibitors use *path-finder floors*, which show you either which way to go, or what you will see when you reach some particular location. At almost all trade shows you will not be permitted to lay out pathfinders along the aisles or the main walk, but you are allowed to use them within your own booth. If you should be allowed to use them in the aisles, they can become a very powerful marketing tool. Many stores use similar techniques with great success. For example, at most Ikea stores visitors are led through the entire store (except for the pick-up area and the check-out) by special markings in the aisles. The marked route is designed so that visitors are encouraged (not forced) to pass through the entire store, that is, all departments. There will be minor opportunities for short cuts along narrow passages, but these are not encouraged by explicit marking and in most cases they are not particularly easy to find or spot. Amusement parks use much the same techniques. These techniques can also be successfully used inside a trade-show booth, especially in larger booths.

Some booths present this in the form a tour, with footstep shapes glued to the floor, showing the visitor which direction to go in. The effective use of pathfinders, which can be created using anything from small pieces of carpet to adhesive tape, will reduce the visitors' mental barriers to entering your booth. The psychological dimension is paramount. This relates to our feeling of security. When we look into a booth, we unconsciously notice or search for a route we can walk along. We don't want to get stuck anywhere where it is difficult to get out. So we want to see the route first, preferably all the way round to the exit, before we go in. Asians, in particular, will be concerned about not losing face, that is, they do not want to let themselves get into any awkward, blocked situation where they might feel foolish and hence less respected. Keeping to the aisles or the main walk is considered safe. If we cannot see how we can walk round within a booth, many of us will be put off entering it.

As one example, a simple form of pathfinder in a booth might be a series of adhesive footprint shapes with large numbers on. We could even use the footprints as another opportunity for advertising or information. Thus, we could show the categories of product we are displaying in each area of the booth, say as "Step 1 (of 74): Radios", "Step 2 (of 74): Radios" . . . "Step 17 (of 74): Mobile phones", etc. The visitor then knows "I am now in the mobile phone display area, and I have 57 more steps, or roughly 19 m, left to walk before I am out again". Being given this information will make some of us feel more secure, and so also in less of a hurry to get out.

With sufficient resources, there is no end of exciting ideas you can work on when furnishing your booth. The low-budget exhibitor might consider other kinds of idea to save money, such as covering a simple table with a cloth hanging to the floor, rather than constructing an elaborate desk. Such tricks are well known to most of us from hotel visits. They make tables look more luxurious, and they are much faster to set up and dismantle. At exhibitions, tables like that can also provide additional storage space. Another cheap addition building on the same idea is drapery. Drapes can be made to hang down from all kinds of high edges in the booth: around the ends of the booth, down from pillars, or even from displays. They do not even need to be specially made. Just make sure they are placed so as to fit. If you know the heights, you might even find that you can take with you some drapery from home. Drapery and table covers make the booth look more dressed-up and warmer.

Another low-budget furniture item is a *literature rack* for your marketing material, such as brochures, or for competitions. The more expensive packs (press packs, and packs for strong leads) you might want to keep under the counter/table. Other marketing material you can place where it is clearly visible. That will save you time and money, too. Many visitors use trade shows principally for information gathering, and are not there to buy your products – not then, and not in the future. If they can see the information they need and take it without needing to ask for it, then this will save us time, time that we can instead use on our genuine prospects. You have probably had the following experience. The exhibitor hurries to finish up with one visitor at the counter, because there are two other people waiting and they look impatient. When it is finally their turn, they just ask for a brochure. We then feel a bit bad about the first visitor, who at least had some questions and might have been a good lead. If we had had a literature rack at the entrance, this situation could have been avoided.

Moving objects can be an excellent way of attracting visitors' attention at trade shows. In an environment where large objects in different colours and shapes are competing to capture visitors' attention, movement can be very effective. As human beings we are primed to notice movement more immediately than most static shapes or colours. Movement can be in the form of standard rotating platforms on which we can place our products. A large-size logo slowly rotating on top of our booth is a good eye-catcher, even from a distance; or how about a fountain system with cool fresh water? If the show is about wine or food, you might even fill the fountain with your beverage products, if that kind of humour works in the local culture.

Ideally, you want to bring your products to the show. If that is not possible, then audiovisual techniques like television, VCRs, and laptop computers can be used to display more advanced products – products that require a more extended form of demonstration. Aeroplanes are one example, but so also are many kitchen appliances, cruise holidays, or construction machinery. Ask yourself the question: will it make it easier for my customers to understand our products if we display them audiovisually? If the answer is yes, we should not hesitate to invest in this kind of equipment. (Alternatively, most of it can be rented.)

Nothing is less excusable at a trade show than exhibitors who do not manage to explain their products to visitors, especially if they are doing everything else right. After all, that is the main reason why we are here. There are two elements to this. One is having the right people at the booth, with the right range of competence to answer most questions. The other side is more pedagogical, and about how we present our products in the booth so as to support the task of communication. These two efforts need to be co-ordinated.

Lighting is a whole chapter in itself. Some lighting is already provided by the organizers, the *hall lighting*. After all, trade-show halls are not normally completely dark. However, the problem with this light is that it is usually too dim to be much use. It is common to see smaller booths set up in relative darkness, sometimes accentuated by the fact that the lighting in neighbouring booths is bright. So, you stand there with your roll-ups and your table and you have spent all morning making yourselves presentable, but no one can see you. "Who is that woman in the dark?", passers-by ask themselves. There is a psychological mechanism which holds us back from walking into a dark booth. It is not that we cannot see the person or that we are afraid of what could happen to us if we walk in, but we might be worried about what other people will say when we stand in the dark with this nicely-dressed member of booth staff. It may be that some people will not care much about this, but for most people at least there will be a sense of awkwardness. A situation which would have been perfect in a bar after the show day is over suddenly seems wrong. If your lighting is poor, or you have forgotten to bring it, at least have staff stand out next to the aisles where people can see them.

Find out in advance what lighting is provided and where the lamps will be located. Then, based on that information, try to work out what you need. Too much lighting in your booth is not good either. That creates excessive heat, which will only make the life of your exhibitors and visitors uncomfortable. Laser shows and halos are also very expensive. Don't use lighting all over the booth. Lighting should be used to highlight something you want the visitors to notice, such as your company name and logo or a new product. Use varied lighting, toning down some areas and making others bright. That will give the best contrasts, hence the best overall effect.

In this part of the book, we have shown why it is worth thinking about how to use simpler forms of booth furnishing. Closely related to this topic is what we call *marketing materials*, which we will discuss next.

3.4 Marketing Materials for the Trade Show

Marketing materials, in sales, are the collection of media used to support the sales of a product or service. These sales aids are intended to make the salesperson's job easier and more effective. Common examples include:
- Sales brochures and other printed product information
- Posters and signs
- Visual aids used in sales presentations
- Web content
- Sales scripts
- Demonstration scripts

Marketing materials differ from *advertising* in that they are most often and most effectively used later in the *sales cycle*, after we have identified our prospects and our staff are making contact with them. The idea behind marketing materials at trade shows is simple. We all love getting something for free when we visit a booth. That something should not be meaningless, worthless, insignificant, but it should also not be too expensive – unless we are giving it to a strong potential customer, but in that case we could give him other kinds of thing, like a dinner, free hotel, or the like.

It is good if we can combine the marketing materials with information about the company or product. Information is communicated in a number of ways apart from face-to-face speaking:
- Printed documents
- Samples
- Demonstrations
- Slide presentations
- Film/movies

The most important item is still the business card, despite the introduction of e-mail. Don't run out of them during the show. Bring more than you think you will need. If you can provide yourself with a scannable business card, then even better. An attractive card is still a special thing to receive, so you may want to have it designed by a graphic artist. However, it does not need to use finest-quality printing and the best paper. That may be too expensive. The card should be designed with clear lettering, and no fancy colours. The company name should appear in ordinary lettering, not merely in the form of a logo. Alternatively, you could have a few luxury cards made up for special customers. They will impress some visitors who recognize the difference.

Not everyone appreciates "yet another brochure". Analysts, journalists, and people of influence may want to download all the relevant information from a company website instead, or get everything on a CD or a USB stick. It has been estimated that 60–85 % of all brochures are thrown away.[7]

---

[7] See Center for Exhibition Industry Research (CEIR) (2003).

Marketing materials do not need to be expensive. The best marketing I saw at the CES 1 year was an inexpensive black cloth bag with the title "XM Satellite Radio" written in large yellow letters on each side. The great thing about this item was not that the handles were comfortable enough to let you wear it on your shoulder as you would wear a gym bag, even though that was a nice side to it. It was not the colours by themselves, or the quality of the bag in general, but the fact that the item was given out free at the entrance. So visitors would start collecting everything in this bag from the word go. Since it was better than most bags given out on other booths, they did not replace it. Suddenly thousands of people were walking into all kinds of booths with the "XM Satellite Radio" logo clearly visible. This was quite a *marketing stunt*, particularly since no one else had thought of it.

Try to think in terms of what can be useful. Hand out business-related giveaways, things that potential customers can use, either there at the show or when they get home. The more closely tied the giveaway is to the business, the better the chances of keeping the *freebie-hunters* away.

Add a message to your giveaways to remember you by; for instance, people might not have known that XM is a satellite radio service available on the internet. You should also include a way to contact you, nowadays preferably a website. Avoid items that will be passed on to children. If possible, your booth number should be clearly printed on your promotional material. (However, if you participate in a large number of smaller shows, that may not be practical.)

Tie-ins often create opportunities to apply good marketing ideas. The best programmes are ones which relate to our basic needs. Ask yourself, what needs do people have at trade shows which you could fulfil. Perhaps you can incorporate the answer into something you do at the show. Of course, many of these needs are difficult for us to fulfil and must be left to others, to experts: say, food, polished shoes, internet connections, or muscle tone. But there are also a number of needs we can satisfy, for instance thirst and relief of fatigue, and there are needs we can help prevent. A brief consideration of the issue might come up with a list like this (Table 3.3):

In the first example, we can put our logo and information on the foot product. In the second, we can put it on the water bottle. Instead of just showing the way to the food stands we can hand out a practical map (better than others have provided) with our information on it, perhaps even with coupons attached and as part of a competition. "Try out all three of these food stands and win a new television set." We will even give a dollar away to charity if you do this. Tie-ins are a fine marketing tool, since they bring the visitor's needs together with a good cause and our aim of selling or marketing.[8]

Uncomfortable shoes have ruined and will continue to ruin many a trade show. We like to buy new things when we go away and do something special, in order to look our best: hence the idea. Most new shoes become uncomfortable after a while

---

[8] I owe most of what I know about tie-ins to Burnet D. Brown while working in the late 1980s at a Los Angeles marketing company, Marketing & Financial Management.

Table 3.3 Needs and solutions

Needs	Solution at our booth	Preventive solution
Tired feet	A chair or bench, or a foot product such as Tiger Balm	Wear comfortable shoes
Thirst	Water, water bottle	Drink water before you start
Better food	No, but we can provide directions on an attractively-produced map	Bring your own, have food delivered
Clamminess	A wet tissue	Wash your hands and face often

if you wear them a lot. And since we have to walk or stand a lot at trade shows, we end up with sore feet. What at first seemed like no big deal becomes a real problem. When our feet are really sore it is difficult to think about anything else. An alternative is to bring several pairs of shoes, especially for women who wear high heels. It can be a good idea to have one pair for standing in the booth and one for walking around. If the worst comes to the worst, bring a pair of back-up shoes.

There are a number of ways to present your message to visitors at the show. The commonest mode is the *one-to-one dialogue*. A mode which is becoming more popular is the *one-to-N dialogue*, using a stage and a guest speaker. For it to be a dialogue, you need a microphone which can be moved around, and you cannot have too many chairs if everyone is to be given the chance to participate. Alternatively, you might consider a *one-to-N presentation* instead of a dialogue. For this, you need some extra furnishing: a small stage, a microphone, a couple of loudspeakers, and a number of chairs. When people leave at the end, give them something that reminds them of the talk, perhaps including a link to a podcast. If you do record anything, make sure that everyone is aware of that in advance. Sometimes the level of professionalism will rise when a presentation is recorded; speakers will be on better form, since everyone wants to appear from their best angle. For those who do not venture to make a comment during the talk, give them a chance to ask questions afterwards. If the speaker is well-known, perhaps you could put that on the marketing materials: "I listened to … at the …", or the like.

Minicase 2: Using One-to-N Dialogues

Company: THX, USA
Trade show: CES, South Hall

THX (a subsidiary of Lucasfilm, now in turn a subsidiary of Disney) is a company selling sound certifications, based on a sound production standard used in cinemas, computer speakers, and screening rooms. The company guarantees that a film shown in cinemas sounds the same as it did when it was mixed.

Half the booth was constructed so that it had a stage with rows of chairs facing out towards the main walk. Company and industry presentations were given with short intervals between, as in a cinema. The sound from the microphones was good, as would be expected from a company dealing with sound (anything else would have been embarrassing). There was also a one-to-one presentation, and booth staff displayed great professionalism towards incoming visitors.

The problem most new visitors had was to know what THX was actually selling, or what kind of company they were (the answer being a certification company for sound). In the booth many stereo components from a large variety of producers were set up for demonstration use, but it was unclear what visitors were actually listening to. Nothing told them.

A small cinema was built into one section. But none of that really helped the visitors to understand what THX was doing, what business they were in, what their work looked like, except that it had something to do with better sound. The market mechanisms were never explained (for instance, that producers want what THX provides because customers ask for it). The logo and company colours were not sufficiently prominent. It was as though the booth staff had worked in the company for so long that they had started to take for granted what they were all about. An item of marketing material could have served both as information and as a reminder.

Conclusion: Less effective use of resources than could be expected from this company. Companies whose business is not readily understood by the general public need to take time to explain what they are all about. They have also more work to do to ensure that they stick in their visitors' memory. Score 6 out of 10.

Most exhibitors follow the *me-too marketing approach*. That is, whatever they do in terms of booth design and marketing materials will be the same as what everyone else is doing. This is usually because everyone is watching everyone else and everyone tends to listen to the same few experts and consultants. When you walk along the aisles you will find that there is little making individual exhibitors stand out, and that is a pity.

There are many ways to be different, and we have already offered a number of suggestions in this book. One way to avoid being like everyone else is by not only displaying your product, but turning it into an experience. For example, rather than just showing your mobile phones, get people to use the phones to play a game against one another. They can compete with video games or quiz-like set-ups, all in a spirit of sport and fun. Get the winners to come back for a special ceremony in your booth to receive a prize and have a glass of sparkling non-alcoholic wine. Perhaps the glass itself could be a marketing giveaway.

Include a *competition* in your booth show. Give passers-by a chance to win something. You can also do a competition with a twist, combining it with market research. Thus, ask visitors to suggest which booth they liked best and list their three top reasons. Or ask them to put down two things they do not like about your booth. This self-criticism will not be perceived as negative; it can be a positive thing. It shows that you are objective about yourselves as a company, and that you want to improve by listening to your customers. It shows that you trust the opinions of others, your visitors. You are letting them be the experts. That in itself has a smack of good marketing.

Pre-show Planning

Once the trade show starts, there are few opportunities to change anything. It is like a roller-coaster ride. Once you are strapped in, all you can really do is enjoy the ride (or not). Whatever you might have liked to do differently before you started, it is too late now.

The pre-show phase is all about planning. *Marketing planning* has been defined as a process that is rational, incremental, and intuitive, which guides a company's marketing towards its future (Saunders et al. 1996). McDonald (1999) and Simkin (2000) have illustrated the advantages of marketing planning.

Pre-show planning is all the marketing activities we undertake in order to prepare for the trade show. Most companies do not think of these preparations specifically as pre-show activities, but simply as marketing, or sometimes as *exhibition planning*. Pre-show planning is the most important part of the trade show, as it ensures the success (or failure) of the exhibition experience for the company. When we are at the show, it is too late to undertake any planning. For a company that has already been around a few years, the *post-show phase* is a question of managing the experience that has already been gathered. In the case of failure, our post-show phase will be mostly about *damage control*.

Planning is always important, but especially for trade shows, for the simple reason that there is so much to prepare. Without proper planning, our trade show will be at best a simple failure, or at worst a disaster. Putting it differently, often it is better not to attend a trade show than to come unprepared, specially if we would be investing time and money in a large booth.

Most companies today prefer to attend *vertical* or *specialized trade shows* with a narrowly targeted visitor base. Once the registration fee has been paid, the pre-show planning stage begins. The closer we get to the show deadline, the more activities there will be to handle, as one might expect. This is referred to as the *bottleneck theory of organization planning*; it is not specific to trade shows, but applies generally to most managerial processes with clear deadlines. At a certain point in the planning activities, commonly from 6 to 3 months ahead of the show, things begin to escalate. We have now entered the bottleneck. At this point we need to focus down, and we can only make minor changes to what we have already

K. Solberg Søilen, *Exhibit Marketing and Trade Show Intelligence*,
Management for Professionals, DOI 10.1007/978-3-642-36793-9_4,
© Springer-Verlag Berlin Heidelberg 2013

arranged. Much of the work will be about logistics (transport) and contracting people to set up and dismantle the booth. This will also be a time for fine-tuning the competences of the staff, the final rehearsal.

Nowadays, organizers register and keep in close touch with exhibitors and visitors, through online registration and e-mail, long before the actual show starts. Internet techniques open up great possibilities in this respect, not only with respect to registration: detailed and updated information can now be checked in advance, and participants can get their activities under way long before they are physically at the show, joining discussion and interest groups, planning meetings with other participants, registering for special events, and determining which talks to attend.

For example, if we visit the CES home page in September, 4 months before the show begins, the keynote speakers are already listed. The full programme will be displayed on 1st October, 3 months ahead of the show. The website already allows you to arrange meetings, even though so far this year only one company has taken advantage of that. The exhibition directory is already searchable. We can select product categories, find company names and booth numbers, check whether a company is a member of CEA (the Consumer Electronics Association, which runs the show), watch videos about the company, and we can begin compiling a list of those companies we are interested in visiting, by ticking their names and saving our search. Each company will also provide a fact sheet. We can sign up for RSS (Real Simple Syndicate) feeds. The deadline for submitting CES speakers has already passed at this point, but CES still allows us to enter names on a back-up list. More than 72,000 people already "like" the forthcoming CES on Facebook. Information about the show is updated continuously, and the quantity of information compiled will soon reach a size where it is no longer possible to read everything in advance. That is just the nature of information on the internet these days. When a site grows that large in terms of quantity of information, it is no longer a matter of reading it, there will never be enough time, but of knowing what kind of information is there.

It is difficult to know in advance how much participation in a given show is going to cost. And empirical research suggests that companies do not normally have a *tailor-made budget* for trade shows.[1] Rather, most companies have a *general marketing budget*, which covers trade shows among other things. Of course that does not mean that we should not try to establish a budget for a trade show that is as precise as we can make it. It just means that there are so many variable costs related to the show that it is difficult to stick to the various budget entries, however hard we try. Sometimes it can be more practical to work in terms of a *budget ceiling*, a maximum spend. There will always be some activities that can and will be cancelled, and others that have to be added. Even for a well-organized and experienced team, it is hard to forecast all items in advance. A rigid budget can even get in the way of being creative. The purpose of the budget is not to achieve complete

---

[1] See Luse and Mau (1999). None of the Swedish SMEs discussed in this book had a clearly-defined trade show budget.

control, but to get some degree of control over costs. It is difficult to get a clear idea of actual costs incurred before we are back at the office. Top management's worries about trade-show costs are often justified, but they should not demand exact budgets. These do not exist. It is better to go for ballpark figures.

According to the Trade Show Exhibitors Association (Vanderleest 1994: 41), the major budget items at a trade show are (i) display construction, (ii) transport costs, (iii) space rental, (iv) specialist advertising, and (v) the setting-up and dismantling processes, in that order. When it comes to transport we need to decide carefully what is needed, as there are normally several options. Furthermore this may not be the best area in which to economize. Many haulage companies have satellite communication systems, so that you can see where the goods are at any point. When time is short this may be a reassurance. Instead of worrying where your kit is, you can see it directly on your smartphone in real time. Perhaps you need special pad-wrapped services, air suspension, or climate-controlled lorries? It is better to ask these questions beforehand (Table 4.1).

We see that most of the budget costs will not be spread over future shows but relate specifically to a single show. That certainly applies to transport, space rental, setting-up and dismantling, personnel, and display maintenance, i.e. about 50 % of the budget total. Thirty-five percent relates to items which may in part be shared with future shows, and 15 % is not accounted for in the above Table. There is also a question about what we include in the budget. For example, in a well-planned show, much of the actual cost in terms of man-hours will relate to the pre-show phase rather than to the show itself.

In the pre-show phase we want to presell our exhibit. For this phase, *pre-show direct mail campaigns* have been shown to be effective (Walls 1998: 52). This could be a postcard in the mail, inviting the recipient to come and visit our booth. That has also been described as *lumpy mail*: an envelope containing something, it doesn't matter what, but nothing that takes long to read (Friedman 2008). Preferably it should be combined with some sort of *freebie*, a small gift or a discount. Perhaps you could give away free passes to some of your best customers or prospects. This might be to an evening show, a special conference, or some other event that is held while the trade show is on. Just make sure you have an idea of whether they are interested in coming before you hand out the passes. We do not want to give free tickets out to visitors who are not going to use them.

Trade journal inserts (postcard-sized advertisements tucked inside the journal) are another idea; another is *smart e-mails* sent out to target potential customers – not too early, so that visitors have time to forget about the contents before the show is on (Friedman 2008).

Unfortunately, the pre-show phase is also beset with checklists. Checklists are necessary, since there are so many things to remember and so little time to get them right. As the points are often the same for every show, checklists tend to be a practical way of dealing with trade-show planning. It is easy to overlook one or two points, and the consequences can be dire. Some of these items, like a forgotten extension lead, light bulbs, or a water cooler can probably be obtained at the show, but to get hold of them will take time, time we have not got. It is scary to see how

Table 4.1 The international trade show budget

Components	Percent of total budget
Display construction	17
Transportation costs	14
Space rental	11
Specialty advertising	11
Set-up and tear-down	10
Personnel	9
Miscellaneous	7
Display maintenance	6

Source: National Trade Show Exhibitors Association

quickly things get out of control once an exhibitor realizes that he has forgotten a few things. The sheer feeling of irritation will often disturb the booth manager psychologically before the show has even opened. It is then likely also to affect his performance during the show. When things go really wrong, some booth staff can even break down psychologically. It is not uncommon to see exhibitors in an incomplete booth sitting with their head in their hands. Using a checklist is probably the best way to avoid a situation like that. Hence, checklists are unavoidable, as with any complex business process which recurs with some regularity. As you attend more shows, your checklist and the way you work with it will improve.

When you hear about a new trade show, start by asking a number of fundamental questions (this list is based on Friedman 2006b):

1. How well does this show fit our marketing needs?
2. How convenient are the show dates?
3. What other events are scheduled on those dates?
4. How convenient is the show location?
5. What percentage of attendees fall into our target market?
6. What percentage of attendees comes from our major service areas?
7. What does show management do to promote the show?
8. What is the show's past success rate?
9. Which of our competitors also exhibit at this show?
10. Will show management provide a list of previous exhibitors to contact about the show?
11. Has anyone from our organization visited the show?
12. How much will our investment need to be in this show?
13. What type of promotional assistance does show management offer?
14. What audience-quality information can show management provide?
15. What return on investment can be expected from each show?
16. Where does this particular show fit into our present marketing strategy?
17. Do we want to increase sales of existing products/services in existing markets?
    (a) Introduce new products/services into existing markets?
    (b) Introduce existing products/services into new markets?
    (c) Introduce new products/services into new markets?

(d) Introduce company into existing markets?

(e) Introduce company into new markets?

18. What products/product lines need to be displayed?
19. Who is our target audience at this show?
20. What are our objectives in exhibiting?
21. Do we have a written exhibiting plan?
22. Has an exhibiting budget been established?
23. Has our space been reserved?
24. Has the necessary deposit been paid?
25. What booth design will satisfy our objectives?
26. Can we refurbish/use our current exhibit?
27. Do we need a new exhibit?
28. Do we need new graphics?
29. What show services/items need to be ordered?

    (A) Signage
    (B) Electricity
    (C) Floor covering (e.g. carpeting)
    (D) Audio-visual equipment
    (E) Plumbing/air/water/drainage
    (F) Booth-cleaning services
    (G) Plants/floral decorations
    (H) Telephone
    (I) Computer
    (J) Printer
    (K) Waste bins
    (L) Furniture

30. Are security arrangements necessary?
31. Has booth installation/dismantling been organized?
32. What transport arrangements need to be organized?
33. Are there any union restrictions we need to know about?
34. Has insurance been arranged?
35. Do we have a toolkit organized to take to the show?
36. Have the necessary hotel arrangements been made?
37. When is final payment due for our booth space?
38. Are credit-card services needed for booth sales?
39. Is a vendor's licence needed?
40. Has a lead card been designed and printed?
41. Has a lead-logging system been organized for visitor requests?
42. Has a daily debriefing session been scheduled?
43. Will thank-you letters be sent to every registered visitor?
44. How will show leads be handled?
45. How will sales from the show be monitored?
46. What kind of reward/recognition will the exhibition staff receive?
47. How will the show be evaluated with respect to future participation?
48. Did we manage to keep within the estimated show budget?

49. Does the budget need revising for next year?
50. What other shows opportunities could be explored nationally/internationally?

   This is a checklist for the whole show process, from pre-show planning to post-show follow-up. The idea here is not to go through answering all the questions, but to get us thinking about making our own list. If you just follow the lists that someone else has devised, you are sure to overlook factors that are important in your particular case.

   Refurbishing is often overlooked in trade-show budgets. The stands we use and everything they contain are handled very roughly, by visitors, by ourselves, and by those who set them up, dismantle them, and transport them. Their life expectancy will be short. It is not like the furniture in our office. We cannot afford to ignore this point. Broken items, whether parts of the exhibit itself, or a piece of glass or furniture, create an unfavourable impression of the company as a whole.

   Another point on the list that is often forgotten is a good toolbox, which we shall need for the setting-up and dismantling; hammer, pliers, screwdriver, tape, hooks, velcro tabs, touch-up paints and brushes, not forgetting extension leads and adapter plugs.

   Once we have completed all our preparations and packed our goods we are ready to go.

   In the following three sections we shall look at three aspects of the planning phase in more detail: budget, sales promotion, and staffing.

4.1   Planning the Budget

When working with a budget, sometimes this will just use the same numbers as last year, with minor changes to reflect changes in general price levels. For instance, if the company expects no major changes, there might be an adjustment for inflation, say a 5 % increase on last year's budget to cover everything. On other occasions we will be asked to come up with an entirely new budget. If this is our first time, the budget will be drawn up from scratch.

   A good way to begin working on a trade show budget is to list the costs in two columns, one for *estimated costs* and one for *actual costs*. That way we can follow up on each entry, and get a good sense of the accuracy of our estimates as we finalize the entries one by one. That is a good way to bring past experience to bear on forecasting costs for next year's show.

   There are no rules about what the budget should look like, nor are there rules about its total. This is ultimately an investment decision. The costs of participation are the investment. Your expected sales stemming from the show are your income. Sometimes it may be a good idea to make the budget generous, at other times you will do fine with a smaller one. One rule of thumb says that you can expect total trade-show costs to be three times as large as the cost of renting your exhibition space. Better indications of costs can be found by doing some simple calculations:

- Work out how many hours the trade show lasts.
- Then decide how many visitors to your booth you can expect per hour. (Some will be there only to look around; they will not take much of your time.)
- Based on the number of conversations you anticipate having per hour, you can calculate what size of staff you need for the show.

A more detailed list of costs can be broken down as follows:

- Booth costs (the booth itself, furnishing, storage)
- Transport costs (shipping, customs, insurance)
- External labour (installation and dismantling, electricians, plumbers, riggers, etc.)
- Promotion costs (advertising, mailings, postage, giveaways, brochures, etc.)
- Services at the show (space rental, other rentals, utilities)
- External events (event costs)
- Booth staff (including hotel accommodation and travel)

Again, a budget provides information which is valuable for next year's show too. We should therefore spend some time drawing up a detailed, well-presented budget on a spreadsheet. After we have done this exercise we will encounter a steep learning curve. If that first spreadsheet was well made, we will want to retain it and improve it year by year. It then becomes a valuable marketing tool, which we may even want to incorporate into our marketing plan.

4.2 Pre-planning of Sales Promotion and Public Relations

"Promotion" in marketing covers personal selling, advertising, sales promotion, direct marketing, and publicity. We need to plan these activities ahead of the show. Promotional opportunities typically need to be planned 6–8 months ahead. We can start by setting up a list of questions, like:

1. What pre-show promotion needs to be organized?
   (a) Personal invitations (e.g. with incentive and response form)
   (b) Advertising (e.g. trade publications, local media)
   (c) Direct mail
   (d) Company visits
   (e) Telemarketing
   (f) Public relations
   (g) Website
   (h) Sponsorship
2. Has our booth number been included on all pre-show promotional pieces?
3. Do extra literature/catalogues/price lists need to be printed?
4. Have press kits been prepared?
5. Do other PR opportunities (e.g. press conference) need to be planned?
6. Has our show guide entry been completed and sent in?
7. What promotional giveaways will best enhance our message? Should we go with (plastic) bags, pens, mugs, or instead get something more useful and/or unconventional?

8. What on-site promotion do we want to organize?
   (a) Airport advertising (excellent first impression when you leave the airport, it looks as though your company owns the town)
   (b) Hoardings (along the route to the show; again, you are king)
   (c) Hotel television advertising ("they even own the hotel")
   (d) Advertising on local transport
   (e) Daily advertising at the show site
   (f) Hotel room promotions
   (g) Show directory advertising
   (h) Sponsorship
   (i) Aerial advertising, using aircraft, balloons, or dirigibles
   (j) Advertising costumes for handouts (outside the show, along the route[2])
   (k) Inflatables (for example arches, inflatable costumes, or product look-alikes)
9. Do we want to organize a visitor competition? (Perhaps we can even run one in co-operation with the show organizers)
10. Is our competition or giveaway in line with state/national lottery laws?
11. How many tickets need to be ordered?
12. Have hospitality functions been planned?

Our promotional efforts should be creative. As there are so many competitors all struggling to get noticed, all doing more or less the same things, only something that is truly different has a good chance of attracting any real attention. If we are a larger company, we might consider doing something outside the exhibition halls also, as an extension of our presence inside. It could be something that has to do with physical activities, relaxing or eating (basic physical needs), as a break and an alternative to what is going on inside. We might want to co-operate with a food stand, or do a tie-in, along the lines "Buy a Sony hotdog and we will donate fifty cents to charity".

The quality of our promotional products should not be neglected. For example, the price difference between photocopied and printed flyers need not be great. The difference in the impact they make is significant. You do not want to look cheap, or be associated with cheapness. Photocopies make you look as though you do everything in a rush, without forethought. Ultimately, everything we do reflects back on our company and its products.

Magazine reprints can be used to create a sense of quality and industry respectability. If you have been cited by a top magazine or newspaper as a leader, display a blow-up of the article on your stand; it gives you plenty of credibility at no cost. The film and entertainment industry has used this technique with good results for decades.

The press is an important participant at a trade show. They have their own particular needs, most of which can be fulfilled in what we call a *press kit*, a folder

---

[2] There are normally restrictions on these items inside the show and outside your own booth. Even if there are no legal restrictions, many people see these promotional techniques as unethical, since they intrude on a space that is regarded as neutral, which no particular exhibitor has paid for.

with specially targeted information which will help them to do their job and satisfy their readers, not forgetting their editor. The press kit should cover questions like:

1. What the company is all about
2. What products are being displayed at the show
3. What is new or important at the show
4. What has been done specially for the show
5. Where they can obtain further information during the show

Editors like stories about people, and they must be timely and unique. According to research by Marken (1989: 22), these are concerns which very few exhibitors actually identify. Those who prepare the kits should focus on "what's new", because that is the focus of the journalist who is going to be looking for the information. Make sure the press releases in the folder are genuinely new, not 3–4 months old. In most industries today, what is new normally means what has happened or has been announced during the past few weeks, preferably the last week. Try to turn announcements into events, as Apple has been so successful in doing when launching its new products to the world. This is more a marketing achievement than a technical achievement. With due respect to Apple, the company manages to get people to believe that its products are new even when the technology inside is not, and indeed is just the same as in other devices designed by their competitors and manufactured by third-party companies. The explanation for Apple's success has more to do with excellent design and marketing.

Preferably the folder should contain some information that is new at this trade show, and has never been published before. It is not the quantity of information in the press kit that matters, but the use journalists can make of it. Journalists are not impressed by attractive colours or glossy paper these days. Instead we should focus our effort on the textual content. The idea is to do as much of the journalist's job as possible for him, which includes providing company background material and photos. As my father used to say when he was still working: "Journalists just want to go home, so you try to help them". If you provide everything on a USB, or make the text downloadable via the web, so that the journalist only needs to edit the story and add his angle, you will have made his day.

Many editors want exclusives. If the newspaper or magazine is big enough and influential enough, we should consider offering such arrangements. That does not mean we cannot hand out ready-made material to other journalists in the form of press kits. In fact we might set up a series of one-to-one meeting with journalists. In the pre-show planning phase we should identify key journalists and invite them to the trade show for a special meeting. The easiest way to spot them is to see who writes about the things that interest your company, about your competitors, and about the industry at large. An article is always so much more effective as publicity than an advertisement in the same paper. (And while it may cost something to give a journalist a complimentary pass to the show, advertising in his paper would probably cost more.) This is largely a question of planning our PR efforts.

4.3   Pre-planning for Staff

A large part of our pre-show planning will revolve round training our staff. We should make sure we begin planning with our booth team 4–6 months ahead. Again, a list of questions will be useful to start the process rolling:

1. How many people are needed to staff the booth?
2. Is there room for them all in the existing booth? If not, can we work with different shifts, perhaps having one person working outside the booth at any time?
3. Who are the best people to represent the organization? (Identify each key task.)
4. Has a booth manager been appointed? (Make sure he has experience, i.e. has done it many times before.)
5. Has staff training been organized?
6. Has a pre-show meeting been scheduled?
7. Is the booth team familiar with the products/services being displayed?
8. Has a practice demonstration session been organized?
9. Will a technical representative be available to answer questions? (What kind of questions do we expect?)
10. Has a dress code been established?
11. Have badges been ordered for all booth personnel?
12. Do the booth personnel have the necessary quantity of business cards?
13. Has a booth schedule been planned?
14. Who will oversee booth installation and dismantling?
15. Does that person understand the move-out procedure?

It may seem unnecessary to make the point, but the number of people going to a show should be determined by the tasks we shall be performing at the show – not by who would like to go or who can go, or who deserves to go this year, all of which unfortunately are considerations that companies use in practice when they decide who should attend. For many companies, participating in a major trade show in their industry is going to be their single most important marketing effort during that year. If someone who is needed cannot go because of another commitment, time and resources should be allocated to that person so that he can give the show priority. On the other hand, we should not fill the booth with so many staff that it limits the number of visitors who can come in. Trade shows are not events for employees to get together. For those purposes we have other kinds of event, such as annual outings, field trips, Christmas parties, or kick-offs.

When visitors come to our booth they expect to get their questions answered. If visitors do not receive a satisfactory answer, or if they are asked to come back later, they will be surprised – and justifiably so. That is particularly true for B2B shows, where a lack of answers will immediately reflect on the company's products. So, we want to send people who can answer all possible questions about our products and services. It may even be a sensible idea to try to anticipate what those questions will be, so that we can really feel sure we are bringing the right competences to the show. If there are questions that booth staff cannot answer – which can always happen, after all, especially for more advanced technical products – then we should at least be able to explain how an answer can be got. For instance, it may be that we can quote the phone number of one of the company's engineers, or we might look it up on a website together with the customer. With today's interconnectedness there are few excuses for not knowing where to look for an answer. That is one aspect of living in the *Information Age*. We are not expected to know everything, but we are expected to be able to find out.

Who should be chosen as booth manager? Well, preferably someone who has participated in a number of trade shows already, who knows what kinds of problems can arise, and has shown that he can solve them. It should be someone who can deal with many different kinds of people, both within and outside the company. It is not enough simply to be sociable or extraverted; the candidate should be someone who is highly organized, who is not stressed by the idea of multitasking, and who can motivate and engage staff. In short, Superman.

Simulations can be a good way to prepare for the actual show. There are two kinds of simulation, *booth simulations* and *booth staff simulations*. If there is time, we would like to set the booth up before we go to the show, to check that it actually looks and performs as it should. It also makes it so much easier to do the setting-up and dismantling at the show if we have already done it at least once before. When the booth is installed at the training facility, this makes an excellent opportunity to do some staff training as well, to see how we "man the battle stations". We could make this lead into role play, where some staff members act the part of various kinds of visitor with different needs and personalities. Then afterwards we can sit in a circle and discuss what kinds of problem occurred and how we responded to them. Sharing experiences and talking about them is not only an excellent way of addressing future problems, but also a way for staff to get tuned in to each other, so that we learn to act as one group or body, and our visitors come away not only with the awareness of having received satisfactory answers to their questions, but with a sense of consistency, and ideally even of harmony.

There are many aspects of booth staff simulations. We can practise what to say, how to say it, how to move around, how to dress and change our clothes for different roles during the day. Decisions about what we choose to simulate will ultimately be limited only by what feels useful and meaningful, given the constraints on what we can simulate. For example, it would hardly be meaningful to simulate our competitors' booths, or to simulate how we would walk round and conduct surveys. The first would cost too much to set up, and the second situation is too complex to replicate. What will be useful, though, is to test out in advance any surveys we plan to use, by asking a few persons to fill them in so that we can check whether our questions are understood and check that they cover all dimensions of the marketing research project.

So far as possible, we want to prepare our various post-show activities before the event. Not all questions can be answered in-house, so we will probably also want to conduct some *market research* on our own. Sometimes it will be enough to prepare some frameworks for analysis to be carried out at the show. That may be anything from a *competitor analysis*, to *benchmarking* or a simple SWOT analysis. In most cases the organizers will be able to supply some useful statistics, but we will seldom be able to rely on that material alone. The data we get will be incomplete in one way or another, or they will raise new questions. This will spur further activities on our part.

Nowadays there are numerous shows for any industry. Sometimes it is obvious which ones to choose – the ones where our competitors are – and at other times a series of questions can help to kick off the process of choice:

1. What kind of trade show is this? Is it well known? If it is a minor show, we might consider sending another team.
2. What kind of people and companies go there? Get hold of a list of previous participants. Will our major competitors be there? If not, perhaps we will send another team.
3. Who is running and organizing the trade show? What are their objectives? That will determine what we can achieve at the show, which in turn decides who we should send.
4. What were the results from this event last time we took part?
5. How much media attention is the event likely to receive?
6. What are the costs of participating, and how could this show contribute to our overall marketing objectives?

Based on our answers, we can set up some goals for the show. These should be realistic and if possible quantifiable (numbers of orders, usable leads, etc.).

Once a show has been chosen, we can begin drawing up a *booth schedule*. This is an hour-by-hour timetable for all activities at the show. It should answer the questions:

1. WHAT is happening
2. WHEN
3. WHO should go
4. The WHY should be explained in the marketing plan for the exhibition.

The schedule should start with who will oversee the installation of the booth and who will oversee the dismantling. Make sure those responsible understand the move-out procedure.

Once we have been included in the catalogue ourselves, we should check that all information printed about us is correct. We should also check out the exhibition geography. Try to be clear about the following, including locations:

1. The avenue system
2. Fire regulations
3. Toilets
4. Exits
5. Competitors' stands
6. Exhibition rules
7. Exhibition office
8. Trade associations
9. Stand photographer (if needed)
10. Information points
11. Banking facilities
12. Food and drink

13. Staircase and lifts
14. General display area
15. Security considerations
16. Car parks

This information is normally available on the organizer's website several months before the show. Very often it will be more or less the same as last year.

We need to set up a series of pre-show meetings with staff to make sure everyone knows what to do and what is expected of each person. These meetings can in part be arranged as simulations, as we saw above. The meetings should include the following elements:

1. Involving staff in budget
2. Reading through the exhibitor manual together, making sure everyone knows how to use it and can find key information (toilets, food, location of competitors, administration, electricity assistance, etc.)
3. Going over the booth schedule together; who does what when?
4. Going over the marketing plan together.
5. A quick course in boothmanship:
   (a) How to behave: theory first, then practice.
   (b) If you can, set up the booth somewhere, or just draw some lines on the floor for simulation purposes.
6. A quick course on the know-how associated with each of your products and services.
7. Practice demonstration session. Rehearse difficult situations: "What do you do if ...?" Discuss reactions in the group.

Organizing three or four meetings of 2–4 h each will make a tremendous difference to the actual performance of your team once they are at the show. Sixteen hours may sound like a lot to many managers, but when you consider what is at stake for most companies, this is only a small investment to make for a major show. Begin 6–12 months ahead. Many shows require space to be booked a year in advance.

We can also engage booth staff in the PR work, especially if we are a small or medium sized company. In that case we need to develop a *media kit* and a *public relations strategy*. Arrange to have special *press briefings* and a special *press reception* at your booth, and lay on some social events. *Press conferences* are reserved for major announcements. Try to organize all your press events between Tuesday and Thursday, provided that fits in with the period of the show. This will give the press the possibility of getting the story out the following day, without any clash arising with weekend material.

Most companies try to get their new products ready just in time for the trade show. That is months too late. Industry analysts and editors need to be briefed in advance, so that they know what they can expect to see at the show, so that they have an idea of what they are going to encounter in the press room, but more importantly so that they can tell their audience what to expect at the show. Unless you are Apple Inc., it is not enough simply to say "be there". It may of course be difficult to have the product ready months ahead, but we ought to have an idea of what is in the pipeline. Of course, sometimes we do not want to disclose what is on the way, just because that is a valuable strategic signal for our competitors. In that case we have to try to create interest among journalists in some other way. If we are lucky, it will be enough simply to say that there will be a "major product announcement". If we have pulled this off before, they will buy it.

There is always the question of the quality of the information we send out. Editors are not interested in a bundle of our old press releases and general company material. They want to know what is new, explained in plain English. It is the quality of information which should be the focus for PR staff, not the quantity. Here are some tips by Marken (2004: 30–33) on how to write a press release for a trade show:

1. Note down all contact names, phone numbers, e-mail addresses. For trade shows let the press know your hotel and mobile phone number.
2. Write with the editor or reporter and his audience in mind, not your managers. Avoid all kinds of management-flattering "fluff".
3. Start with the essentials: who, what, when, where, why, and how, expressed in newsy style.
4. Write so as to help the reporter to move from the summary and into the details.
5. What you write should be well formatted, to make it easy to read.
6. It should be simple, factual, complete.
7. It should be written to position the company and/or the product quickly, clearly, and concisely.
8. Use complete sentences with active nouns and verbs.
9. Include contact information, details on how the press can get more information, photos.

Do not include sales information in the press kit. Kerin and Cron (1987b) distinguish between two types of trade show: *selling trade shows* and *non-selling trade shows*. Non-selling shows comprise promotional activities, for instance. At the same time, we know that selling has become an increasingly important aim for companies participating in trade shows, as company executives demand greater returns from their marketing budgets.

Some remarks to conclude this chapter: Tanner (2002: 229–239) has shown that (contrary to what many consultants would have you believe) spending huge amounts of money on exhibition marketing may not yield the results desired. Rather, it is good answers to organizational questions like how responsibilities are delegated, and tactical decisions relating e.g. to pre-show promotion, that give the best results. Planning for a show carefully does not necessarily imply many additional costs. But the rewards of pre-show planning are substantial. That is the main reason why exhibition marketing deserves our attention as a study.

Post-show Follow-up

5

Post-show marketing covers the activities we perform once we are back from the trade show. These consist mainly of two kinds of activity, follow-up and assessment. The aim of these activities is increased sales through relationship improvements, as shown in the model offered by Lee and Kim (2008: 786) (Fig. 5.1):

Getting back from a trade show can be quite a shock. You have moved from a hectic environment, with thousands of people and plenty of stimuli, to the office. You are trying to work out what to do next, and at the same time asking yourself what really happened at the show. The effects of that shock have led many commentators to refer to this phase and mood as the *post-show blues*. The most difficult thing now may be how to get started on moving forward.

By now we should have a database of prospects. What is important is that we act on them straight away – leaving a prospect a couple of days to get the whole trade-show experience out of his system, but not long enough to forget us or forget the show. This is harvest time. The names, phone numbers, and additional information in that computer are our crops. They are there to pay for the whole cost of going to the trade show and our salaries, and they should therefore be treated with utmost attention.

Leads are like fresh fish: if we leave them too long they become bothersome. The chances are that it was not only us who acquired the good leads. They will also be our competitors' leads, since they were probably at the same show. If we do not act upon these leads within a reasonable time, someone else will.

Furthermore, we now have a great advantage in making our *cold calls*. We have already met the individuals we are about to call, so there is no real breaking of the ice to get through. For that reason it is important that the same person who met the visitor at the trade show should also be the one phoning or making the initial contact. "Mr Olsson, we met at the *X* Booth at the *YZ* Show last week". Even if Mr Olsson does not remember, he will probably say yes, so as not to come across as a fool.

Many companies write a post-show report for top management, for their colleagues, or for themselves. Sometimes it looks rather like a diary, with pictures

K. Solberg Søilen, *Exhibit Marketing and Trade Show Intelligence*,
Management for Professionals, DOI 10.1007/978-3-642-36793-9_5,
© Springer-Verlag Berlin Heidelberg 2013

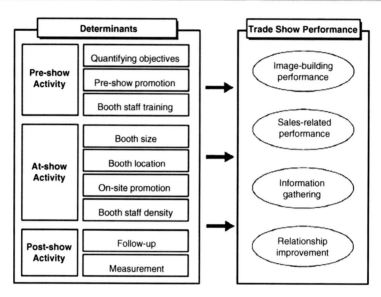

Fig. 5.1 A conceptual model of determinants and outcomes of trade show performance

of people, exhibitors' booths, and activities. The same format is also typical of industry and trade-show magazines. The report will give us the essentials about the trade show: major exhibitors, new products, keynote speakers and their topics. The following figure (from *Beverage Industry*, vol. 99 no. 8, August 2008, p. 46) is an example:

Special Topic 2: Example of a Post-show Report

▷

IFT post-show report

Beauty, health solutions on display in New Orleans

The Institute of Food Technologists held its annual convention and trade show in New Orleans June 28-July 1, and if ingredient trends are predictors of future beverage trends, beauty products, superfruits and digestive health beverages are on the horizon.

DSM Nutritional Products, Parsippany, N.J., used the show to launch "Beauty from Within" ingredient solutions for healthy skin. The portfolio of ingredients includes carotenoids in the form of beta-carotene, Redivivo lycopene, Optisharp zeaxanthin and FloraGlo lutein, as well as vitamins A, C, D and E, B vitamins; polyphenols such as Teavigo EGCG, Resvida resveratrol, Hidrox olive polyphenols, Bonistein and genistein; Ropufa omega 3 and omega 6 ingredients; and All-Q

coenzyme Q10. The ingredients are intended to nourish the skin from the inside, and several have been studied for their ability to protect the skin from UV light and oxidative stress.

Fortitech, Schenectady, N.Y., focused on mood-enhancement, cosmeceuticals and heart health. with premix examples such as good-mood/stress-reducing chocolate bars and cosmeceutical beverages. Fortitech incorporated GABA, magnesium, l-theanine, l-tryptophan and ashwaganda extract in its mood-enhancing chocolate bars. Its beverage is designed to promote better overall wellness as well as a better appearance, included collagen, coenzyme Q10 and lutein. L-carnitine, l-arginine, zinc, fiber, copper and selenium made their way into bars formulated for heart

health and diabetes prevention.

Nutragenesis discussed its Sensara skin-enhancing cosmeceutical ingredient made from a blend of two GRAS-affirmed standardized herbal extracts. The ingredient is water-extracted without solvents, is heat-stable and water-soluble, vegetarian and kosher. Sensara is thought to help with skin aging by preserving collagen protein, inhibiting oxidative stress, slowing pro-oxidative cellular damage and stimulating non-collagenic proteins. In addition, it is said to promote emotional well-being and a calm, relaxed state of mind.

Cargill displayed beverage prototypes such as a Heart Healthy Juice Beverage with Barliv barley betafiber as a source of soluble fiber, and Milk with CoroWise Plant Sterols. Chipotle Chocolate-

Flavored Milk used bold flavors to target older consumers with a diminishing sense of taste, as well as Cargill's Chana Lightly Alkalized Cocoa. In addition, the company featured Peach-Cinnamon-Flavored White Tea, with 4 grams of protein per serving in the form of BT100, as well as Zerose erythritol for fewer calories, and Aubygel ABN 4000 carageenan from Cargill Texturizing Solutions. The hydrocolloid was used to stabilize the cocoa and provide a homogeneous texture. For digestive health, the Ginger-Apricot-Flavored Smoothie with Probiotics contained Oliggo-Fiber

In the report we learn what new products were launched, what was included in the companies' product portfolios, what the products do, and what their benefits are. This is a quick and easy way to get an overview and update one's knowledge of the industry.

5.1 The Sales Call

Not everyone enjoys making sales calls. According to research by Verbeke, Belschak, and Bagozzi (2000), more than 60 % of salespeople suffer from *sales call anxiety* (SCA) on occasions. Previous research had given an estimate of up to 40 % (Ray 1995), which may mean that anxiety levels have increased. The best way to cope with SCA is to focus on *sale perseverance* and *task concentration*, ultimately reducing dysfunctional protective actions. Sale perseverance refers to attempts to press ahead actively with the sale despite one's feelings of anxiety. Task concentration means freeing up thinking in relation to the task at hand (Belschak et al. 2006).

There are basically two aspects to successful sales calls: *product knowledge*, and *selling skills*. There are a number of steps to closing a deal with a trade-show visitor, and no single approach can be said to be the right one for all situations, but most procedures includes elements such as (i) establishing customer receptivity, (ii) assessing the customer's needs, (iii) offering some examples/telling a story, and (iv) recommending actions/closing the deal (for an example, see Hubbard 1988).

Let us imagine a hypothetical conversation, and add some reasoning between the lines:

Hello, Mr *N*. I am *PQ* from the *XYZ* company. I believe we met when you came to our booth at the *X* trade show in Messeburg.
 This is a good start. It was he who came to see us, not the other way round. Now, we are coming to see him. That means that he will at least listen to what we have to say. He owes us that much. This is also the time to show that we have gathered more information about the visitor than just his name and phone number:
 I understood that you were looking for a product *P*, is that right?
 If he said so in our booth, he is probably not going to deny it now, unless someone else has beaten us to it. From his "yes" to our questions a whole range of possibilities opens up. The best thing is to continue with the information we obtained from him during our conversation, until he becomes sufficiently comfortable and cordial:
 Do I remember correctly that you were particularly concerned about the function *F*?
 Then we can go on to give a few examples, if appropriate. When we break away from this pattern and move on to our selling points, we should do so very carefully.
 Would you mind if I came over at a time of your convenience and showed you the product which meets the requirements we have talked about?
 Now we are closing in on the moment of truth.

No sales situation is exactly the same. It is a question of sticking to some basics and being flexible in the conversation, adapting to the situation. Above all else it is about showing empathy, about being sympathetic without overdoing it. Good salespeople are like pals.

5.2   The Post-show Evaluation

Management is going to want to see a post-show evaluation. The report should answer questions and topics such as:

1. Number and quantity of sales
2. Number and quality of prospects
3. Number and quality of press releases
4. How well we kept expenses within budget (explaining deviations)
5. Booth staff evaluations
6. Opinions about other exhibitors
7. Results of market surveys among customers and potential customers

We may want to initiate the whole process with a short debriefing session once we are home. What went well and what less well overall, and why? We should also use the opportunity to thank people for taking part and ask them for feedback. What could we have done better? What should be changed for next year, or next time? Don't forget to do an evaluation of your giveaways too. Did they work? Did people see them? Were they useful? Were they consistent with our corporate values and the identity we want to portray? This is a time to be self-critical. If we are not, the chances are that someone else in the company will be critical in our place.

Ultimately the purpose of evaluation is not to point fingers, but to ensure improvements for the next show. That said, each staff member's performance should be evaluated and the evaluations should have consequences, in the form of rewards and penalties.

Trade Show Intelligence

6

Trade shows are primarily a knowledge sharing activity. In the 1980s and 1990s, when systematic research on trade shows began, the focus was mostly on sales and costs. The implications of the information age for the trade show profession first became a topic within the past 10 years (see e.g. Reychav 2009, Solberg Søilen 2010).

What we call "intelligence" is different from information: it relates to *need-to-know*, as opposed to *nice-to-know*. With ever more information, managers have stopped asking for information. In fact, information has become part of the problem: it is what all companies are drowning in, even after they have installed machines and software to handle it. What managers want is not information, but knowledge about what is really important – that is, what affects the company's strategy. This means that gathering intelligence is impossible if we do not know in advance what the strategy of the company is.

Few things affect our strategy more than the entrance of a new competitor or the introduction of a new competing product, especially if it is priced more keenly. Exhibitions provide an excellent opportunity to take a good look at what our competitors are doing, and what products and offers they have. Thus there is a natural connection between trade shows and *intelligence studies*.

Now, as soon as we broach the topic of *trade show intelligence* (TSI), we need to begin a discussion about methods. The question of methods, in this context, is the question about how we can gather information without (i) breaking the law, or (ii) violating our ethics (whether our company's ethics, or our own personal moral code). The first issue is legal, the second belongs to the study of business ethics. We cannot solve the problem by getting someone else, a third party, to handle our dirty laundry for us. It is true that that is a way to reduce the probability of being caught (by police and/or by journalists) and hence it reduces the risk of bad publicity, but the offence and the dilemma are just as real.

Some readers will feel that it is unethical to "nose around", especially if this includes lying about one's identity. Paying someone to lie on our behalf does not eliminate the ethical problem, only the embarrassment when something goes wrong

K. Solberg Søilen, *Exhibit Marketing and Trade Show Intelligence,*
Management for Professionals, DOI 10.1007/978-3-642-36793-9_6,
© Springer-Verlag Berlin Heidelberg 2013

(and it does not always achieve that). So we must make it clear to whoever does the job what sort of conduct we regard as acceptable.

Trade show intelligence is a speciality; it is sometimes even regarded as a profession. Some companies will get their own people to go around and take a look at what their competitors are doing and offering. Others will commission a *competitive intelligence* (CI) professional or a market researcher to conduct the analysis, i.e. they will outsource this particular service. Many larger companies have their own staff journalists. If we can get hold of a press pass, this will admit us to a number of interesting forums, such as invited gatherings and presentations. Arriving as a journalist not only will make it easier for us to ask hard-nosed, direct questions, but also people will commonly tell us things without our even needing to ask.

No one can prevent you observing the booths and taking notes. However, this should be done discreetly. One approach is to observe first, and then go somewhere else to write up your notes. Some shows and exhibitors do not approve of outside people taking photographs in someone else's booth. One way to approach this is to ask permission first. Some longer-established shows, and some exhibitor companies whose managements are more senior, particularly family-run businesses, are more likely to disapprove of in-booth photography.[1]

To begin with, we might want to gather together all the documentation we can get hold of from our competitors. This will teach us first about their marketing strategy, and secondly about their products. What kind of *marketing-material mix* are they using (brochures, flyers, giveaways?) How new are their products really? How much money are they spending on documentation?

We might also look at which competitors our customers and prospects are visiting. We do not have to follow them about to do this; we can get a good idea of the answer by using a questionnaire.

There are many techniques for doing *exhibition intelligence*. It will often include drawing up a route plan. Start by studying the catalogue. Where are our competitors sited? Who from our company will visit which booths? If we do not have outside people to do this job for us, we can share out between us the main areas of intelligence we are aiming to acquire, ultimately in order to identify specific competitors and trends in the market.

Our next objective may be to work with a large number of ready-made analyses and compare these with our own observations. If it is a major international trade show, then we can probably draw conclusion for the global market. If it is national, then we can only draw conclusions for one country, or if regional, then only for that part of the country.

---

[1] Other constraints at a trade show may include no children under the age of 10, no dogs or other animals, no heavy or bulky bags, or a prohibition on bringing still or cine cameras into the showground. By enquiring in advance we can learn what is both ethically and legally acceptable. Note that it is not considered good form to make sales contacts outside our booth area, in the aisles for instance.

Table 6.1 Types of question for each intelligence category (Solberg Søilen 2010)

Product intelligence	Trade show software intelligence: the people	Trade show hardware intelligence: the booth
Technical specs (weight, size, colour, design, etc.)	Number and composition of staff (age, sex, experience, etc.)	Booth spec (size, design, material used, etc.)
Product demonstration	Quality of boothmanship	Booth location
Price	Estimated staff cost	Estimated booth cost

One way to begin the process is first to walk briskly through the whole show to spot what is of particular interest to us and our company. On a second pass we shall want to collect written material, gathering information from brochures and handouts. Based on this information and a careful study of its contents, we can prepare questions to be answered on our third and final tour of the show. The whole process, if done effectively, will take us most of a day. This in itself is an argument in favour of outsourcing at least some part of the function.

While walking round and gathering information it will sometimes be enough just to observe. In other situations, we might want to engage in conversation with booth staff or experts. In most cases, our main focus will be the competitors' product. At a trade show we have an excellent opportunity to see them demonstrated. We might also want to gather intelligence about the behaviour of booth staff and about the quality and appearance of the actual booth. That was in fact how this book got started, when I was working for groups of companies, travelling round the world with them and learning alongside them. See also Minicase 1 below.

The table below distinguishes three different of intelligence gathering and some key dimensions (Table 6.1):

The estimated booth costs and our observation of personnel and activities will give us an idea about any one exhibitor's total marketing budget for the trade show. This gives us an indication of the belief the company have in their new products, hence it is also an indication of what sort of competition we can expect to face. In some cases it will be a false assumption to suppose that a company which is putting heavy resources into its exhibit will be successful; but in general, and assuming that companies are not only rational but well-organized, it is fair to assume that resources used reflect their current and to some extent also their future strength.

6.1   Using Focus Groups in Trade Show Intelligence

A *focus group* can be defined as a form of organized discussion, and is a well-established technique in social-science research. A group of 5–10 individuals are selected by the analyst, or "moderator" as he or she is often called, to discuss and comment on an issue or on a set of selected questions for which the participants have had relevant personal experience. The participants then interact with each other, and the results are logged and analysed.

Focus groups are different from *group interviews*, where the participants answer the analyst's questions. The advantage with focus groups is that the analyst can make observations of the participants' feelings, attitudes, and reactions which are unavailable when various other techniques such as *surveys* or *telephone interviews* are used. To be successful, the technique assumes that participants are able to let go of the idea that they are being observed, and will become as involved in the discussion as if the situation had arisen in real life. In a focus group the moderator does not control the activity, which rather is left to the social dynamic of the group. The role of the moderator is to make sure that participants do not drift too far away from the topic. He or she should otherwise remain in the background.

Minicase 1: Using Focus Groups for Exhibition Intelligence

Company: a selection of high-design furniture companies
Trade show: **Salone Internazionale del Mobile,** *Fiera di Milano, Milan*

A number of executives from six small and medium-sized furniture companies from the Swedish province of Skåne (Scania) were asked to go and study a group of their high-design competitors. A list of targets was worked out in advance and a floorplan of the trade show was marked up accordingly. The executives took with them a list of specific variables to examine, like their competitors' product design, any new products, the booths, and booth staff behaviour.

On their return the executives sat in a circle and a general discussion began. Each observer presented his or her findings over a 5–10 min period. The others could respond to each individual's observations and remarks. Thus a discussion started, which turned out to involve strong opinions on certain issues. The whole conversation was recorded, and a transcription of the audiotape was later distributed to each participating company together with an analysis of the discussion. The exercise was carried out in a conference room hired for the occasion at the show and immediately after the observations were made, while impressions were still fresh in people's minds.

As a result of the exercise a number of unexpected changes occurred at the companies. They not only came up with ideas for new furniture products, but also learned about the level of interest in techniques of making new furniture look old. One company was even asked to manufacture Venetian gondolas.

Conclusion: The companies concluded that the quality of their products was still significantly better than that of their competitors, but that the competitors' new designs made their products attractive to a wider foreign market. Realizing this gave some of the companies the courage to make radical changes to their business plans after they returned home.

The quality of our analysis will determine the value of our conclusions. It is necessary, therefore, to know how to carry out various kinds of analysis before attending a trade show. Depending on the nature of the analysis to be carried out on the competition, there are a number of appropriate technical alternatives to choose from. The topic is covered in Solberg Søilen (2005: 97–110) and Jenster and Solberg Søilen (2009).

Table 6.2 The industry and the macro environment (Jenster and Solberg Søilen 2009: 67)

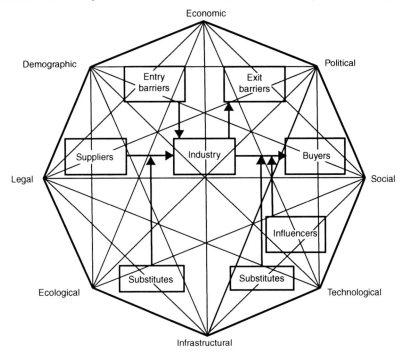

A good way to begin thinking about analysis is to follow a model of the aggregate forces influencing our business. The basic idea here is not to forget any one perspective or player. For example, there are many cases of companies that are very good at carrying out analyses of their competitors and their industry, but forget to take into account the political considerations which influence their business. The model below is an extended version of Porter's five-forces model (Table 6.2).

At a trade show we will not only gain information about our micro environment – about competitors, customers, and suppliers – but we will also learn a great deal about the macro environment which constantly impacts on our business. This includes information about political decisions, new technologies, changes in the macro-economy, new laws being planned or coming into force, ecological concerns, infrastructural limitations, social trends, and demographic concerns or opportunities. We will learn this from speakers, but also from the people of influence and the journalists present at the show. Much of this information will also be picked up during the evenings, at social gatherings. We should then find a way to register these pieces of intelligence, which today often means that we use some sort of business intelligence system (Table 6.3).

Table 6.3 Choosing the most appropriate analysis (Solberg Søilen 2005: 68–69)

Variable	Subject/Function	Analysis
Micro environment		
Customers	Marketing	Focus groups
		Questionnaires
		Trend analysis
		Forecasting
Competitors	Marketing	Benchmarking
		SWOT
		Game theoretical approaches
		Simulations
	Finance	Ratio analysis
		Cost analysis
Suppliers	Industrial management	Benchmarking
		Game theoretical approaches
	Finance	Cost analysis
	Marketing	Simulations
Entry barriers	Finance	Spread sheets
		Cost analysis
Exit barriers	Finance	Spread sheets
		Cost analysis
Substitutes to suppliers	Industrial management	Devil's advocate
		Spread sheets
Marketing		Simulations
Substitutes to customers	Marketing	Devil's advocate
		Spread sheets
		Simulations
Macro environment		
Economic	Economics, Macro	
Political	Political Science	PEST analysis
Social	Sociology	
Technological	Technology-Sociology	
Infrastructural	Technology-Sociology	State-of-art reporting
Ecological	Ecology	Power analysis
Legal	Law	
Demographic	Political geography	Statistical analysis

When we have an overview of all the forces influencing our business, we can move to the second step of selecting the analytic techniques. It is recommended that we do more than one analysis for each dimension, since this can confirm tentatively-formed conclusions. We call this *redundancy in method*. If we carry out two analyses and they lead to different conclusions then we may consider doing a third analysis, etc. To keep things simple it will be an advantage of we can use the same business intelligence system we started with above also for this part of the process.

In the following sections, we shall look in more detail at a few of these types of analysis which may be specially useful at trade shows. These are: benchmarking (Sect. 6.2), trend analysis and forecasting (Sect. 6.3), and questionnaires (Sect. 6.4). For a more detailed overview, see Solberg Søilen (2005), Jenster and Solberg Søilen (2009).

6.2 Trade Show Benchmarking

It is said that when Boeing brought out their 707 model in 1958, Airbus bought one and flew it to Toulouse, where it was taken apart for the purpose of comparison, or benchmarking.

In *benchmarking* we define a number of Key Success Factors (KSF) for any given product or service, and compare them quantitatively as between a company and its competitor(s). Usually companies benchmark against companies within their own industry. But there can also be great advantage in benchmarking against so-called *companies of excellence* within other industries. Many operations are the same, even though companies are in different industries. (Examples would include the handling of customers, outsourcing of services, and the rewarding of employees.)

Benchmarking is extensively used in technological industries, e.g., in car manufacture, not least in order to ensure that one's products are *state of the art*. Benchmarking may be conducted secretly, in co-operation with competitors, by an independent outside company, or in a mixture of these ways. In theory, you can benchmark anything that is easily comparable, that is, quantifiable.[2]

6.3 Trend Analysis and Forecasting for Trade Shows

A *trend analysis*, a cousin of the *scenario analysis* to be discussed below, is more descriptive than the latter. The focus is less on putting values on outcomes, and more on painting whole pictures of what the future might look like and what consequences this could have for consumer behaviour. Trend analysis is not only important for any industry concerned with design or fashion, but is used for describing all sorts of areas of life, from political opinions to people's hobbies and choices of education and profession. Its time frame is often longer than that of a scenario analysis; it may cover a period from 5–10 years, depending on the

---

[2] For more on benchmarking see Solberg Søilen (2013).

industry. Trend analysis within a specific sector is often called *industry forecasting*. The use of the term "forecasting" often implies use of quantitative techniques, as in *weather forecasting*.

These analyses are often carried out by finance or accounting departments, whose focus is standardly on quantitative analysis. The focus is often on financial performance or market demand, and may be linked directly to a company's plan or strategy via specific metrics. Forecasting often involves carrying out statistical analysis on historical data, e.g., *regression analysis, time series, univariate* and *bivariate statistics, Theil's U statistic, forecast errors, least squares estimates*, and adjustments for inflation and population. This may in some cases give us a detailed prediction for the 6 months to come, or perhaps even up to 2 years ahead, depending on the situation and the industry we are dealing with. But, whatever we arrive at we are seldom able to express ourselves with much certainty. That is just the nature of the future, it is uncertain.

Many customers want to know what the world will look like 20 years or more from now. Such questions are better left to *futurologists* and the subject of *futurology* or *future studies*. In the study of futurology, the requirements of social-science methodology become more relaxed, with relatively creative thinking substituted for rigid chains of cause and effect. That does not mean that futurology cannot get things right, but it does mean that it cannot clearly show its reasoning. Hence there are no real proofs, and everything depends on the individual consultant and his or her experience. In other words, it very much depends on the credibility of the futurologist. Futurologists often become like *management gurus*: either you believe in them or you don't. Very often your belief may stem from sympathetic feelings, which may not be the best indication that someone is correct. A trend analysis, on the other hand, ought to be answerable to rigid tests of cause and effect.

There are hardly any consumer products that are unaffected by trends; they apply to everything from toothbrushes to mobile phones. What products we buy depends largely on what they look like, their design and their features. As the social beings we are, we tend to want what our role models have. In modern societies these role models are often selected from *popular culture*, whether music, films, or sport.

6.4   Questionnaires for Trade Shows

A questionnaire is probably the commonest way of gathering first-hand information outside the boundaries of an organization. In simple terms, a *questionnaire* is a sheet of paper containing a number of unbiased questions to be answered by a target group of people. The art of using questionnaires is a matter of defining the right questions, choosing the right group of people, and carrying out the appropriate analysis of their answers.

For example, we might want to know what our visitors think about our exhibit. This information might be used to check whether our prior expectations were correct, and whether we could or should change anything for next year's show. The first thing we need to do is to capture all relevant dimensions of what we want to measure in our questions, making sure not to leave any variables out. Then we need to construct the questions in such a way that they do not lead respondents to give a particular answer. And finally we need to be sure that we have actually found the target group we are aiming at, rather than some other group of respondents. For example, if we ask people just outside the conference hall whether they visited our booth, they might give a positive answer out of politeness, or because they had intended or wanted to go. Including these answers will distort our survey; our analysis will be wrong, and ultimately it will lead us to incorrect conclusions. To avoid this, we should first identify and list all the different kinds of *bias* which our survey risks encountering. Then we should plan how to avoid each type of bias. If we cannot avoid some particular types of bias, we should discuss these explicitly, and try to compensate for them, in our final analysis.

Mastering the art of questionnaires takes a long time and is often underestimated. What looks easy conceals great complexity. People will often not answer honestly, and questions will often involve bias. There are whole ranges of questions to which we often give false answers, for various reasons. We can categorize these biases into classes or types. It may be, for instance, that a question is too sensitive, or we may want to represent ourselves as superior to our true reality. For example, it is easier to ask a person to state his annual salary using wide income bands (say from US$100,000 to 150,000) than to ask for the exact figure. Sometimes people do not really know, or they give a higher figure to look better or because they are unable to distinguish between what they would like and what they actually have.

A questionnaire usually begins with a series of formal questions which it is easy for the respondent to be honest about, such as age, sex, number of years of experience, etc., followed by groups of questions for each area of information being investigated. It is important that the choices available to the respondent cover all possible opinions.

The hardest part of designing a questionnaire is constructing specific forms of words that succeed in expressing the questions we are actually interested in. It can be a good idea to provide a few lines at the end to allow for "other" as a multiple-choice response, or for "comments" (*open-ended question*) where the respondent can give a free-form answer. When respondents are asked to rate things numerically, a *Likert scale* is preferred, using a scale of 5 or 7. Odd numbers allow for neutral answers.

In surveys, it is not so much the results themselves that primarily interest us, but issues about the technique used. Only if the technique is bias-free will the survey be worthwhile, and we can put confidence in the conclusions.

When the analysis is done we write a report and pass it on to decision makers in our organization, all according to their needs. The best reports are often those made on demand, but we can also pass on reports to those we think may need it. The form of these *intelligence reports* vary greatly. However, if we are to do a thorough analysis it is difficult to get under 50–70 pages. If the report gets too long we can provide an *executive summary*.

6.5   Intelligence on Trade Shows

There is not only the phenomenon of intelligence at trade shows, but of course there is also intelligence on trade shows. A few final words therefore about that topic.

There is no doubt that the best way nowadays to assemble information about trade shows is to use Google or another search engine. The information available through these sites is overwhelming, and it is improving every day. To examine a particular show you might want to use a special service such as the Trade Show News Network at www.tsnn.com. According to their own website they have been the world's leading online resource for the trade show, exhibition, and event industry since 1996:

> TSNN.com owns and operates the most widely consulted event database on the Internet, containing data about more than 25,000 trade shows, exhibitions, public events and conferences.

For international trade shows I found more hits at BizTradeShows.Com. This site claims to list "19,000+ Live Upcoming Business Trade Shows World Wide". It describes itself as:

> The largest directory of trade fairs and business events bring[ing] you an exhaustive coverage of exhibitions, trade shows & expositions, conferences and seminars for various industries worldwide.

Rather than getting trapped by the offerings of any one site, always try Googling some keywords and concepts in order to optimize each of your searches. A single site is not usually ideal for answering a range of diverse questions.

Then there are also books, of course. Books often seem to be underestimated as a source of business information today. While the internet is often good for easy questions about what, where, and when, I find that books still offer the best explanations of the how and why. If the book is available as an e-book, of course, you get the best of both worlds: deep coverage and instant accessibility.

The present book will be accompanied by a website containing additional materials. Perhaps it may even be an e-book in due course, if the publisher so decides.

Concluding Remarks on the Future of Trade Shows

What can we say about the fate of trade shows in the future? Will they disappear as internet technology becomes more advanced? Will people prefer virtual shows? So far, internet technology has been used successfully as a supplement to traditional shows, enhancing them rather than replacing them.

In general, we can say that the more difficult it is to get an overview of an industry, and the more dynamic the market is, the more important trade shows will be. We can also see that trade shows are preferred in industries where the impact of a specific market is important, e.g. in telecomms. We could say that the more crucial personal contacts are, the greater the need to arrange trade shows where people can meet face to face (cf. Müller-Hagedorn 2003: 24). That means that trade shows will continue to be more important for business-to-business (B2B) than for business-to-consumer (B2C) marketing, and more important for countries with a strong commitment to increased exports, such as Germany and China.

Trade shows are important for building trust, without which all commerce becomes impossible in the long run.

Whatever the future may bring, there are lessons which will always hold true about how to organize a successful trade show. The essence of marketing is accurate *segmentation*, that is, we need to know who our customers are so that we can know how to go after them. Secondly, we need to focus on what we want to say at the trade show. How do we plan to communicate what we have to offer? Then ultimately we need to try to make our exhibit an interesting experience for visitors, to present ourselves in a way that will attract visitors into our booth. If we can only hold these three ideas clearly in our mind while working with everything else at the show, we will never be completely lost in the details.

Some readers may have expected me to round this book off by wishing them good luck. But, as you will understand by now, luck actually has very little to do with successful trade shows; they are mostly down to planning. So: good planning!

K. Solberg Søilen, *Exhibit Marketing and Trade Show Intelligence*,
Management for Professionals, DOI 10.1007/978-3-642-36793-9,
© Springer-Verlag Berlin Heidelberg 2013

Bibliography

Allen, J. (2002). *The business of event planning*. New York: Wiley.

Allen, C. W. (2005). Put the "show me" into trade shows exhibiting. *Successful Meetings, 54*, 4.

Arnold, D. (2000). *Messepraxis: Die professionelle Unternehmenspräsentation bei Messen und Ausstellungen*. Frankfurt am Main: Deutscher Fachverlag.

Arnold, M. K. (2002). *Build a better trade show image*. Kansas City, MO: Tiffany Harbor Productions.

Axelson, B. (1999). Trade shows gain larger share of marketing budgets: Computers help make manufacturing top category. *Advertising Age's Business Marketing, 84*, 14–15.

Barker, J. (2004). Show time. *Sales & Marketing Management, 157*(6).

Bello, D. C. (1988). *Attendee purchase behavior at a consumer show: An analysis of the Atlanta home show*. East Orleans, MA: Trade Show Bureau.

Bello, D. C. (1992). Industrial buyer behavior at trade shows: Implications for selling effectiveness. *Journal of Business Research, 25*, 59–80.

Bello, D. C., & Lohtia, R. (1993). Improving trade show effectiveness by analyzing attendees. *Industrial Marketing Management, 22*, 311–318.

Belschak, F., Verbeke, W., & Bagozzi, R. P. (2006). Coping with sales call anxiety: The role of sale perseverance and task concentration strategies. *Journal of the Academy of Marketing Science, 34*(3), 403–418.

Black, R. (1986). *The trade show industry: Management and marketing career opportunities*. Denver, CO: Trade Show Bureau.

Blurton, J. (2001). *Scenery: Drafting and construction for theatres, museums, exhibitions and trade shows*. New York: Routledge.

Blythe, J. (2000). Objectives and measures at UK trade exhibitions. *Journal of Marketing Management, 16*, 203–222.

Bonomoa, T. V. (1983). Get more out of your trade show. *Harvard Business Review, 61*, 75–83.

Bremshey, P., & Domning, R. (2001). *Event marketing*. Wiesbaden: Gabler.

Briere, D. (2006). Trade show tips that make life easier for all. *Network World, 23*(10), 41.

Brückner, M., & Przyklenk, A. (1999). *Event-marketing*. Wien and Frankfurt: Ueberreuter.

Center for Exhibition Industry Research (CEIR). (2003). *The role and value of face-to-face interaction*. Chicago, IL: CEIR.

Chapman, E. A., Jr. (1993). The autopilot syndrome. *Sales & Marketing Management, 145*(5), 36–38.

Chapman, E. A., Jr. (1995). *Exhibit marketing* (2nd ed.). Maidenhead: McGraw-Hill.

Christman, C. (1991). *The complete handbook of profitable trade show exhibiting*. Englewood Cliffs, NJ: Prentice Hall.

Clausen, E. (1997). *Mehr Erfolg auf Messen*. Landsberg/Lech: Verlag Moderne Industrie.

Clausen, E. (2005). *Messemarketing: so führen Sie Messen zum Erfolg*. Göttingen: Business Village.

Clausen, E., & Schreiber, P. (2000). *Messen optimal nutzen: Ziele definieren und Erfolge programmieren*. Würzburg: Schimmel.

K. Solberg Søilen, *Exhibit Marketing and Trade Show Intelligence*, Management for Professionals, DOI 10.1007/978-3-642-36793-9, © Springer-Verlag Berlin Heidelberg 2013

Dallmeyer, R. (1998). *Cold facts* (p. 4). Chicago, IL: Hot Tips, Center for Exhibition Industry Research.

Dornscheidt, W. M. (2003). *Handbuch messemanagement*. Wiesbaden: Gabler.

Edwards, D. M. (2002). *Fair days in the 'zone of plenty': Exhibit networks and the development of the American West*. Ann Arbor, MI: UMI.

Ford, D. (1980). The development of buyer-seller relationships in industrial markets. *European Journal of Marketing, 14*, 339–354.

Friedman, S. A. (Ed.). (1999). *Still more secrets of successful exhibiting*. Lake Placid, NY: Avia Publishing.

Friedman, S. A. (2002). Ten steps to a successful trade show. *Marketing Health Services, 22*(1), 31–32.

Friedman, S. A. (2004a). The guru reports: Survey reveals most exhibitor staff training is hit or miss. *CSP*, p. 23.

Friedman, S. A. (2005). Put show biz into your trade show. *Successful Meetings, 54*(2), 17.

Friedman, S. A. (2006a). Changing your trade show routines. *Successful Meetings, 55*, 6.

Friedman, S. A. (2006b). *75 dynamic ways to increase your trade show success*. http://www. thetradeshowcoach.com/article02.html. Accessed 07 July 2006.

Friedman, S. (2008). Making pre-show promotion stand out. *Successful Meetings, 57*(33), 35–36.

Gaedt, C. H., & Müller-Hagedorn, L. (2003). *Messen und Ausstellungen für Dienstleistungen*. Köln: Institut für Messewirtschaft und Distributionsforschung, Universität zu Köln.

Gartrell, R. B. (1988). *Destination marketing for conventions and visitor bureaus*. Dubuque, IA: Kendall-Hunt.

Gesteland, G. G. (2005). *Cross cultural business behavior*. Copenhagen: Copenhagen Business School Press.

Godar, S. H., & O'Connor, P. J. (2001). Same time next year – buyer trade show motives. *Industrial Marketing Management, 30*, 77–86.

Goldblatt, J. (2002). *Special events*. New York: Wiley.

Gopalakrishna, S., & Lilien, G. L. (1994). *A dynamic model of business trade show effectiveness*. University Park, PA: Institute for the Study of Business Markets, The Pennsylvania State University.

Gopalakrishna, S., Lilien, G. L., Williams, J. D., & Sequeira, I. K. (1995). Do trade shows pay off? *Journal of Marketing, 59*(3), 75–83.

Gruben, K. H. (2003). *The effectiveness of promotional products in trade show settings: Recipient perceptions of recall, usefulness and company image*. Irving, TX: PPAI.

Hansen, K. (1996). The dual motives of participants at international trade shows: An empirical investigation of exhibitors and visitors with selling motives. *International Marketing Review, 13*(2), 39–53.

Hansen, K. (1999). Trade show performance: A conceptual framework and its implications for future research. *Academy of Marketing Science Review, 3*, 1–12.

Hill, M. (1996). *Trade show survival guide: A tongue-in-cheek sales handbook*. San Jose, CA: Hill Group.

Hough, J. (1986). *Corporate executives' perceptions of trade expositions: Factors which influence attendance decisions*. East Orleans, MA: Trade Show Bureau.

Hoyle, L. H. (2002). *Event marketing: How to successfully promote events, festivals, conventions, and expositions*. New York, NY: Wiley.

Hubbard, J. (1988). How to make better sales calls. American bankers association. *ABA Banking Journal, 80*, 78. 10(Oct).

Huckemann, M., et al. (2005). *Messen messbar machen: Mehr Intelligenz pro m2*. Berlin: Springer.

Jensen, R. (1999). *The dream society: How the coming shift from information to imagination will transform your business*. New York, NY: McGraw-Hill.

Jenster, P., & Solberg Søilen, K. (2009). *Market intelligence: Building strategic insight*. Copenhagen: Copenhagen Business School Press.

Johansson, U. (2001). *The role of trade and consumer show participation: A national tourism organisation perspective*. Thesis, School of Economics and Commercial Law, Department of Human Geography, Göteborg.

Kerin, R. A., & Cron, W. L. (1986). *The exhibit management function: Perceptions of exhibit management and marketing executives*. Orleans, MA: Trade Show Bureau.

Kerin, R. A., & Cron, W. L. (1987a). Assessing trade show functions and performance: An exploratory study. *Journal of Marketing, 51*, 87–94.

Kerin, R. A., & Cron, W. L. (1987b). Assessing trade show functions and performance: An exploratory study. *Journal of Marketing, 59*, 87–94.

Kirchgeorg, M., Klante, O., Jung, K., Hochheim, H., & Tornier, J. (Eds.). (2007). *Messewirtschaft 2020 – Zukunftsszenarien*. Berlin: Auma.

Kleemann, A. (2006). *Event marketing-Lexikon*. Frankfurt am Main: Deutscher Fachverlag.

Konikow, R. B. (1984). *Exhibit design: The graphics of trade show communication*. New York, NY: PBC International.

Kotler, P. (1988/2000). *Marketing management* (1st ed. 1988) Chapter 18. Upper Saddle River, NJ: Prentice Hall.

Kreuter, D. (2002). *Der Messetrainer*. Wiesbaden: Gabler.

Lee, C. H., & Kim, S. Y. (2008). Differential effects of determinants on multi-dimensions of trade show performance: By three stages of pre-show, at-show, and post-show activities. *Industrial Marketing Management, 37*(7), 784–796.

Leitner, G. (1980). *Messegestaltuing aus didaktischer Sicht*. Klagefurt.

Levinson, J. C., Smith, M. S. A., & Wilson, O. R. (1997). *Guerrilla trade show selling: New unconventional weapons and tactics to meet more people, get more leads, and close more sales*. New York, NY: Wiley.

Li, L.-y. (2006). Relationship learning at trade shows: Its antecedents and consequences. *Industrial Marketing Management, 35*(2), 166–177.

Li, L.-y. (2010). Antecedents and effect of internet implementation for trade shows. *The Journal of Business and Industrial Marketing, 25*(4), 272–283.

Luse, I., & Mau, M. (1999). *International trade show participation: Experience of Swedish SMEs*. Thesis, Luleå.

Lynn, J. (1998). *Trade show gymnastics: Jumping through hoops without getting hurt*. Ann Arbor, MI: Fairview studios.

Mangelli, P. J. (1995). Trade shows: helping to drive the bottom line. *Advertising age's Business Marketing, 2*.

Marken, G. A. (1989). Courting the press: The dos and don'ts of trade show press. *Public Relations Quarterly, 34*(2), 21–24 (Summer 1989).

Marken, G. A. (2004). Trade show PR....It's time to focus on goals, substance, results. *Public Relations Quarterly, 49*(3), 30–33 (Fall).

McDonald, M. (1999). *Marketing plans*. Oxford: Butterworth-Heinemann.

Miller, S. (1996). *How to get the most out of trade shows*. Chicago, IL: NTC Business Books.

Miller, S. (1999). *How to get the most out of trade shows*. Chicago, IL: NTC Business Books.

Miller, S., & Sjoquist, R. (2002). *How to design a "wow!" trade show booth without spending a fortune*. Federal Way, WA: HiKelly Productions.

Montgomery, R. J., & Strick, S. K. (1995). *Meetings, conventions and expositions – an introduction to the industry*. New York: Wiley.

Morrow, S. L. (2002). *The art of the show*. Dallas, TX: IAEM Foundation.

Müller-Hagedorn, L. (2003). *Messen – Wirtschaftsforen der Zukunft?: Chancen in einer Welt des globalen Network*. Köln: Institut für Messewirtschaft und Distributionsforschung, Universität zu Köln.

O'Hara, B. S. (1993). Evaluating the effectiveness of trade shows: A personal selling perspective. *Journal of Personal Selling & Sales Management, 13*(3 (Summer)), 67–77.

Pegler, M. M. (Ed.). (2001). *Contemporary exhibit design*. New York, NY/London: Visual reference/Hi Marketing.

Pepinski, K. E. (2003). *Wirkungen von Messen auf die Standortqualität einer Grossstadt: Dargestellt am Beispiel Duisburgs.* Stuttgart: Ibidem.

Pitta, D. A., Weisgal, M., & Lynagh, P. (2006). Integrating exhibit marketing into integrated marketing communications. *Journal of Consumer Marketing, 23*(3), 156–166.

Ray, D. (1995). Confront call reluctance. *Personal Selling Power, September,* 46–51.

Reychav, I. (2009). Knowledge sharing in a trade show: A learning spiral model. *Vine, 39*(2), 143–158.

Robbe, D. (2000). *Expositions and trade shows.* New York: Wiley.

Roberts, E. (1995). *The complete manual for exhibiting in trade shows: A guide to planning and organizing an effective and profitable trade show program for your company.* Colorado Springs, CO: A-Way-with-Words Publications.

Rogers, E. M. (1962). *Diffusion of innovations.* Glencoe: Free Press.

Rosson, P. J., & Seringhaus, R. F. H. (1995). Visitor and exhibitor interaction at industrial trade fairs. *Journal of Business Research, 32,* 81–90.

Saget, A. (2006). *The event marketing handbook beyond logistics and planning.* Chicago, IL: Dearborn Trade Publishing, a Kaplan Professional Company.

Saunders, J., Saker, J., & Smith, G. (1996). Afterword: An agenda for research into strategic marketing planning. *Journal of Marketing Management, 12*(1–3), 215–230.

Schäfer-Mehdi, S. (2005). *Event-Marketing: Kommunikationsstrategie, Konzeption und Umsetzung, Dramaturgie und Inszenierung.* Berlin: Cornelsen.

Sharland, A., & Balogh, P. (1996a). The value of non-selling activities at international trade shows. *Journal of Global Marketing, 12*(3), 41–56.

Sharland, A., & Balogh, P. (1996b). The value of non-selling activities at international trade shows. *Industrial Marketing Management, 25*(1), 59–66.

Shoham, A. (1999). Performance in trade shows and exhibitions: A synthesis and directions for future research. *Journal of Global Marketing, 12*(3), 41–57.

Simkin, L. (2000). Delivering effective marketing planning. *Journal of Targeting, Measurement and Analysis for Marketing, 8*(3), 1–16.

Sind, S. (1996). More evidence of the power of exhibitions. *Advertising Age's Business Marketing, 81,* B-2.

Siskind, B. (1993). *The successful exhibitor's handbook: Trade show techniques for beginners and pros.* North Vancouver: Self-Counsel Press.

Siskind, B. (2005). *Powerful exhibit marketing: The complete guide to successful trade shows, conferences and consumer shows.* Mississauga, ON: Wiley.

Skinner, G. W. (1964). Marketing and social structure in Rural China. *Journal of Asian Studies, 24,* 3–43, 25, 195–229 & 363–399.

Skinner, B. E., & Rukavina, V. (2003). *Event sponsorship.* New York: Wiley.

Smith, T. M. (1998). *The effectiveness of trade show efforts for exhibitors of woodworking machinery: A thesis in forest resources.* Doctoral dissertation, UMI, Ann Arbor, MI.

Smith, T. M., Gopalakrishna, S., & Smith, P. M. (2004). The complementary effect of trade shows on personal selling. *International Journal of Research in Marketing, 21*(1), 61–76.

Solberg Søilen, K. (2005). *Introduction to private and public intelligence.* Lund: Studentlitteratur.

Solberg Søilen, K. (2010). Boosting innovation and knowledge through delocalization: Market intelligence at trade shows. *Problems and Perspectives in Management, 3,* 200–208.

Solberg Søilen, K. (2012). *Geoeconomics.* London: Bookboon.

Solberg Søilen, K. (upcoming 2013). Benchmarking innovation, Chapter 7. In Brett Trusko (Ed.), *Handbook of business innovation.* New York: McGraw-Hill.

Stevens, R. P. (2005). *Trade show and event marketing: Plan, promote and profit.* New York, NY: Thomson Texere.

Tafesse, W., & Korneliussen, T. (2012). Identifying factors affecting consumers purchase incidence at retail trade shows. *Journal of Retailing and Consumer Services, 19*(4), 438–444.

Tanner, J. F., Jr. (1994). Adaptive selling at trade shows. *Journal of Personal Selling & Sales Management, 22,* 15–23. Spring.

Tanner, J. F., Jr. (1995). *Curriculum guide to trade show marketing*. Bethesda, MD: Center for Exhibition Industry Research.

Tanner, J. F., Jr. (2002). Leveling the playing field: Factors influencing trade show success for small companies. *Industrial Marketing Management, 31*, 229–239.

Tanner, J. F., Jr. (1996). *Book review. Exhibit marketing* (2nd ed.) by E. A. Chapman, Jr. (Ed.). In *The Journal of Personal Selling & Sales Management, Winter*(16), 1.

Thain, D. H. (1955). Industrial trade shows: An examination and appraisal of the industrial trade show industry and the use of industrial trade show exhibits as a promotional tool. Vol 2. *Dissertation*. Boston, MA: Harvard University.

Thomas, J. (1993). *Le temps des foires: foires et marchés dans le Midi Toulousain dela fin de l'Ancien Régime*. Toulouse: PUM.

Tynan, D. (2004). Tricks of the trade show. *Sales & Marketing Management, 156*, 27.

Vanderleest, H. W. (1994). Planning for international trade show participation: A pract. *SAM Advanced Management Journal, 59*(4), 39–44. Autumn.

Verbeke, W., & Bagozzi, R. P. (2000). Sales call anxiety: Exploring what it means when fear rules a sales encounter. *Journal of Marketing, 64*(July), 88–101.

Walls, K. (1998). Don't overlook the role of exhibiting in your marketing mix. *Medical Marketing & Media, 33*(8), 48–52. 49.

Weintraub, D. K. (1991). *Trade show exhibiting: The insider's guide for entrepreneurs*. Blue Ridge Summit, PA: Liberty Hall.

Weisgal, M. B. (1997). *Show and sell: 133 business building ways to promote your trade show exhibit*. New York, NY: American Management Association.

Weisgal, M. B. (1999). *12 Steps to exhibit success*. Cambridge, UK: Prosemics Press.

Wenz-Gahler, I. (2002). *Big ideas for small stands*. Würzburg, Germany: Max Schimmel Verlag.

Williams, J. D., Gopalakrishna, S., & Cox, J. M. (1993). Trade show guidelines for smaller firms. *Industrial Marketing Management, 22*, 265–275.

Wu, J., et al. (1997). *A model of trade show diversity*. Thesis, Institute for the Study of Business Markets, The Pennsylvania State University, University Park, PA.

Wu, J., Dasgupta, A., & Lilien, G. L. (2003). *An empirical study of trade show formation and diversity*. Thesis, Institute for the Study of Business Markets, the Pennsylvania State University, University Park, PA.

Zwahr, H., Topfstedt, T., & Bentele, G. (Eds.). (1999). *Leipzigs Messen 1497–1997*. Köln: Böhlau. 2 Volumes.

Index

K. Solberg Søilen, *Exhibit Marketing and Trade Show Intelligence*,   145
Management for Professionals, DOI 10.1007/978-3-642-36793-9,
© Springer-Verlag Berlin Heidelberg 2013

CPSIA information can be obtained at www.ICGtesting.com
Printed in the USA
LVOW07*2351010813

345920LV00016B/272/P